Memories of the...

MARKET TAVERN
KIDDERMINSTER
1990 - 1996

Written, compiled and designed by Mark Badgeman with
additional research by Andrew Wolfman.

Thanks to everyone who dredged the depths of their memory
to contribute or kept hold of old memorabilia. Extra special
thanks to all the bands and musicians who took the time to
write down their recollections.

Front cover photograph of the audience at the
first Carter USM gig by Mike Parker.

Rear cover photo of Carter USM on stage at
the Tavern by Mike Parker.

All newspaper cuttings used with kind permission
of Kidderminster Shuttle unless otherwise noted.

Published by Mark Badgeman
ISBN 978-1-5272-7278-1
© 2020 Mark Badgeman

"I told you to call it Cattle & Hum."

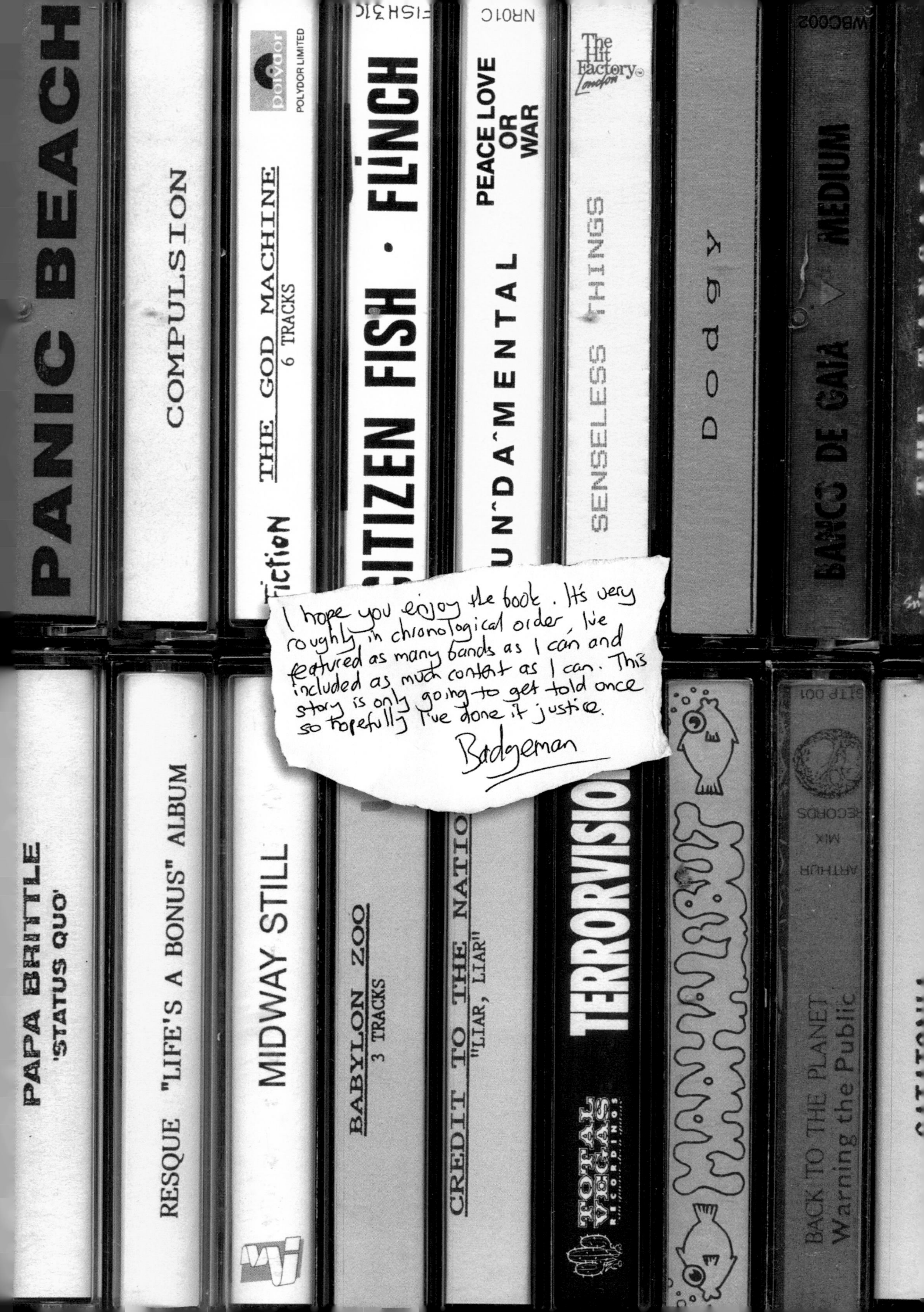

PANIC BEACH

COMPULSION

POLYDOR LIMITED

THE GOD MACHINE
6 TRACKS

Fiction

CITIZEN FISH · FLINCH

FISH31C

PEACE LOVE OR WAR

NR01C

FUN'DA'MENTAL

The Hit Factory London

SENSELESS THINGS

Dodgy

BANCO DE GAIA

MEDIUM

WBC002

PAPA BRITTLE 'STATUS QUO'

RESQUE "LIFE'S A BONUS" ALBUM

MIDWAY STILL

BABYLON ZOO
3 TRACKS

CREDIT TO THE NATION "LIAR, LIAR"

TERRORVISION

Total Vegas Recordings

BACK TO THE PLANET
Warning the Public

ARTHUR MIX RECORDS

SLTP 001

I hope you enjoy the book. It's very roughly in chronological order, I've featured as many bands as I can and included as much content as I can. This story is only going to get told once so hopefully I've done it justice.

Badgeman

# FOREWORD

It would be safe to say there are few music venues that have existed anywhere in the world that can boast having had Radiohead perform 10 yards away from a herd of cattle occupying the same space, but then most venues were not the Market Tavern.

This flat-roofed farmer's market-cum-social club that accidentally landed in a train station overflow car park, found itself conveniently navigable for music-goers from the north and the south of the Midlands and its reputation for touring bands as a must-play venue helped draw countless numbers to visit a town with the funny name of Kidderminster.

Attracting a diverse, and often freakish melee of punters, it was not uncommon to see Rastas brushing shoulders with Metal-heads and Goths, Punks playing pool with Bikers and, as ever, the Indie kids, always in massive numbers, that would swarm inside and around what would became an important cultural hub, where a drunken half-encounter either ended up in romance or, most likely, agreeing to play bass in a newly formed blues-ska band.

For those who were fortunate enough to drink, socialise or even perform there, it was a unique and unforgettable venue. Its reputation for being weird or dangerous only increased its allure for its disciples and heightened its intrigue to the non-believer.

Boasting a pop-up vegetarian cafe before it was cool, politically active in awareness campaigns before social media existed and even managing to have its own indoor summer festivals -its all-dayer events were legendary- the Tavern had everything going on, even its own psychedelic disco.

The reputation of its toilets was a fair one (think Trainspotting and then some...) but this was quickly forgiven when one of the friendly neighbourhood cows would peer longingly at you through the circular window as you exited. It is clear to see, it was not your typical music venue.

In the engine room of the good ship Tavern, its hardworking promoter, Mark Badgeman, had the enviable knack of booking bands that he knew were going to be successful, even before they did, leading to such rising stars as Catatonia, Carter USM, Wolfsbane, Chumbawamba and Radiohead to play for a steal and grace the Tavern's tight box stage to play to sweaty, excited fans who had just read about them in the music press or heard them on the radio that very week.

Gig after gig after gig, flyers, posters, bill stickers, press articles, band after band, load in, set up, soundcheck, hand-stamp, performance, break down, load out, do it again tomorrow night, loud music, dark room, bright lights and the sweat literally dripping from the walls, strobe lights, smoke, beer, fog machines, spirits, weed, laughter, noise, cheering, shouting, merriment and good times all now like a distant lighthouse you can no longer reach and helplessly drift away from.

And just like that, the light is gone forever, a new housing development forced through in the mid-1990s pushed this microcosm of subculture off the map forever with not as much as a street sign to commemorate its existence.

As some small comfort, in its place are the recollections, anecdotes and testimonies of many a regular and musician, collected in numbers and presented to you, the reader, to digest at your leisure.

For the full authentic Market Tavern experience, please read with a torch in a smoky room with some 90's BritPop played deafeningly loud.

Dale Von Minaker

# TAVERN MEMORIES

Lou "One of the coolest things about the Tavern was that you could just be chilling in the bar on an afternoon and then find yourself randomly playing pool with a member of some cool indie or punk band."

Heather Howell Jones "There is nowhere like the Tavern. Wish it was there now, really really do. Best days, best laughs, best memories."

Jo Deakin "What an incredible thing to have a gig venue like the Tavern in our home town, I don't think we appreciated it at the time. I went as much as I could when I was in 6th form ('91-'93) and I remember my Dad coming to pick me up once and waiting outside, leaning on the car, for me to come out later than the agreed time and he was absolutely furious. Memories of the actual gigs are very hazy but I remember much jumping about to Back To The Planet, Chumbawamba and Credit To The Nation, plus secretly fancying most of Fretblanket."

Dr Marc Price "I remember going into a trendy pub for a quick pint of Banks's before closing, and the barman advised me to leave before I got beaten up. He suggested that I might do better at the Farmers Boy or Market Tavern. Both of those options offered a scary-looking but friendlier clientele."

Andy Price (landlord) "I think part of the attraction of the Tavern was it was always on a bit of a knife edge, nobody knew what was going to happen next."

Paul Brockway "I went to a few shows...Radiohead...Fretblanket ...my mate's band Scrash...the Family Cat...Redd Kross...it was great there...really sticky floors...the pit was always manic...sweaty steam worse than JBs...I lost a watch...but found 35 quid...lying on the floor between the barriers and stage...landed on a shitload of bust glass...I went there with some mates from school...all part of the Stourbridge scene at the time...prob about 15...16 years old."

Chip Leong "Aaaahhh where my drinking career started. What a place! Where else could I get served with no ID or hassle at 14 just because I had long hair! That place shaped me for the rest of my life and I'm still suffering for it! Haha!"

Lindsay Smith "Previously we'd been going to Murdoch's for nights out, but they didn't ever play the music I liked. Once I found the Tavern I spent most of my teenage years there. It felt like I'd finally found my tribe of people."

Benny Tovey "Spilt beer and cow shit. My brain still smells it from time to time."

The Head Barman "The cows were always coming into the pub!"

Ian Passey (Jackpot) "The much talked about gigs at Kidderminster Town Hall in the 1960's are often hailed as a time of historical and cultural importance for the area, and rightly so, but the Market Tavern era was equally rich in musical significance and influence. There were so many highlights, but the ones that really stood out for me were Redd Kross, Snuff, The Telescopes, Frank Sidebottom, Fatima Mansions, Carter USM, Top, The Primitives, Bob and God Machine. The fact that I missed the Senseless Things bugs me on an almost daily basis!"

Andrew Wolfman "You can take the boy out of the Market Tavern but you'll never take the Market Tavern out of the boy. I still get the the unique stench of the corridor to the bogs in my nostrils from time to time... Awesome venue. Man I miss 1991."

Leonard Shaw "Went there 3 times. I think I'll always remember hearing the cattle for the first time. I thought what the fuck?!"

Mat Power (Panic Beach) "Yep the smell of cow poo and the hate of farmers was always integral to a gig at the Tavern!"

Sue Costello "Was it my imagination or did the Velvet Underground play there?"

Fiona Gordon "Best pub ever!! Great bands and Red Stripe on tap! Seeing cows on the way to the toilet was different too!!"

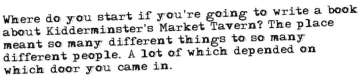

Where do you start if you're going to write a book about Kidderminster's Market Tavern? The place meant so many different things to so many different people. A lot of which depended on which door you came in.

The front door was traditionally used by bikers and boozers who imposed their authority over skiving lunchtime students playing pool. The bar had a great jukebox and sold value for money ploughman's lunches.

The back door was for the music fans. Depending on which night it was, you could either be watching your mate's local band, old rhythm and blues pros endlessly treadmilling the pub circuit or stumbling into a fragrant haze of psychedelia / acid house / headbanging metal grunge.

And, of course, we should't forget that vocal minority who travelled in from the countryside to trample straw and cowshit all over the place whilst moaning about cattle prices. Bloody farmers, thought they owned the place, just because it was attached to a cattle auction.

All the more remarkable then, that for a short period in the early 90s, it transformed into both a matt-black mecca of NME-championed indie bands who, unbelievably, chose to include Kidderminster on their UK tours, AND the closest you could get to a free festival without being stuck in a field. Somehow the Tavern shone very brightly for a few years and all the tribes co-existed in a beautiful harmony. Unless it was one of those nights when the bikers fancied a tussle or the footie boys were on a rampage.

The Tavern was built in about 1960 and had probably hosted bands before I was even born. I remember my classmate, Carl Greybanks, whilst still at school played in a function band that had a weekly Sunday lunchtime residency. I saw lots of great Tavern gigs in the 80's such as Omnia Opera, Wayward Angel, Bitches Bru, Colbert Hamilton and the Hell Razors, the Rockin' Renegades, The Rockets, 3 to Midnight, Jynx, Becky Swan and probably more that I've long since forgotten about. I put on a couple of gigs myself with Spiny Dogfish and Sweet Xtasy.

Even when I booked the first Carter USM gig, there were other gigs in the diary and I wasn't the only promoter using the room. I did hold the diary after a while, but looking back, it's hard to remember which bands I actually promoted. Citizen Fish seemed to already be regulars before I walked in and took over booking them, Hawkwind associates Tubilah Dog too. Martin Pelta had confirmed a string of gigs by the time I'd got involved and he continued to book more in tandem with mine.

So the only way to write a book about the Tavern is to go with what I know and base it roughly on the years 1990 to 1996. The pub closed in about 1997 as far as I'm aware but I don't have any knowledge of those dying days, so it's not included here in any detail. There's liberal use of Straight Elephant articles and cuttings as the magazine was partially used to promote the bands playing the Tavern. I've tried to get as many people involved in this book as possible and by doing so, I hope I've managed to represent the 'other' gigs that took place alongside mine.

It was a long time ago, historical revisionism is undoubtedly rife but I think the book paints a very good picture of what it was like. There's a Market Tavern Facebook group (where a lot of the book's content originated from) so if I've missed something, and you think the world needs to know about it, stick it on there. Just don't grass up whoever put the poppers in the smoke machine!

Mark Badgeman 2020

When you have an unusual job, such as working in the music industry, everybody wants to know how you got started. I always say that I lied my way in but that's only part of the story. You can trace it back to the beginnings with Spiny Dogfish, my mates from school. Unable to join the band on account of not being able to sing or play anything (never saw the problem myself), I became their manager. Not that we had any idea what a manager did. After a bit of head scratching, we decided the manager sorts the gigs, so I went to see Murdochs about using their cellar bar.

SPINY DOGFISH AT THE TAVERN IN THE 80s

I have a feeling the room hire was £20. We booked a date and Craig's mate, Squirrel, from the Rockin' Renegades, asks us which PA we're using. I had no idea what he was talking about because Spiny Dogfish rehearsed with Craig's vocals going through a guitar amp. After he'd explained it, he kindly rented us his PA for a tenner. All our mates came and it was a roaring success. I don't recall who played on the first gig but we had bands such as The Vital Organs, The Time Beings and the Christmas Trees playing on the bills. I roped in Mad Max who was doing an alternative disco there. Those nights were great and always busy.

Then it dawned on me that we could ask the bands we used to go and see in the Birmingham pubs to come down and play, and give them a few quid to cover their train fare. The audience would still turn out for Spiny Dogfish, but we also got to see bands like The Sect or Suicide Blonde, and they played to a new audience. One of the bands I asked to play was Wild and Wandering from Stourbridge. They phoned me after we'd confirmed a date and said they'd be playing under their brand new name of Pop Will Eat Itself. And then rang again a few days later to say they'd been offered some studio time in London so they couldn't do it, but they were sending Yeah God! in their place. Gutted I missed out on promoting the first Poppies gig!

JUST AFTER IT WAS BUILT. THE GIG ROOM IS FACING US

After Spiny Dogfish, I managed Sweet Xtasy in the late 80s. For one of their local gigs we hired the Market Tavern. During the evening, a skinhead got glassed and the landlord was furious. Possibly just over the broken pint glass because he made me pay 50p for it and sweep it up! At the end of the night, he banned me from the venue. I went back the next day to see if he'd calmed down, but he still didn't want 'my kind' in there so that was that, I was banned.

When I heard the Tavern was under new management, and the rumour that it was being turned into a proper venue, I went to see the new landlord, Andy Price, and asked him about it. He said it wasn't but what could I offer. I told him I booked 'big bands' and that I was the main promoter in this town! God knows where I got that level of arrogance from but it seemed to work because he said yep, let's do it. So I trotted back home trying to figure out how I was going to pull this off.

LIVE AT THE MARKET TAVERN

THE VITAL ORGANS

SATURDAY 12th JULY

8 TILL LATE

DOUBLE BILL

SPINY DOGFISH

£1 on the door

Craig's Birthday

2

When you see the nineteen nineties on tv or film these days, it's a technicolour place. All Ninja Turtle greens, smiley face yellows and the popping pinks and purples of a Fresh Prince of Bel Air bum-bag.

It wasn't like that in Kidderminster. In the nineties, Kidderminster still looked like the seventies. It was bus-station brown and dole queue grey, wet, flat and disappointing like a spilled pint of bitter. Kidderminster was a decent place that had seen better days. The carpets from its factories had fallen out of fashion, its town centre had been choked by an ugly ring road and years of Conservative disinterest.

Plus, it stank. This being where the industrial Midlands meets the countryside, a fog of factory pollution mingled with the acrid fug of sugarbeet. Clouds of cow shit from the fields met fumes from the traffic leaving town and the faint waft of urine from the swan-shaped kiddies' slide outside the old Waitrose that people used as a toilet. It was an unlikely home for a musical revolution.

In 1990 if you were a young person wanting to form a band, go to shows, or meet like-minded people (without getting your head kicked in for being a weirdo) there was only one thing to do. You left.

Birmingham is barely fifteen miles and forty minutes away from Kidderminster, but that's a universe when you're a kid. The train was expensive, and if you missed the last one home (which you would, because children are stupid) you'd have to sleep in a bin, with a rolled up Harriers' scarf for a pillow.

Up the A449 interesting things were happening. Thanks to Pop Will Eat Itself, The Wonder Stuff and (I don't care what you say) Fretblanket, neighbouring Stourbridge was fast becoming a centre for indie-rock activity in the UK. A sort of self-deprecating Seattle in a balti-splattered long-sleeved t-shirt, a chummy two-pub Camden with glass blowing. A night out there might net you a nod from a Ned, a passing chat with a Poppie, or, if you were really lucky, Miles Hunt might call you a cunt. Hup! Still, no big bands had actually played there since a stale Sigue Sigue Sputnik pulled in 79 people at the Town Hall in 1988.

Back home, nothing seemed to happen at all. Kidderminster's night clubs: Weavers, The Riverboat (later, Flirtz / Diva's / Elements / Time) catered for a fun-hating crowd of tucked-in knuckle draggers, and Murdoch's (very much the best of a bad bunch) most closely resembled the ex-pat Spanish bar from the TV Show Duty Free (stick with me teenagers!) Taste-free local radio personalities and creepy mobile disco DJs ruled the roost. Thirty two years after I first encountered him, hopeless local DJ Martin Stooke, rather than shoving his bubble machine up his arse, became the first UKIP mayor of Kidderminster. Sadly, he's still ignoring my requests.

No one was putting on bands you'd really want to see in a town with a significant musical heritage: Robert Plant, Stan Webb's Chicken Shack and the roots of Fleetwood Mac. Clifford T Ward, Jowe Head from the Swell Maps, wasn't one of Wishbone Ash from here? Kidderminster's picturesque surrounding villages and rolling Hobbity hills were the perfect place for the great and greasy of the seventies and eighties metal scene to set up a farm, build a golf course or drive their dragsters, but the town didn't seem especially interested in its rock history.

These days, there's a plaque to remind us that Captain Beefheart played at Frank Freeman's Dancing Club on Lower Mill St (next door to Woolwise and the Paradise Balti House). There's a bench opposite W.H. Smiths to commemorate where Underworld's Karl Hyde once sat (presumably having a lager and shouting). Wolverley High School even has a huge mural of Robert Plant and Jimmy Page next to the toilets in the cafeteria - probably not the Physical Graffiti they were originally on about. Strangely, there's also one of Lady Gaga, who I didn't know was local, though I do enjoy saying 'Poker Face' in a Kiddy accent.

Criminally, there is nothing to commemorate the site where the Market Tavern once stood.

In 1990 a bright-eyed indie badge maker (truly the least celebrated of all the frontline workers) approached a cattle-filled biker bar that always seemed on the verge of being completely on fire, and said he wanted to put on some gigs. Six years, and countless seminal shows later, it was replaced by faceless orange flats and, ironically given some of its clientele, a shiny new Magistrates' Court. For a brief period in the early nineteen nineties though, the Tavern was Kidderminster's last stand against the mundanity of modern life. A sort-of iconic, brilliantly chaotic and utterly unhygienic footnote in the history of rock and roll. My favourite place. There ought to be a statue.

Andrew Wolfman 2020

The Ectoplasmic Sonic Stomp Disco was organised by the KCC, Kidderminster Creative Cooperative, consisting of some of the members of Omnia Opera (Andy Jones, Ade Scholefield, Lisa Moraity and Natalie Jones), artists Moggy Morris and Dale Shaw, Karin Owen, Mike Parker and Chas Taylor. They'd approached the Tavern as the back room wasn't being used much in the late 80's.

Andy Jones remembers, "The guy that ran it was very straight but open-minded enough to let us have a go, but also he realised he would make some money over the bar, which he certainly did. The idea was that we would just turn up with all our own records and play them, which is what we did. None of us were DJs and so changing between tracks was often clumsy but it was kind of fun and down-to-earth and added to the whole vibe - very DIY."

In the early days you'd hear Fields Of The Nephilim, Hawkwind, Sisters Of Mercy, Pink Floyd, Culture Shock, basically anything and everything from the alternative scene, or music that you wouldn't hear anywhere else. It was an instant hit, loads of people came.

Andy said, "There was virtually nothing else to do in Kiddy, so it was bound to work. We kept it cheap to enter, it was a very socialist approach, we had stalls displaying animal rights leaflets and political stuff. Any money that was made was just simply pumped back into more equipment, lights, speakers, decks, smoke machine etc."

Mike remembers that the original grand plan had been to raise some money to open a cafe venue in somewhere like Green Street, where properties were likely to be cheaper because a lot were boarded up. Instead they built up a great collection of lights such as Moonflowers, a monster strobe and my favourite, the one that projected a laser style flat beam of light.

# Finding the alternative

I always wonder what people mean when they use the word 'alternative' in an entertainment context such as 'alternative music' or 'alternative theatre' — alternative to what I always ask.

Well now I have my chance to find out because several locals have formed a group called Kidderminster Kreative Co-operative (KKC) because they believe there is a need for more entertainment facilities in Wyre Forest — something I wholeheartedly agree with.

Anyway, they aim to raise money to fund alternative bands, discos, art shows, craft fayres etc, all being done with a view to finding a permanent base for such events and other ambitious projects of benefit to the community.

The first such event has the rather tongue-twisting title of — the Ectoplasmic Sonic Stomp Disco which will be held on Friday, August 26, featuring psychedelic, heavy metal and other sounds, at the Market Tavern, Comberton Place, Kidderminster.

Entrance to this mind-blowing event will cost 75p.

Calling all space aliens. The next Ectoplasmic Stomp Sonic Disco (whaaaat?) will be held as usual (is usual the right word?) at the Market Tavern, Kidderminster, on Saturday.

Now for the bad news — this time it'll cost you £1 to get in; but the good news is the extra cash will be used to buy more equipment and records. And it still sounds like good value — just think of all that ectoplasmic stomping you get for a quid.

4

Moggy Morris did the Stomp posters, which were works of art in their own right. They also produced a fanzine style newsletter to keep people updated with their plans.

Andy told me, "One of my abiding memories from the early days was the great efforts we made to get the atmosphere just right in the Tavern, with the lights and the projectors and the music and the smoke and the darkness, which wasn't easy because it was not a particularly atmospheric building. Then somebody would break a glass by accident. All of a sudden, all the lights would come on, utterly destroying the atmosphere, and the barman would be shouting and trying to find out who broke the glass. He would come round and clean it up and it would take far too long and eventually the lights went off again, much to everyone's relief, and we could get back to being in our world."

KCC branched out and started putting bands on. One of those was a fledgling Neds Atomic Dustbin as Mike knew Mat Cheslin. It turned out to be quite pivotal in their career as it was their first ever gig with the classic five piece line-up.

Mike and Chas started a version of the Stomp in Redditch at the Limelight which was hugely successful. Numbers in Kiddy started dropping off but it had paved the way for me to come in and start putting the gigs on. A solid foundation for what was to come.

"Ade Wilkes ""Newky Brown, hash, whizz, Outcasts and the Stomp... That's some I remember and some I don't."

Tracy Butterfield "Loved the Stomp, always went for a boogie."

Sally Lacy-kerr "Ectoplasmic Stomp was the dog's, and by far the best indie disco ever."

Marc Price "The silly dance competition at The Stomp disco was, well, quite silly."

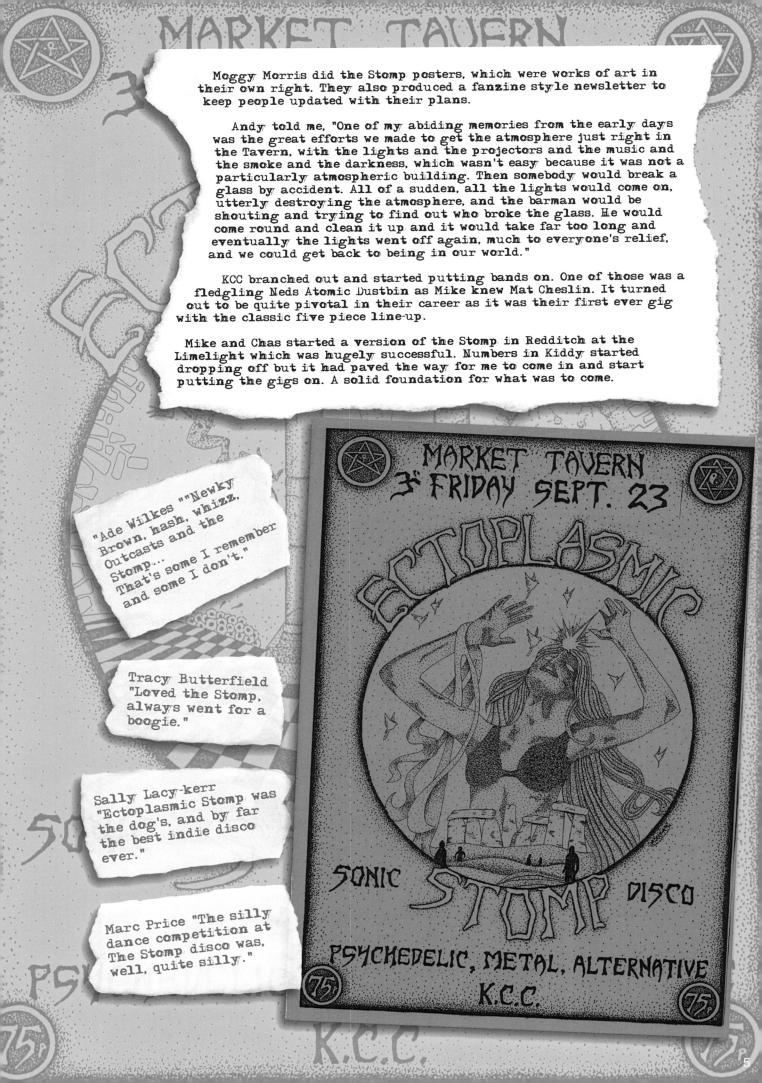

MARKET TAVERN
3ʳᵈ FRIDAY SEPT. 23
ECTOPLASMIC
SONIC STOMP DISCO
PSYCHEDELIC, METAL, ALTERNATIVE
K.C.C.

Mark Badgeman "I first saw Ned's play in February of 1989 at the Mitre, their local in Stourbridge. We had mutual friends and I went to quite a few of their gigs that year.

Eventually, I ended up making their badges as I was still working at Veldonn Printers in the Horsefair and they owned the Button Badge factory. Ned's nicknamed me Badgeman.

I didn't go to their '89 gig at the Tavern because I'd been banned from the pub in 1988. I saw them at JB's the week before.

After supporting The Wonder Stuff on a couple of tours, Ned's signed to Chapter 22 and their first two singles did really well. They secured a main stage afternoon slot at the 1991 Reading festival and it was a packed sea of Ned's t-shirts. You knew something was about to happen.

By 1991 they were on Top Of The Pops and their debut album charted at No 4. The following year they headlined the second stage at Glastonbury."

THE ECTOPLASMIK STOMP PRESENTS

NED'S ATOMIC DUSTBIN

THE MARKET TAVERN
"KIDDERMINSTER"
SAT 19TH AUG
£1·50 IN

Badgeman in Ned's T-shirt at Reading Festival 1991

Jonn Penney (Ned's) "We used to have two vocalists but this was our first gig with just me and I was bricking it. I didn't know if I had the guts to do it on my own as the only frontman.

Unfortunately, on top of all those nerves, we had to contend with the Tavern's resident bikers who'd taken exception to us. It wasn't the usual nutter-at-a-gig, this actually made us fear for our lives. In those days, there was no stage, so we were a bit exposed. Our manager, Tank, had his car on standby for a fast exit!

Luckily it all passed without incident and I also found that I could hear myself better as the only vocalist and that songs like Grey Cell Green were far less busy.

I only came back once after that, to see Fretblanket, and I couldn't believe the transformation. It now had a proper stage, was painted black and the yellow curtains had gone!"

Roy Davies "Cheap n' Nasty were a group put together by Hanoi Rocks guitarist Nasty Suicide... they opened with 'Hello Kidderminster, are you ready to kick arse???' An NME journalist was there and in the review said if ever a town needed its arse kicking, it was Kidderminster..."

Mark Badgeman "I had absolutely no idea Cheap n' Nasty were playing. Even now, I'm still a big fan of Hanoi Rocks so I'd definitely have gone if I'd known about it. Hell, I even saw Cherry Bombz at the Portland and bought the Fallen Angels single Nasty Suicide did with Knox from The Vibrators.

It's likely that Martin Pelta promoted it but even now, it's a truly puzzling thing to have happened. The Tavern wasn't on the national gig circuit and Cheap n' Nasty had only just formed. How on earth did they end up in Kiddy? With the NME there?!

When I found out after it had happened, it felt like it was just a rumour, as I didn't know anyone who'd gone and no one was talking about it. I knew I had to put in a lot of legwork to make sure my gigs weren't going to suffer the same fate."

Martin Pelta was Andy Price's mate from Bath. News clearly travelled slowly in those days as I thought I was getting in on the act really fast by going to see Andy as soon as I heard he wanted to turn the Tavern into a venue. He'd actually had it for months at that point and Martin had come up to visit him and ended up behind the bar and booking some bands. I don't think Martin appreciated the jumped up kid trying to muscle in and he definitely didn't like the bands I was booking. He was either a musician or very musical because he appreciated good musicianship and valued that over everything else. Eric Bell from Thin Lizzy was the perfect Martin gig.

On the other hand, I couldn't care less if the band could play! It was all about selling tickets for me. Why would I be judgemental if 300 people wanted to see the show? But now, when I look back, I wish I'd gone to more of Martin's gigs. I especially wished I'd seen Steve Gibbons or Trevor Burton or even Dumpys Rusty Nuts. The reality was that I was probably out flyering or flyposting somewhere but there was a solid booking policy in the parallel universe of gigs that I wasn't promoting. It's just a shame that they never did good numbers, especially as there was already a built-in biker crowd who would have loved a lot of the stuff he booked.

I wanted to talk to Martin for this book but after a quick internet search to locate him, I found out that he passed away in 2009. He was only 52.

Andy Price "I was gutted when I found out. He had a remarkable personality, so sad."

7", 4 Track 12" & CD (ROUGH TRADE) Out Now.

# CARTER
## THE UNSTOPPABLE SEX MACHINE

### ANYTIME ANYPLACE ANYWHERE

**ON TOUR IN OCTOBER**

3rd **Kidderminster** Market Tavern
4th **Oxford** Poly
5th **Northampton** Irish Centre
6th **Essex** University
8th **Bristol** Poly
9th **Birmingham** Burberrie's
10th **Wolverhampton** Poly
11th **Manchester** U.M.I.S.T.
12th **Treforest** Poly
13th **Southampton** East Point Centre
17th **Wigan** Maxines
18th **Glasgow** King Tuts
19th **Leeds** University
20th **Hartlepool** Borough Hall
21st **Huddersfield** Poly
22nd **Liverpool** University
24th **Brixton** Fridge
26th **Leicester** Poly
27th **Kent** University

'Fun Palace' present –
**CARTER**
THE UNSTOPPABLE SEX MACHINE
+ Support and disco.
**MARKET TAVERN**
**WED Oct 3rd**
Doors 7.30
Music £3·50 005
Band 10.00

Badgeman presents **FUN PALACE** – A NEW INDIE NIGHT with –

# CARTER
## THE UNSTOPPABLE SEX MACHINE

AT THE **MARKET TAVERN, KIDDERMINSTER**
ON **Wednesday OCT 3rd** 7·30 – 11·00
**Adv. Tickets £3·50** From the venue or the music shop, kidd.

THE TERRIBLE HAND DRAWN
POSTER, A 'FORGERY-PROOF'(!)
TICKET AND THE FIRST TIME
I'D HAD A GIG ON A
PROFESSIONAL TOUR POSTER

8

# CARTER
## ■ THE UNSTOPPABLE SEX MACHINE ■

"I almost feel I've exhausted the mileage I can get from this story, but if ever there was place to tell it, it's here. I'd set myself up for a fall by telling Andy Price that I was some sort of local hotshot promoter who booked 'big bands'. My only 'in' to bigger bands was knowing Ned's Atomic Dustbin and I was just hanging around at their gigs after delivering the badges. They weren't going to play the Tavern again because they'd not had a good experience at their previous gig. However, through them, I'd met Jon Beast who did the lights for Carter USM. He also used to introduce them virtually naked on stage and was a bit of a character. I told him I wanted Carter to play this new venture of mine and he said I needed to talk to their booking agent, Lisa at Brag. I'd never heard of such a role before but undeterred, I called her up and told her I wanted to book the band. She wasn't convinced.

I called Jon back the next day and he suggested I phone Adrian Boss, Carter's manager. Adrian didn't seem particularly opposed to the idea but said I needed to go through Lisa, which I took as being fobbed off anyway. So I rang Jon Beast again. Then I rang Lisa, then Adrian, then Jon and I kept on doing this until they caved in. Lisa called me one day and said 'look, we're going to let you book the band, but you have to do everything Jon tells you. He'll tell you what PA to use, which lights to book, you'll need to get a stage barrier, you need to pay us £500, you need to feed us and generally just do as we tell you'.

That was fair enough because I hadn't got a clue what I was doing. I set about making the tiny stage larger and higher using sheets of wood nailed to pallets I'd nicked from the market, and then balanced them on beer crates. Jon booked the PA and lights for me. I rented some crowd control barrier, but not the stuff you get at gigs these days, it was the kind of barrier that lines the road when the Queen comes to town. It was a bit wobbly so I strengthened it with a scaff bar and wedged it between the two pillars that were either side of the stage. It was really ropey, but health and safety hadn't been invented in those days.

Meanwhile, Carter were getting more and more popular. The tickets were selling well and, for the first time, not just to my mates and old school friends. I actually started to worry we might sell out and have to turn people away. To be honest, I didn't really know what the capacity of the room was, so I guessed at 300 by trying to imagine how many blocks of ten people by ten people I could squeeze in. Definitely the days before health and safety!

I booked my mates, Seven Dead Astronauts, as support. Looking back, there were probably better options, but I was banking on them spreading the word in Stourbridge to help get more people in. Carter sent their rider through, which was a novelty for me. They wanted 36 lagers, 3 orange juices, 3 large waters and 2 bottles of lemonade plus fruit, nuts, yoghurts and enough hot vegetarian food for 7 people. I took this to Andy and he asked me what I thought vegetarians really liked to eat. Somehow lasagne got agreed, and he must've made them an alternative too. I certainly remember that on the day there was enough food to feed three times the amount of people. Carter had been used to the poor hospitality of the usual 'toilet circuit' venues and wolfed the lot! It was good too, because Andy had previously run a restaurant in Gibraltar.

The gig itself was chaotic. We had 250 through the door, which put the makeshift barrier under some strain. Then the scaffold pipe bent. Poor old Mike Parker was in the pit taking photos and had to help some of the Carter crew to hold it up. Then some bikers from the front bar came in to help. Nobody even thought for a minute you could stop a show in those days. Then the stage parted because I'd overlooked how energetic the band are, despite having seen them several times before. I look back in abject horror, but it all seemed perfectly reasonable to me on the night.

When I counted the cash at the end of the night, there was £160 left over. Seeing as I'd already quit my job at this point to carve out a career in the music industry (yeah, I know - a little premature), that was a most welcome result. I needed it too because the next few were destined to lose me money!

JimBob "Carter played Kidderminster Market Tavern three times. I know that because there's a list of all our gigs at the back of my book 'Goodnight Jim Bob'. But it feels like we played there a lot more than that, such is my affectionate memory of the place. I say memory even though it's such a long time ago that I don't remember any detail of our first two gigs there. I do recall everyone being so welcoming and nice to us, and I have a vivid memory of the food they gave us being great. According to my book, the first time we played there was on October 3rd 1990. It was our one hundred and second gig of the year and we must have had a good time because we were back just over three months later. It was February 6th 1991, our second album was about to come out and we were playing some of our favourite and smaller venues that we'd perhaps grown out of.

Typically, I remember more detail of our third gig at the Market Tavern. Probably because it's less of a fond memory. We were thirty gigs away from splitting up. The venue had changed its name to The Cage and the stage was inside one. A cage. We were expected to play inside a cage. Like in the Blues Brothers apparently. I don't think there were many people at the gig and somebody graffitied our tour bus. But sod that. It's my lack of any kind of detailed memory of our first two shows at the Market Tavern that tells me we really loved it there. I have a warm feeling about the place that a name change and a stupid onstage cage couldn't spoil"

CARTER THE UNSTOPPABLE SEX MACHINE - KIDDERMINSTER
MARKET TAVERN - 03.10.1990
1990 was a bit of an epic year for gigs and this would prove to be the fourth top notch one in a row. It was also the year a chap by the name of Badgeman appeared and started putting on gigs at the Market Tavern in Kidderminster. Now instead of a 40 minute journey to gigs, it was only 10. The Market Tavern was as rough as they came, but luckily a seperate bar room and gig room with its own bar, meant we could avoid the regulars most of the time. As you might have guessed from the name the Tavern was the pub for the local cattle market. One of the oddest things about the venue was the sound of cows mooing on the other side of the corridor wall that led to the toilet. Even better was watching newcomers become startled by said cows. Although that meant hanging around outside the toilets, which was just weird.
So The Badgeman had booked Carter to play. Anytime, Anyplace, Anywhere was out and the band were at their peak. This gig was intense and frenetic as tune after tune flew by. We dancedand moshed and went crazy for them. It was the perfect intimate sweaty pub gig.

ONE
The Road To Domestos
Everytime A Churchbell Rings
Twenty Four Minutes From Tulse Hill
An All American National Sport
Sheriff Fatman
The Taking of Peckham 123

MY SIGNED CARTER ALBUM AND A REVIEW IN 'LUNCHTIME FOR THE WILD YOUTH' FANZINE

Matt Woolliscroft "My first trip to Market Tavern was in October 1990. A very memorable night out. It was the first date on Carter USM's 'Anytime, Anyplace, Anywhere' tour and about my 8th time of seeing them live. My then girlfriend, her mate and I were the first people to buy the full set of 3 t-shirts the band had done for the single, for which Jon Beast awarded us some bonus badge sets - which I still have today. We were pretty proud tbh.

The gig was chaos. Carter were really starting to take off regionally at this point and their shows were pretty insane and the never ending flow of stage divers was such that the stage started to come apart mid set, much to the band's alarm - tho the audience didn't really care. Their lighting show at this point was a smoke machine set to 'heavy fog' and a bunch of strobes set to 'stun' which made the whole experience pretty exceptional! That show, outside of London, for me felt like a real momentum in their rise had kicked in, a rise that would see them second on at Reading Festival within the year (and steal the festival from the actual headliners) and headline Glastonbury themselves less than a year after that."

(Matt later promoted Carter for SJM Concerts)

Dave Lane (Seven Dead Astronauts) "The support you gave us for the Carter gig in October 90 was an experience. I mainly remember Jon Beast coming on to introduce Carter saying 'thanks to the support band, nice bunch of lads, shame they were shit'. He was right on both counts."

Ed Steelefox "The Carter USM gig was one of my first ever and my main memory is that everyone started dancing from the off - I lost one shoe in the first song and pogoed on one leg until I found it at the end of their set. Great gig!"

Russell Barker "What a great night. Had so many ace nights at the Tavern"

Daz, Carter USM crew "The Market Tavern! Absolute legend, I remember the gig there, me in the pit with the bikers propping up the makeshift barrier whilst also trying to stop crowd surfers and stage divers."

Andy Price "Mark started off by saying he thought it would be busy, and as the day got nearer, got more and more worried about how many people would actually come. I wasn't worried at all, I have had many busy nights, how busy could it get?

There has only been one other time the Market Tavern had been as busy as that!"

Paul Standen "The barriers caved in due to the millions of people who came."

Richard Brookes "I stole Fruitbat from Carter USM's cycling hat and drew a large spunking Hampton on his shirt."

Mike Parker "I thought I was going to die holding that barrier at the Carter gig and then the stage started to lift because it was only balancing on the beer crates!"

CARTER AT THE TAVERN BY MIKE PARKER

Back in those days I was a young trainee reporter on the Kidderminster Shuttle, the local weekly newspaper. As a trainee you were expected to turn your hand to whatever was thrown at you, which was great training, and as part of that training I was given the entertainments page, which meant you were writing about anything from the Birmingham Royal Ballet to karaoke nights. As I remember it, Mark rang me up to say he was going to be putting on bands at the Market Tavern and would I be able to give them a plug?

The Tavern had a bit of a reputation as a rough pub, although in fairness that description could be applied to most of the pubs in Kidderminster back then. But I said sure, it sounded interesting. My musical tastes back then were honed by growing up in the late 70s/early 80s, so I was into New Wave acts such as The Jam and The Undertones. But in the early 90s anyone with a passing interest in music could see that there was a thing called the indie scene that was really taking off. Up the road from Kidderminster is Stourbridge and the Black Country, where the likes of The Wonder Stuff, Pop Will Eat It Itself and Ned's Atomic Dustbin were attracting serious attention.

Mark was as good as his word, he fed me regularly with biogs of forthcoming acts. I'd be lying if I said I'd even heard of half of them. Most of them sank back into the obscurity from whence they had come, but some did not. Apparently an outfit called Radiohead played there at some point - I missed that particular gig but I gather they went on to do OK.

However there was one act who carved their name into Tavern legend. I remember when I saw the material Mark had give me and wondering if I was going to get the name Carter The Unstoppable Sex Machine past the editor, given some of the more elderly

readers didn't approve of that sort of thing. "Don't worry, you can call them Carter USM. But I think you really need to speak to these two, they're going places", said Mark. So, deal sealed, a telephone chat was arranged with the band ahead of the gig. The contents of said chat are lost to the mists of time I'm afraid, but it would have been along the lines of 'How did you meet', 'Where did you get the name from', all that sort of stuff I'm afraid. NME it wasn't. I spoke to Jim Bob and we actually got on OK. I remember him as chatty, if slightly wary about speaking to a bloody journalist. But he said 'come to the gig, we'll talk beforehand'. So I did. I went straight after work, and there I met him and Fruitbat backstage. My chat with Fruitbat consisted of: "Alright?', to which I got 'Alright mate' and then he walked off. So it was me and Jim Bob. Again, we had a good chat. Sadly I remember little of the gig that night. But I did see them again a couple of times after, notably at The Hummingbird in my native Birmingham. By then they were probably as big as they were going to get and bloody brilliant.

I can't claim any credit for making the Market Tavern what it became. That was down to Mark and his hard work. There was a buzz about the place and that was all down to what they were doing. My part in it came from promoting what was coming up. A lot of local bands were being formed, and I took the view that if they had a gig booked then I'd get them photographed and in the paper ahead of the date. If it gave them that little springboard and first bit of publicity then job done.

The Market Tavern sadly is long gone, but I think it's safe to say for a couple of years there was a real vibe there. I moved on in my career to Birmingham, London and then to Suffolk where I now live but those Kidderminster days were great fun.

# Giant International

From Straight Elephant: Giant International release their second single in January 1991. 'The Beat That Kicks My Head' bursts into life with a riff ripped straight outta Purple Haze and a throbbing bass that pumps the groove into the heart of the song. 'Beat Metal' and Jesus Jones are obvious yardsticks but the Giants don't rely on studio wizardry or gimmicks to deliver the goods. They can do it live too. A recent rave-style gig saw the ravers continue dancing for a full five minutes before they realised the records had ended and the band were on stage.

This song is a cacophony of all things groovy merging a dub-stylee bass with spacey vocals and echoing guitars topped off with funky drumming, Manchester style. Once the guitars thunder back in we're on a magic carpet ride over a vibrant city with Hendrix, Sly and Robbie and the Stones providing the influences and the soundtrack. This is a worthy follow up to 'Do The Right Thing' which was criminally ignored, and should see some serious interest coming the band's way.

Mark Badgeman "I really liked Giant International but they sound a bit dated now, all wah-wah guitar, Ned's drumming, funky grooves, heavy guitars and samples. Very of its time, a 1990 time capsule. You can find a video of The Beat That Kicks My Head on YouTube. They played three times, twice at Stomp discos and once with Cake."

# Helter Skelter & Paintbox

Andrew Wolfman about Paintbox: "When I was at school, I didn't think anyone else really liked music. Sure, some of the bigger boys would moo on about Simple Minds, or Big Country or some other big blokey bagpipe band, but nobody thought to mention that Kidderminster's answer to the Pastels were quietly beavering away on something magical over in tutor group 4MR. The band's debut 7" flexi-disc featuring Dean Morbey's 'Hatebomb' is the single greatest Kidderminster record ever released (number two is probably Physical Graffiti)."

Mark Badgeman "I honestly couldn't remember Helter Skelter so I had to look them up. They released an album called Consume on Island records and they must have been touring in support of this. I paid them £50 and put my mate Ted's band, Paintbox, on as support. I suspect that's how we managed to get 100 people through the door!"

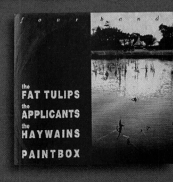

13

# Shark Taboo & Bathchair Suicide

## Wed 7th Nov 1990

Mark Badgeman "I don't know where the obsession with Shark Taboo came from, especially as I don't seem to have any of their four albums. Spiny Dogfish had supported them at the Mermaid in Birmingham in 1987 which must be where I first met them. They were a London based goth band and were the first non-local act I booked for Murdochs, so I'm calling that my first proper gig! At some point, I even made their badges. They must have been an obvious booking for my new venture at the Tavern. Looking back, I should've put more supports on to help get the numbers up, even though this marks the first of many supports by Bathchair Suicide. Midweek wasn't a smart move either. It was a steep learning curve."

Neil from Shark Taboo "Oh I remember the smell! I was also in The Primitives and played lots of the same venues with both bands. The audiences though were different in numbers. Great memories and still got a badge somewhere."

SHARK TABOO AT MURDOCHS IN 1989

Shark Taboo's keyboard player is now the leader of Croydon Council. Guitarist John Triteos was on the front page of the national papers for his charity efforts when he fought a losing battle with leukemia, searching for a donor and encouraging more Greek Cypriots to come forwards.

MALC & ASH IN THE FRONT BAR. NOTE THE FRANK SIDEBOTTOM POSTER

# The Family Cat

Tue 13th Nov 1990
w/Polarbug & The Kilbaines

Wed 6th Feb 1991
supporting Carter USM

Fri 18th Oct 1991
w/Bill Pritchard & Elegy

'The Family Cat - All other bands are dogshite' proclaimed their t-shirts. Highly tipped but never quite making it, perhaps they should have put their record label codes onto a t-shirt - after all FCUK eventually proved popular for French Connection. Their third Tavern show was in support of the 'Colour Me Grey' single whose backing vocalist, one PJ Harvey, eventually achieved the level of success that ultimately eluded The Family Cat.

Simon Holder "We (Spiny Dogfish / Polarbug) supported The Family Cat there, a band we saw several times and bought their records. How exciting!"

John Young (Family Cat tour manager) "Whenever I got the tour dates through, the Market Tavern was always one of the first I'd look for as it was always a highlight... great venue and Mark always looked after us and promoted the show properly... Good times."

Andrew Wolfman "Al from Cake did the most spectacular stagedive to 'Steamroller'. Everybody moved and he was suitably flattened."

THE FAMILY CAT ON STAGE AT THE TAVERN

Andrew Wolfman "For 30 years I was sure that we saw P.J. Harvey with The Family Cat and I've always maintained that she was, "definitely the real reason we went." I have just been shown a picture of me in a bright orange Family Cat t-shirt and learned that the support was a bloke called Bill Pritchard from Lichfield, so don't listen to me."

Polarbug were Spiny Dogfish with a new name and new material. The Murdoch glory days were long gone, but it's worth remembering that in the mid 80's, Spiny Dogfish were chalking up some decent achievements. They had a good set of original material, they were supporting name artists such as The Meteors, their cassingle outsold every other local band in Virgin and they got played on daytime Radio One. Yep! Probably the only band to have a 4-track demo (recorded in a church hall with the drum mic gaffa'ed to a broom handle) played on the Breakfast Show. DJ Mike Smith had requested some material to play on air after reading out a letter insisting Spiny Dogfish were better than Rouen. He played about a minute, adjudged it to be 'overproduced' and then lowered the volume and left it playing in the background whilst he carried on talking. Spiny Dogfish were my stepping stone to becoming a promoter, so it's only right I gave them one of the first available supports. Still gutted I missed their 25th anniversary reunion show."

SPINY DOGFISH

Beached at Last
6 TRACK CASSINGLE

POLARBUG SUPPORTING THE FAMILY CAT IN FRONT OF THE TERRIBLE TAVERN CURTAINS!

ABOVE: THE FAMILY CAT AND POLARBUG IN THE CAFE / DRESSING ROOM

Craig Lewis (Spiny Dogfish) "I have fond memories of a venue that gave my home town/area somewhere credible that new and old bands could play as part of their national tours. Best memories include when the rebranded Spiny Dogfish, Polarbug, supported The Family Cat, Carter (the second gig) and the first all dayer (eating chips on Comberton Hill). The other great thing was the Friday night gigs Top, Scorpio Rising and The Primitives to name a few. This was a throwback to our Friday visits to JB's in the mid/late 80's."

# LUNCHTIME FOR THE WILD YOUTH

Before I'd thought of writing this book, Russell Barker was already retrospectively reviewing the shows he'd seen in his youth and publishing them in a fanzine called Lunchtime For The Wild Youth. Quite a few are reproduced throughout the book. They're available to buy on Bandcamp at https://lunchtimeforthewildyouth.bandcamp.com/

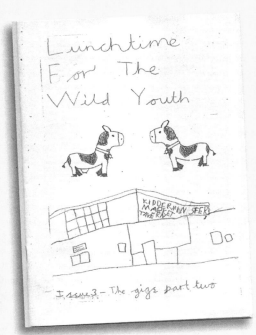

Issue 3 - The gigs part two

**What prompted you to start a fanzine that reviews gigs from 30 years ago?**
I'd been reading a lot of fanzines and enjoyed the anecdotal way of writing about music, rather than the sometimes dry, analytical way you get in the press. Eventually it came to me to look back to the fanzines I loved in the 80s, but also the music from those times and onwards too.
It followed from this that it should be devoid of modern technology, so it's a proper cut 'n' paste affair. The first issue was actually about albums from the 80s that I hadn't heard for ages. Then I found my gig book, where I keep all my tickets and had the idea of seeing what I could remember about them. Sometimes it's odd things, seemingly irrelevant to the gig, sometimes it's loads, sometimes nothing at all!

My daughter drew the first cover, so she then came on board to do the illustrations.

**How has it been received?**
It's not been an overnight success! We've been doing it for almost 4 years now and it sells but a handful of copies. The thing that is nice is that the people who buy it absolutely love it. I've made some good friends through doing it. It's good fun to make too. It probably would sell more if I spammed social media, but I can't be bothered with that. I give a lot away, Billy Bragg has copies too.

**What was your favourite gig at the Tavern?**
Probably the Carter ones, for differing reasons obviously! So many great nights there though.

**What do you think made the Tavern so unique?**
It was my first experience of something so small. I had been to gigs in Birmingham before, but probably nothing smaller than the Powerhouse. So it was great, up close and personal with the bands. I'm from Bewdley, so all of a sudden there are all these great bands playing a few minutes down the road. It was such perfect timing too, just what we wanted and at a time when so many cool bands were on the road.
The cows too, they certainly made it unique.

**Favourite gig of all time?**
So many great gigs I could pick, for different reasons, so here's a few:
My first gig - The Cult at the Odeon, 1985 (so this is what it's all about)
First big road trip (with someone I barely knew) to a gig - The Stone Roses, Spike Island, 1990
First big road trip (on my own) to a gig - The Cure, Crystal Palace Bowl, 1990
The most fun - The Lemonheads - Sydney University, 1994
The most intense gig ever - 60ft Dolls - Flapper & Firkin, Brmingham, 1996
Taking my parents to a gig - The Divine Comedy - Birmingham Irish Centre, 2001
Dancing onstage dressed as a kangaroo - The Flaming Lips - Birmingham Academy, 2003
Putting on the Wombats (supporting I, Ludicrous) in a pub - Oxford Port Mahon, 2006
Putting on a gig for one of my heroes - Robert Forster - Quaker Meeting House, Oxford, 2015

I could go on, but...

**Are you still regularly going to gigs?**
Yep. I also started promoting again last year, doing all ages matinee gigs.
In recent months before lockdown I'd seen Peaness, Fresh, The Divine Comedy, Pip Blom and some great local acts like Lucy Leave, Pandapopalyse and Max Blansjaar.

**ELEGY**
Side A:
Why Don't You Notice Me
Anymore?
© ELEGY, 1990.

Produced by John Harris and Elegy
The Fishy Smell Record Company
Catalogue Number: COD1

**Which town were you based in?**
We had members in Malvern and Worcester and regularly played in both

**What years were you active?**
1988 - 1992

**Who was in the band?**
When we played we were a three piece – Ben Willmott (guitar / vocals), Craig Wood (bass) and Tony Lee (drums). Prior to that we had a keyboard player called Mark Edwards.

**What kind of music did you play?**
Guitar-driven indie rock with a hint of psychedelia.

**Who were the influences?**
Pixies, Wedding Present, New Order, Joy Division, Wonderstuff, Cardiacs, Pink Floyd

**What level of success did you achieve?**
We played a lot around the Worcestershire and Herefordshire areas, and occasionally further afield, such as Birmingham and Manchester. We supported The Family Cat, Senseless Things and Bleach – who were John Peel favourites at the time – at the Market Tavern and supported The Bible in Worcester, but probably our biggest success was at a festival in Worcester High Street where local tramp and street celebrity chicken George gave us the thumbs up by dancing to us. He totally upstaged us but nevertheless it was praise indeed. We took a coachload of mates up to Manchester and played Isadora's nightclub, which was more notable for the fact that MC Tunes was in attendance than anything we did! We also released a 7" single 'Why Don't You Notice Me Anymore? / It's Not Enough' and had a neat line in t-shirts. But everyone did in those days.

**What do you remember about playing at the Tavern?**
I don't think you could ever visit a venue with a bigger disparity between its exterior – drab polytechnic concrete – and a truly magical interior which sparkled with lights, backdrop and interesting people from all the local sub-genre tribes to match. You didn't have to walk far from the main room to be reminded that this was still a fully functioning cattle market – not a metaphor, it really was one!

**Any memories of the other bands you played with at the Tavern?**
We weren't involved except as audience members, but seeing Pop Will Eat Itself coming down to DJ on one occasion. They were the biggest band in the Midlands at the time and a huge influence on music in the long term. Can't remember what they played – Motorhead and hip-hop possibly? - but they were great.

**How did the band end?**
Tragically, heroically, drunkenly.

**Did anyone go on to further success or have a career in the music industry?**
Ben Willmott and Tony Lee went on to be two thirds of Slang (with Ben Crosland being the third third), and remixed Aphex Twin, Mike Flowers Pops and Stereolab and released records on Lo, Sprawl, Spiky, !K7 and others. Craig Wood plays to this day with the mighty Stuntdog. Ben Willmott went on to be a music writer for NME and many others, Tony Lee worked for many years with HMV.

**What else do we need to know about the band?**
There was a riot after one of our shows at the Malvern Winter Gardens that got bands banned from the venue to this day.

# Dr Phibes & The House of Wax Equations

Wed 21st Nov 1990
(support unknown)

Fri 21st May 1993
w/Tomorrows Joy

Mark Badgeman "For the Carter gig, I'd used a very good PA from Worcester. But it was expensive (actually, it wasn't in reality - I just thought it was at the time!) so I'd located a cheaper one. However, for the first Dr Phibes gig, I had the bright idea of just using a very, very cheap vocal PA on dry hire. With no engineer. Did I say somewhere it was a steep learning curve?

So, there I am, sat on the door with an ice cream tub full of pound coins, the band are busy playing their set, when the unmistakable whine of feedback started crescendoing through the PA. What do I do? I'm on my own, I can't let go of the ice cream tub, or someone will nick the meagre door money, and the 12 channel basic mixing desk is about 15 feet away at the side of the stage. So I just ran over, pulled the faders down and pushed them back up to slightly below where they were and ran back. That'll do, eh?

I don't think the band were overly impressed at this early attempt at production managing. As a financial business decision, I justified it to myself because only 45 people paid to get in and the band had cost me £150, putting me £80 out of pocket. They didn't hold a grudge over the vocal PA fiasco because they came back when they were bigger. Or maybe they just felt guilty at overcharging me! The second gig sold 134, making £33.70 profit, so it still didn't balance.

I don't fancy a 3rd attempt to balance the books as the singer killed his mother with an axe and was only recently released from jail. Nice! Maybe I got off lightly?"

## Doc's spacerockin'

Funky psychedelic spacerock is the description which best matches the highly promising three piece Dr Phibes and the House of Wax Equations.

Formed five years ago after meeting at college, Dr Phibes have built up a very solid following on the Indie circuit, which culminated in an appear-ance at last year's Glastonbury Festival.

Their music incorporates blues, metal, ambience and funk and has also made the band big favourites in France.

Dr Phibes will be appearing at Kidderminster's Market Tav-ern tomorrow (Friday May 21), Admission is £3.50.

### DR PHIBES AND THE HOUSE OF WAX EQUATIONS
#### Kidderminster Market Tavern

By the time you read this you should know who the band are. They will be the new name on the cover of every music paper. God knows I've tried to pigeon-hole them, but to no avail. Imagine the Jimi Hendrix Experience on 'E' jamming through some out-takes from Faith No More's latest. Throw in a couple of Chilli Peppers, add a dash of Pink Floyd and slowly bring to the boil.

"Lucifer Sam" is an embracing swirl that quickly stabs you in the guts given half a chance. Guitarist/Vocalist Howard King bellows each line from that cavernous mouth of his and you think that the mic will surely be swallowed up. When he rolls his eyes, head to one side, the man is genuinely scary!

From the precision drumming, through the thundering, funking bass, to that wild guitar, Dr Phibes are a marvellously mesmeric event. Their new EP, recorded "live in the studio" and featuring "Sugarblast" and "Marshmallow Madness" is a stunning debut but merely a foretaste of what the band are surely capable of creating in the months to come : good, good, good, good Phibrations......
By Dave Hingley.

## DR. PHIBES AND THE HOUSE OF WAX EQUATIONS
### DEADPAN CONTROL FREAK

DEADPAN CONTROL FREAK (Club Mix)
DEADPAN CONTROL FREAK (Dr Dub's Ambient Phibes Mix)
DEADPAN CONTROL FREAK (Dub Haze)
Remix and additional production : SIMON POSFORD FOR BUTTERFLY
DEADPAN CONTROL FREAK (Part 1)
Remix and additional production : THRASH

DR PHIBES and THE HOUSE OF WAX EQUATIONS

DEADPAN CONTROL FREAK

## DR. PHIBES AND THE HOUSE OF WAX EQUATIONS

+ support

# Friday 21st May
## MARKET TAVERN
### KIDDERMINSTER
£3.50
7.30 -

Danyul Organ "Got to be one of the most memorable gigs for me." (1993)

Andrew Wolfman "The Dr Phibes story is as depressing as it is distressing. Their live show was anything but, a heady, high-octane, joyful occasion."

Johnny Vinyl "Acid/Trance and techno seeped into the scene and Dr Phibes and the House of Wax Equations, nailed it. New sounds Deadpan Control Freak got played by me at sooo many house parties. 12"... bought at the gig Ah... the merch table. I still have the 12" but the memory of the gig is long gone."

# Snuff + Sink + Psychedelia Smith

## Wed 28th Nov 1990

### SNUFF
#### Kidderminster Market Tavern

It's ten o'clock as Snuff take the stage, and the atmosphere has nearly reached fever pitch. There are no set lists - Snuff make it up as they go along, inviting requests which include a 400 mph dash through "Rockin' All Over The World"!

Their brilliantly brainless pop thrash confusion (complete with lead-singing drummer) sees the crowd whipped into a snarling frenzy. Several tracks from the "Snuffsaid.." album are present and are even more manic than their vinyl versions. The undoubted climax to the set - a frantic version of "I Think We're Alone Now" is the perfect example of what Snuff are all about - brutal bubblegum pop that manages to bite your hand off while resting it's head in your lap.

Tonight, Snuff are at their screaming, snarling best - hurtling through a vicious set with the energy of a rabid rottweiler, and for once, no-one minds being savaged.

By Helen.

SNUFF - KIDDERMINSTER MARKET TAVERN - 28.11.1990
Ah, Snuff. What a wonderful, hilarious, frenetic, exciting band. Sometimes you just need a band like this, who have an inate sense of fun. Obviously I would have been drawn to the band through their wonderful cover versions, which they were quite adept at. The Snuff Said album showed they had more to them than this, inculding the fantastic original, Not Listening, but as an immature twenty year old, I wanted to hear stuff from the Flibbiddydibbiddy-dob 11 track covers EP. It was a tremendous sweaty gig, with songs flying past in a blur. Sink and the wonderfully named Psychedelia Smith had opened the night but I don't recall them.

SNUFF
+
SINK
+
PSYCHEDELIA SMITH
MARKET TAVERN
Comberton Hill Kidderminster
wednesday
NOV 28th ONLY £2.50

Snuff came to prominence following their 1988 Peel Session so they were well established by the time the played the Tavern, pulling 150 midweek punters. Reviews from Straight Elephant and Lunchtime For The Wild Youth. Another hand drawn poster!

Fri 23rd Nov 1990
w/Swamp Donkeys

Fri 24th May 1991

Fri 13th Mar 1992
w/Real Simon Pure
& The Flimmers

Originally International Resque, they shortened the name after their first Tavern gig. The Straight Elephant article is all you need - they were the eternal Carter USM support act. You'll easily find them online to have a listen. Drummer, Wez, actually joined Carter USM in 1994 and they became a trio until 1996 when they filled out to a 6 piece, including Wez's brother.

# RESQUE

Things are looking up for Reading's biggest Beatles enthusiasts, Resque. They are about to release their debut album "Life's A Bonus" on Musidisc, and they are tour support on the first half of the Carter USM tour. This will be the third time they've toured with Carter, and should be the one that breaks them in this country.(They spent most of the summer touring with them in Europe, camping out because they couldn't afford guest-houses).

Since forming many moons ago, the band have released three cracking singles (Yeah, So Way Down,She Drives My Train) gigged/partied remorselessly and taken their clothes off at every opportunity. Incredibly they now have over 1100 names on their mailing list, so it costs a small fortune each time they send out a newsletter.

Guitarist Mark's parents run the mailing list, and even make it to some of their gigs. They were a bit shocked however at Jon Beast's antics at a recent Carter show. "Yeah, we're thinking of sending Mole (roadie/t-shirt seller/PR person) on stage before we go on. People can shout "You little cunt!" instead of "You fat bastard!" But don't print that - my mum doesn't know I swear!" (VERY ROCK'N'ROLL - ED)

Despite the number of gigs Resque play they've had a dismal amount of press attention, blaming this on their lack of a press plugger. This should change after the Carter tour, and they plan to release a new single before Christmas. "It'll be new material - not anything from the album. We don't want to rip off The Kids! We're writing new songs, so I'll have to buy a new Chord-A-Day book!"

Hailing from the festival town of Reading you'd think that they'd have lots of groovy places to go to when they're back home, but not so. "The best place is your own house. There's one place called "Cartoons" that's full of builders on drugs. Reading's full of builders on drugs.If you look in the least alternative and want to go somewhere where people shout "Oi! Girl!" then Cartoons is the place for you. The best thing to do in Reading is stay in with loads of booze and drugs and keep away from buiders."

Resque will be out touring and avoiding builders for the rest of the year, so get Resqued at a venue near you.

# Joolz & Rev Hammer

Mark Badgeman "In an earlier attempt at bringing some decent acts to Kidderminster, I'd tipped off Joolz about the Riverboat in Kiddy. I was a bit miffed when they went direct to the venue themselves in 1989 and did a Red Sky Coven gig with Slade The Leveller from New Model Army, but I still bought a ticket for it. It wasn't sold out which should have told me something.

The Tavern gig was minus Slade The Leveller, thereby reducing the appeal, but you were always guaranteed a hardcore of the clog-wearing NMA kit bag brigade would turn up. That included some of my mates at the time, so I thought I'd be ok.

The biggest problem was that Andy Price had previous with Rev and he was banned from the pub. I had to convince Andy to lift the ban, telling him that he'd bring people through the door. Unfortunately, not enough of them and I lost £150 on this one.

Rev doesn't remember any of this and didn't remember being banned. Joolz couldn't remember it either!"

Joolz is a poet and Rev is a folk musician. They still play Red Sky Coven gigs with Justin from New Model Army

Helen Hipkiss "Joolz's opening line was something like 'I've never played a gig where the toilets are labelled Ladies, Gents, Cattle!' Classic"

Andy Price "I hardly ever banned anyone because my rule was a ban was permanent. I've seen pubs where being banned was a challenge to see how long you could get. It was normally over money or drugs. Rev owed me for a room hire."

THE OLD SIGN

THE BACK DOOR

# The Telescopes & Slowdive

Matthew Kettle "I did the sound at this gig for The Telescopes. It was very early in my career. I'd become mates with some members of Bark Psychosis when I was in college and done some bits of (somewhat dodgy) recording with them. They'd invited me to a party where I met Nick & Vinita who ran their label but also managed The Telescopes. The band were looking for someone to do sound on their tour, so somehow I was put into the picture. I had some familiarity with sound gear, but totally new to live gigs... so I figured it out as I went along.

They were lovely people and I couldn't have hoped for a better bunch of people to start down this path with. They were also very influential in my early musical taste. I used to stay over at Stephen & Jo's house all the time, and we'd sit around listening to obscure underground records for hours and hours. It was a great education!"

Badgeman "I feel me and Matt started out at roughly the same time and we're both still in the industry. Matt's won a Grammy and now mixes sound for acts such as Artic Monkeys, Niall Horan and Mark Ronson."

Wikipedia calls The Telescopes an English noise, space rock, dream pop and psychedelic band. The Music press tagged them 'shoegazers'. Slowdive were also part of the 'scene that celebrates itself' and had just released their first single.

1. NEW SONG
2. CATCH THE BREEZE
3. BEACHSONG
4. SLOWDIVE
5. DOLLY
6. SHE CALLS

Christian

Rachel

SLOWDIVE'S SETLIST FROM THE TAVERN GIG

SLOWDIVE SUPPORTING THE TELESCOPES IN FRONT OF THE TERRIBLE CURTAINS
PHOTO BY KATHERINE GREAVES

FUN PALACE PRESENT
The Telescopes
+ SLOWDIVE
MARKET TAVERN
DEC 1st £3.00 Adv

Andrew Wolfman "Just after they played their hit 'The Perfect Needle' the singer from The Telescopes attempted to kick Al from Cake in the face. Alan requested that the fragile noise-rockers 'Play some fooking Abba!' until their Lou-Reedy singer took a punt. Less 'To Kill a Slow Girl Walking' more 'kick a big lad talking'. He had really long pointy boots on, so he didn't have to swing that far."

"Our good friend David Stanton enjoyed Slowdive's glorious pedal-hopping performance so much that he would, forever more, be called SlowDave."

Sue Gardner "I was so excited about this gig, and just enraptured by the whole thing. It's a very hazy memory, but what a gig. Amazing!! I was weirded out by the fact that one of my all time fave bands was playing 3 miles away from where I lived. (Nearest gigs were usually 20 miles away in Brum.)"

Andrew Wolfman "James from Cake spent three hours trying to convince Rachel Goswell's Mum, that he should be allowed round to cook Sunday Lunch."

James Mitchell (Cake) "I remember nothing (about inviting himself around to Rachel from Slowdive's Mum's house to cook dinner) except cheap Red Stripe."

Sand Palmer "I asked Andy if I could have my wedding thing there... He said no as didn't believe in marriage... So booked Murdochs... had a wicked night. Andy turns up later with loads of beer as Tavern was dead lol xxx"

Paul Fielding "KIDS DON'T DO DRUGS... But saying that I remember doing my first ever acid tab as an 18 year old at The Market Tavern during a gig... Can't remember the band but the tab was £2.50 and was a White Lightning....

Great days. (strictly straight and responsible now)"

# TAVERN MEMORIES

Dr Marc Price "I saw a number of local bands at the Tavern, including Salem's Lot, Omnia Opera, Wayward Angel, etc. I even played there (with The Christmas Trees - Big Willy and the Dobber didn't make it). I played bass with Salem's Lot briefly, they fired me shortly before the Tavern gig. I don't blame them, I can't play. I also saw Neds Atomic Dustbin at the Tavern, but sadly missed Carter USM."

Mark Badgeman "Andy used to do these legendary ploughmans lunches where you'd get enough cheese to last a week. They must have been a loss leader! A good chunk of bread and some pickle. Loved those!"

Gary O'Dea (Love Hounds) "We played in 1990, one of our last gigs... I remember we robbed the fridge... so I'll probably owe somebody a bag of frozen veg, some beers and a tub of ice cream... times were hard in the rock n roll world then!"

Debbie Jones "We met Badgeman and Mike Parker at the first Carter gig there. Then Alison convinced them to let us do some nights. I feel like it was more like an Indie disco than a gig & think we only did it for a few weekends. Definitely played Soup Dragons & Stone Roses. Can't remember much more!"

# Frank Sidebottom + Bathchair Suicide

## Thu 6th Dec 1990

**FRANK SIDEBOTTOM**

Frank had been around since the mid-80's and had done lots of TV and radio. He later had his own ITV show in 1992. Although this gig has since become a Tavern legend, there were only 127 people there and his fee had to be hastily re-negotiated on the night to avoid bankrupting Badgeman.

Steve Cooper "Somebody got on stage and tried to remove his papier mache head. It passed without a result and Frank took it very well."

Ian Passey "Someone tried to pull Frank's head off at one point during the gig. Is anyone going to own up..?"

The Head Barman "I was serving pints that day. This guy came in hours before the gig and sat on his own. I hassled him for two hours accusing him of being Frank. Really gave him a hard time. It wasn't him."

Andrew Wolfman "Stan the Sound Man had a hard time getting Frank Sidebottom to soundcheck.
"What sort of set up do you want mate?" He asked.
Chris Sievey, Frank's comic creator, ignored him, "Dunno, you'd have to ask Frank."
Stan was riled (Stan was usually riled) but persisted, "Do you need a mic stand, or what?"
"I'm sorry, I don't know. You'd have to ask Frank".
"I am asking Frank," he fumed. "What do you want in the monitors?" Sievey shrugged and Stan stropped off to the bar. He returned an hour later gruffly threatening to pack his rig up and go home, when in walked Frank Sidebottom, as seen on TV.
"Hiya Stan," he trilled nasally, thumbs aloft, "I don't need anything fancy thanks, I've got a microphone in me' head." You know he did.
He really did."

Jonny Stancill "I can only say that I didn't get him and I never will... however it didn't stop one of the most famous actors on the planet playing him in Frank"

Roy Davies "I recall Frank Sidebottom was an Altrincham FC fan...they were (still are) rivals to the Harriers!!"

Jon Pardoe "I very much was looking forward to the Frank Sidebottom gig at the Tavern, having seen him on Match of the Day (in his very big shorts).

My recollection of events is a little hazy, as it is of 1990 in general, however I do recall that he opened with 'Guess Who's Been On Match of the Day' and that I was very much enjoying the whole affair.

What I wasn't expecting however was a mid-gig pitch invasion. It was particularly unexpected as it came in the form of the little brother of an ex-girlfriend, now in full-on Jim Morrison mode with wild beard and, what I since learned, was a lysergically-altered point of view. I could only imagine that he had somehow taken umbrage to Frank's papier-mache bonce in a similar manner to Iggy when Elton John joined him on stage in a gorilla suit.

I don't really remember how the issue was resolved, but I do know that Frank's privacy remained intact somehow and the rest of the gig proceeded without incident, and to much hilarity. Little Frank's head remained undisturbed throughout.

22 years later I found myself at a christening with Chris Sievey's (Frank's alter-ego) daughter, who it turns out is one of my mate's sister's best friends. Thankfully I chose not to mention the incident to her.

The protagonist of the head-removal attempt now lives at the bottom of my road and we are still in touch. Ivan is a lovely fella so I won't name and shame him here. Oh, wait..."

# Senseless Things + Elegy Genius Freak

Fri 1st Feb 1991

HELLEN'S SIGNED 7"

Mark Badgeman "The phone rang. 'Is this the venue with the nice food? We've heard about it from Carter. We'd like to play.' And that's how I got to book Senseless Things. For me, it was this one that opened the floodgate and started the trend of agents calling me instead of me pestering them. I'd seen Senseless Things loads of times so I knew I'd do ok. Final score on the door was 205 tickets.

Senseless Things were part of the scene that included Carter USM, Mega City 4 and Snuff. Their poppy punk sound scored them a couple of Top 20 hits in 1992 and appearances on Top Of The Pops.

Andrew Wolfman "As one of the Pop Kids they shouted about on their shirts, I had no idea who The Replacements or The Only Ones were until I heard Senseless Things. I will always be grateful to them for pushing me in the right direction. 'Too Much Kissing' is a perfect song."

Hellen Nim "It was within the sweaty walls of the Market Tavern that my love for the Senseless Things was born: their perfectly chaotic pop punk melodies... and the (then) angel face of singer Mark Keds. I can feel my teenage hormones moshing even now!"

Kev Wheeler "They were one of my favourite bands of the time along with Carter USM, I bought all their EPs and albums. Not sure if I still have a T-shirt around, as I wore them pretty much constantly and they ended up threadbare."

*By Tim Allen*

**Which town were you based in?** Stourbridge

**What years were you active?** 1988 to 1993/4 ish

**Who was in the band?**
Tim Allen vocals/guitar
Tim Bailey drums
Tim Hogg bass
Stuart Wilson guitar

**What kind of music did you play?**
According to our interview in Raw magazine "It is a fusion of funk- rock with chundering grebo-style bass and a subtle blend of psychedelic overtones and melodic swirlings" but we were probably taking the piss. The reality was that I started off wanting to be a mix of The Cure and early Bunnymen with the rest of the band making it more early 90s contemporary. We did a pretty damn good white noise shoegaze wall of sound. Thanks hearing loss.

**Who were the influences?**
Cure, Bunnymen, Ride, Slowdive, My Bloody Valentine, Wedding Present, Smiths, Velvet Underground, Bowie, Beatles, Stones

**What level of success did you achieve?**
Nothing too spectacular. Played loads locally and Manchester where Tim B was at uni. Made it to the rounds of the Our Price 'Hit The Right Note' competition with a gig at the Marquee. Released The Ress E.P. the title was influenced/play on Ned's Ingredients EP. I think the biggest support other than Frank Sidebottom was Every New Dead Ghost at The Barrel Organ in Digbeth. They were another proper goth band. We seemed to play a lot with Ambelian, I guess we had a similar vibe.

**What do you remember about playing at the Tavern?**
Playing at the Tavern was always ace, a really good atmosphere and people were really into music in a big way. There was quite a scene going on in Stourbridge at the time and lots of rivalries probably. We all used to drink in The Swan and The Mitre and would regularly make the journey to the Tavern.

**Any memories of the other bands you saw at the Tavern?**
I remember seeing Radiohead possibly pre-Pablo Honey. The Bunnymen, minus Mac and got to go backstage to chat with Will Sargent who was my guitar hero. And obviously Frank Sidebottom nearly getting decapitated. I think I might have been at Carter. Didn't their tape machine fuck up?

**How did the band end?**
The band kind of fizzled out in the end. People wanted different things musically. Once Stu decided to leave we carried on for a bit but it was never really the same and we lost momentum and enthusiasm with lack of real progress or interest and then real life called with proper jobs. Plus my flanger ran out of batteries.

**Did anyone go on to further success or have a career in the music industry?**
No one has gone on to do anything else as far as I am aware. I lost touch with the other Tims. I didn't do anything again musically until a few years ago I got my guitar out the loft and have started writing and recording again. I have since produced 3 solo albums, the latest Dark Days Are Here is on Bandcamp with two others on Soundcloud.

Andrew Wolfman "After playing The Market Tavern almost hourly, Bathchair Suicide recorded an enigmatic EP that changes hands for big bucks online, and promptly disappeared off the face of the internet. The most mysterious of local acts, the hunt for the band's three Tims would have made a decent documentary: a patchouli-tinged Searching for Sugarman.

I like to think that somewhere under the newbuild flats where the Tavern used to stand, Bathchair are still playing, impervious to change and oblivious to the fact that there hasn't been an audience in for thirty years because of the hurricane of dry ice they've got coming off stage."

# CARTER

## ■ THE UNSTOPPABLE SEX MACHINE ■

**30**

WED 6TH FEB 1991
W/ The Family Cat
& Pop Am Good
The legendary one!

# SOMETHING

## MARKET TAVERN - 6th FEB

## TICKETS HERE

**LP CD**

**CASS**

**OUT**

**NOW**

6/2 KIDDERMINSTER Market Tavern ■ 7/2 EXETER University
8/2 TAUNTON The Priory ■ 9/2 BRIGHTON Sussex University
10/2 PORTSMOUTH Sth Pararde Pier ■ 12/2 AYLESBURY Civic Centre
13/2 BRISTOL Bierkeller ■ 14/2 London U.L.U.
15/2 NORWICH Waterfront ■ 16/2 IPSWICH Caribbean Assoc
18/2 BIRMINGHAM Goldwins ■ 19/2 Teeside Polytechnic
22/2 LANCASTER University ■ 23/2 BOLTON Inst Higher Education
24/2 HUDDERSFIELD Polytechnic ■ 28/2 BRADFORD Queens Hall
1/3 SHEFFIELD University ■ 3/3 NOTTINGHAM Polytechnic
5/3 HULL The Tower ■ 6/3 MANCHESTER U.M.I.S.T.
7/3 LEICESTER Polytechnic ■ 9/3 READING University
11/3 CHELTENHAM Shaftesbury Hall ■ 12/3 CAMBRIDGE Junction
13/3 SLOUGH COLLEGE ■ 14/3 COVENTRY Tic Toc

Mike Moore "2nd Carter USM gig - heavily oversold(!), I was DJing, ended up watching the gig from behind the bar helping myself liberally to the optics."

Andy Taylor "Seem to recall Jimbob telling the audience that it had been a shit day."

Paul Standen "It's funny how quickly it all descended into kids chanting, Carter need a drummer la-la-la-laa and then fuck off back to London la-la-la-laaa."

"EPIC!!!"
Mervyn Weaver

Matt Woolliscroft "This gig shows how the Market Tavern really was setting the pace for bands in those days."

Lindsay Smith "I remember seeing Carter there a few times - we were in 6th form and someone had a tape of their album '101 Damnations' which got copied and passed around. Couldn't believe they were actually coming to Kidderminster - I heard that they loved Andy's veggie lasagne so kept coming back."

"Helen Smith "I remember the night the tapes broke. That was funny, yet I really liked how they sounded that night. I remember my feet sticking to the floor and loving what I was hearing. I felt that everytime I went to the Market Tavern."

Fruitbat "The second time we played the Market Tavern was so full and raucous that the condensation from all of the excitement caused three of our tape machines to break down. The cassette player that we had brought along in case of absolute emergencies was our last resort and the only cassette tape we had with us had songs on that we hadn't played for ages. Then the cassette machine broke down and for the first time ever we heard the crowd chanting 'Carter need a drummer, Carter need a drummer'. I still remember that gig with great fondness :) "

I can't tell you how thrilled I was when Carter said they wanted to come back! They were clearly too big for the Tavern as most of the other dates were on the university circuit. This was to promote their second album and we were the opening night. Things had changed a bit and the crew arrived ahead of the band and spent the afternoon setting up a stage set of old televisions that most of the audience had no chance of seeing.

The band missed the soundcheck because they hadn't left London on time. Normally, the crew would do it but the backing tapes were in the car with the band. I was conscious of getting the doors open on time because we were sold out. SOLD OUT! My first sell out (I might have accidentally let 335 in). So we couldn't wait for the band to arrive and test the tapes.

When they finally turned up, it was packed and it was almost time for them to go straight on stage. The gig was in February, so it was cold outside but my word it was hot inside! And that's where the problems started. That's what caused the condensation on the DAT tapes. They simply wouldn't play.

Carter just stood there, on stage, isolated, whilst the good natured crowd chanted at them. It was so funny! They tried a couple of songs without the tapes and to be honest, they were great. Meanwhile, at the mixing desk, they'd tried the cassette version of the backing tracks but the machine chewed the tape. Then, as I recall, the DAT fast forwarded to the encore so they played that. Then it died forever!

I remember Jim lying on the sofa in the dressing room afterwards, worried the audience were going to kill them or at least want their money back. Nope! It was one of the best gigs anyone had ever seen. What's a gig if it's not a shared experience? This was brilliant. Not one person complained!

LUNCHTIME FOR THE WILD YOUTH FANZINE

THE FIRST TAVERN AD OF THE ANDY PRICE ERA. FROM STRAIGHT ELEPHANT

The stage had been turned into a permanent fixture after the success of the first Carter gig, albeit with the drum riser built in so you couldn't move it. We took the cladding off the two pillars that flanked the stage only to find they were hiding twin concrete-encased storm drains for the flat roof. They looked terrible so we paid a local graffiti artist to paint them. I also took him into town and wallpapered the flyposting rotundas with lining paper and got him to spray paint a giant Tavern ad. A copper came over and this lad already had a conviction for graffiti so he was a bit worried. I asked the copper if he knew flyposting was permitted there and he did. So what's the difference if I have this spray painted on the floor and then pasted up versus doing it in situ? Obviously he had no answer and trotted off, leaving us with a massive spray-painted what's on ad on the rotunda!

# Enter Soundman: Stan The PA Man

Stan "If you ask anybody who ever went to the Market Tavern for their most vivid memory, then it would be of shit! Cow shit to be precise as the pub was primarily there to service the cattle market. There was a corridor which linked the market to the pub, which on a good day with a run up, you could skid the full length of - like some kind of perverse water slide! The market and pub may now be gone but the smell will be etched on my memory until my dying day.

I was employed to supply PA for Mark's cheaper shows initially. He did have a much more professional company who did his bigger gigs but when he wanted to save a few bob, he called us. But as time went on we became more involved with all sorts of things to do with the venue. If you were a band with a name you got to use the nice cafe room as your dressing room, but if you were the support or one of the local artists you got changed in the kitchen! The kitchen/dressing room would be furnished with whatever we could find in the skip at the general auctions at the end of the road. Many a night, Mark and myself, aided and abetted by 'Diesel' Dave Watkins and Alan 'Doof' McCann, could be found hauling old sofas over the gate.

We would also spend many afternoons re-fitting ceiling tiles above the stage as it was very low and it was a regular event for bands to throw their mic stands or guitars in the air and get showered with, in hindsight, what I suspect was asbestos.

One time the newly fitted CO2 fire extinguisher fell off the wall and went off all over the mixing desk, leaving me looking like I was at a of Sisters of Mercy show.

The front of stage barrier was some old pedestrian barrier and on bigger shows was manned by whoever was not doing anything else. I remember one occasion where a kid came over and got his leg stuck in it, a tug of war ensued where we pulled him one way, trying to free him, while his mates pulled the other way, trying to pull him back into the crowd, all the time with him screaming that we were breaking his leg, and I'm not entirely sure how we didn't.

Many local bands that played bought their own radio mics, which I remember with particular amusement, as there was a taxi office on Comberton Hill and it would be a regular feature of band's sets to suddenly get taxi conversations coming through the PA, causing much hilarity to all.

Another thing that sticks in my mind is the drummer who built his own kit. I forget which band it was, but when they were playing their big local show and he decided it would be good to build his own frame for his drum kit. Rather than use the lightweight tubular steel that racks are made of, he chose thick box section steel, which made it incredibly heavy. This was not the main issue though. The stage of the Tavern had a 9 inch high drum riser and, much to the annoyance of many a stage manager, it was screwed to the rest of the stage. This meant if you built a drum rack 7 feet wide and tried to put it on a 6ft 6" riser, you had a problem. Finally, after much messing about and a couple of house bricks, the kit was in place. This sticks in my mind, not because it was a complete pain to deal with, but mainly because the drummer was, when it came to the big solo, so bloody awful."

Mike Moore "I remember 'Car Blackwell' 'Five 6s' coming over the PA all night"

David Watkins "Stan testing the PA with 'Enter Sandman'. Every. Single. Time."

John Dennehy
"Pop Am Good originally started out as just me and Dermot in Bow, East London in 1989. We didn't have a drummer at the beginning. We'd been writing songs and making demos on a four-track Fostex using a drum machine and, although we had originally intended getting a drummer, we just wanted to start playing gigs as soon as possible and so we just decided to use the drum machine live as well.

At first, we just played around London. We'd play anywhere. After one gig this guy called Steve, who Dermot knew, came up to us and said he really liked us and wanted to join us on drums. We were happy with the drum machine at that stage but he kept turning up to our gigs and asking.

Because he played standing up, we thought it would look pretty cool with the three of us in a line at the front of the stage so in the end, we gave it a go and that's how we became a three-piece.

Lots of the venues in London at that time were 'pay to play' where the band would actually have to pay for the 'privilege' of playing. We refused to go down that route so we were always looking for venues to play where we didn't have to pay... We even moved into a pub called the Bird in Hand in Bow on the Mile End Road after it closed down. The beer pumps were still working so we bought loads of barrels of beer from the brewery and played gigs in the basement and sold pints at cost price.

Right from the start we did EVERYTHING ourselves. We were so into playing live that we wanted to try and get gigs outside London. In those days, the music weekly 'Sounds' used to run listings of all the gigs in the country. So we would look for venues all over the country and send them demos and then keep pestering them on the phone asking for a support slot.

I guess that's how we ended up playing the Market Tavern. At one of our first gigs, we went into the bar to let everyone know we'd arrived. Steve and Dermot were round by the back door waiting for someone to open it so we could load in the gear while I went to bring the van round.

We heard the chanting as the mob approached the pub and then the windows smashing. I was lucky as I was able to hide in the van but Dermot and Steve were not so fortunate. The back door then burst open and people started piling out and scattering.

Somebody shouted, "Run!" They started running but were surrounded. Steve got a few punches and kicks and Dermot was curled up with his hands clasped over his head and one of them bashed him a few times with a brick.

It turned out that they were 'Zulu Warriors', the football hooligan firm that followed Birmingham City, who were playing a pre-season friendly against Kidderminster Harriers. Because of Dermot's hand injury and the state of the venue, we had to cancel that night.

I don't know why but we always had a great connection with the West Midlands. We played at quite a few different venues in the area such as Worcester Arts Centre, JBs in Dudley and some others I can't remember. After signing with Damaged Goods, we even recorded our first EP in Redditch at Workshop Studios where The Wonder Stuff had made their first record.

We were the first band that Damaged Goods signed after the Manic Street Preachers and our EP actually did better than theirs. As a result, Damaged Goods gave us more money than they'd ever given a band (before or after) to record our second EP. We spent the recording budget on a great studio that Pixies had recorded at with a good engineer but he wasn't an experienced producer and the results were pretty poor, so Damaged Goods let us go...

We decided (a bit too late, in retrospect) that we needed a manager. Mark had a fanzine that he ran with a guy called Conal. Mark had introduced us to him at one of our shows at the Market Tavern and Conal booked us to play at a venue he promoted in Hereford and later got us some gigs in Bristol, Newport and other venues in the south west. When we

**POP AM GOOD**

CONAL:
MARK:

## TOP 20 INDEPENDENT SINGLES

| | | | |
|---|---|---|---|
| 1 | (4) | MESMERISED | Chapterhouse/ Dedicated |
| 2 | ♦ | BLACK SPRING EP | Lush/ 4AD |
| 3 | ♦ | WORDS THAT SAY | Mega City 4/ Big Life |
| 4 | (13) | COLOUR ME GRAY | The Family Cat/ Bad Girl |
| 5 | (12) | SPEEDING MOTORCYCLE | The Pastels/ Paperhouse |
| 6 | ♦ | GO (RAINFOREST MIX) | Moby/ Outer Rhythm |
| 7 | ♦ | SUPER-ELECTRIC | Stereolab/ Too Pure |
| 8 | (1) | BOO UP EP | The Boo Radleys/ Rough Trade |
| 9 | (2) | TEENAGE WHORE | Hole/ City Slang |
| 10 | ♦ | DRESS | PJ Harvey/ Too Pure |
| 11 | (6) | SUCH A FEELING | Bizarre Inc/ Vinyl Solution |
| 12 | ♦ | THE LATEST THING EP | Pop Am Good/ Damaged goods |
| 13 | (11) | WATER MELON | Scorpio Rising/ Chapter 22 |
| 14 | (15) | BLACK RABBIT | The Del-Bloods/ Seminal Twang |
| 15 | ♦ | MENTASM | Second Phase/ R&S |
| 16 | (7) | ENERGY FLASH EP | Joey Beltram/ R&S |
| 17 | ♦ | GROOVE POWER | |
| 18 | ♦ | ENDLESS ART | |
| 19 | (20) | GO OUT BE HAPPY | |
| 20 | (3) | LOVE TO HATE YOU | |

Lou "Haha the lads from Funbug changed Pop Am Good's backdrop before the gig started, to spell out 'Do a poo' instead and I'm pretty sure they left it like that for the full set. This was so much fun - all the bands were great and got the crowd going and Pop Am Good were always a crowd pleaser. They were genuinely nice people and it was good to see a drummer out front with a standing kit!"

Andrew Wolfman "Pop Am Good must have known where Badgeman buried the bodies, they were on ALL the time. For a while there you couldn't even sing in the shower without having them politely waiting outside to go on after you."

decided that we needed a manager, we wanted someone up and coming that we could work with, rather than an established manager who would tell us what to... so we asked Conal if he'd be interested and he said yes and he asked if we minded if Mark helped out too, which was fine by us.

After playing a couple of shows at the Tavern, we got support slots with Carter USM, Redd Kross and Crazyhead. We also carried on playing headline shows.

In retrospect, as a band, we didn't really go as far as we should have because we didn't have a manager... we were pretty stubborn and we were probably a little bit too worried about losing control, so that by the time we realised that we needed a manager, it was too late.

We signed a new record deal with Trunk Records and released our second EP 'This Year's Models'. After that, we recorded another single, 'All Wound Up' with Trunk Records but we split up before it got released. By the time we called it a day we'd played just under 180 gigs."

↓ NME 5/10/91 ↓

## ON ON 'AM IT UP

"One of the first gigs we ever did was with this really posey band. They walked in with this, 'Hey, we don't talk to other bands' attitude and they had a drumkit that had so much scaffolding it looked like a building site. When we saw them we just thought, we don't wanna be anything like that . . ."

Singing guitarist John Dennehy has nothing to worry about – several universes removed from the Cool Rock Band norm, **POP AM GOOD** are a tatty but nifty alternative. Formed by John, a beatbox and broadly Irish bassist Dermot Mullan at the end of 1989, Pop Am Good were called Seven Deadly Sins until A N Other band of the same name took offence, whereupon the duo changed their name and had their arms twisted into several painful positions before Steve Brice convinced them that he could sing marginally

better than the drum machine.

He was right, too. Now Steve is firmly ensconced as the stand-up rhythm person with his fair share of vocal duties, and the bedraggled, Fraggle-tinged, Violent Femmes-gone-punk Pop Am Good are garnering a reputation as a Martini outfit: anytime, anyplace, anymoney. Rumour has it they travelled from their East End homeland to play Newcastle for 25 quid.

"That's a very slight exaggeration," admits Steve amidst the hubblebubble of the Bull & Gate bar (honestly!). "We did go to Widnes and played to four people in a place the size of ULU, though."

"But it had backstage showers!" shouts John. "We were like pop stars when we arrived! And it was a Liverpool Council-run venue, so we got paid £100: we could have ferried the entire crowd down to London for that!"

One of the best nights of Pop Am Good's career was supporting Carter USM in Kidderminster. One of the worst just happened to be in the same town, when they fell foul of a posse of Midlands soccer dickheads out for a bit of

pre-season 'friendly' fun. Things could be worse – their debut single 'The Latest Thing', a hectic blast of punk attitude, early Wonder Stuff riffs and mammoth melodies, is out on Damaged Goods.

They'll play for a bag of marbles and a dead mouse. They admit to being totally skint but middle-class. Their music is (like Serious Drinking) an example of studied stupidity, but they don't want to be perceived as 'idiots'. They're fun, funny and play as though they're making it up as they go along. Bingo!

When you sing "We're the latest thing", are you being ironic or optimistic?

"Well, we're certainly not being sensible!"

Welcome to the Treasuredome.

**Simon Williams**

● 'The Latest Thing' is released through Rough Trade this week. Pop Am Good play London Kentish Town Bull & Gate on October 2 (with Thee Headcoats) and London Tufnell Park Dome on October 3 (with Nutmeg and Disneyhood).

## POP AM GOOD

Neil Archer "One day a lot of football hooligans turned up and threw everything at us, pint glasses, some wasps and a concrete bench, (Aspro got a broom and swept up while all this was happening). They came back a few hours later and chased us through the glass doors (they opened inwards unfortunately) into the old Market, trashed the bar and attacked the band that had just turned up."

Ian Hill "They came sweeping around the corner further down the road and covered the entire width of the street (including pavements lol) and were six or seven people deep."

John Peutherer "It was Birmingham City's Zulus, there for a pre-season friendly. Stop The World were meant to be on supporting our friends, Pop Am Good, who had the misfortune of turning up at the exact time. They got out of the van & got beaten up. The bassist had his wrist broken. They got back in the van & went home.

I'd popped home for some forgotten piece of equipment at exactly the RIGHT time... I was driving back, unaware of all the shenanigans to see Pud, Ian Hill & several others running around by the dual track... I arrived at the Tavern to see Andy armed with a broom trying to make sense of the devastation!"

Roy Davies "I recall a guy called Jimmy Price got pushed through the glass in the doors at the back in the stampede to escape and needed stitches in his gashed arm. His girlfriend at the time couldn't find him after the trouble and I found her stood by the Farmers Boy afterwards in tears clutching his blood stained sweater!! He arrived back at the Tavern stitched and dosed up with painkillers later that night and unwisely started drinking again, with the result four of us had to carry him home!!"

Neil Archer "The Police phoned around 10.30pm to say that the hooligans were on the way back. Colin started sawing pool cues up and giving us instructions on how best to use them, we didn't really care by then and they didn't turn up."

Andy Price "We were done over by the Zulus. Years later I met a Zulu in Birmingham Airport and he said it was because of the cops. I was told by the cops to close the pub and refuse to serve them. That was their response."

Market Tavern regulars will be saying hello to some familiar faces this week with the return of the Metal Monkey Machine and Ambelian.

First on are the Monkeys, who can be seen tonight with the Tavern's own Martin's Marauders in a gig scheduled for last month but snowed off.

Things have been moving for the Manchester lads since they last appeared in Wyre Forest.

Tomas, Jake, Jeremy, Steve and Jerry are on tour to promote their EP *Thrashing The Funk Out Of Our Souls*, which is available from March 18 on Psi Records.

They have also been supporting The Ramones and Atom Seed, while in April they will be backing the Lunachicks, an all-girl American thrash-funk outfit — and after that is a mini tour of Germany with fellow Mancunians Mad Jacks.

As for Ambelian, you can see them on Saturday night with Your Icon from Walsall as support.

If you want details on either of these, ring the Tavern on Kidderminster 752590.

Thu 14th Mar 1991

● Manchester's Metal Monkey Machine.

34

# Fatima Mansions + King Woderick & The Yogots

## Sat 2nd Mar 1991

David Watkins "They were really really great!"

Andrew Wolfman "Fatima Mansions were immense, real combat rock. Cathal Coughlan came across as the sort of bloke who could start a fight in a phone box or offer out an entire football stadium. The indie rock Roy Keane."

Andrew Wolfman "King Woderick and the Yogots were from Tamworth and would definitely get a slot at the Tavern's Terrible Band Names festival."

Mark Badgeman "Little known fact - they had a proper Top 10 hit by being on the B-side of the Manic's 'Suicide Is Painless' charity single."

Surely Microdisney should have been massive? Instead, Sean Hagan took his pop classicism to the High Llamas and Cathal Coughlan formed the uncompromising Fatima Mansions. I only paid them £200 but I've no record of how many people came.

Dave Morgan (Melon) "The best band I saw at the Tavern were Fatima Mansions. Blew the lid off. Nice blokes too. Although Cathal Coughlan wasn't too flattered when I said they were 'even better' than Carter."

THE FATIMA MANSIONS - KIDDERMINSTER MARKET TAVERN -
02.03.1991

A year before the band supported U2, on a tour that
included a confrontational performance in Milan,
where frontman Cathal Coughlan swore at the audience
and simulated shoving a Virgin Mary shampoo bottle
up his ass, the band were appearing at the far less
salubrious surroundings of the Market Tavern, to
promote their Hive EP.
Coughlan may have been slightly less confrontational
at this gig, but he was no less in your face.
I'd gone to this with my mate Pete. Pete was great
like that. He knew little, if anything about The
Fatima Mansions, but he was always up for going to
gigs. He was often unlucky or unfortunate, with a
tendency towards the clumsy. So it was hardly
surprising that as we pushed forward towards the
front, Pete entered the mosh pit at just the right
moment to receive a Doc in the face from a
stagediver. Ever the trooper, he dusted himself
down and got on with it.
The gig was immense. The band was harsh and intense,
Coughlan a wonderful provocative frontman. The
energy from the band was given back by the crowd as
the venue turned into a sweaty, writhing mess. It was
an exhausting night, both mentally and physically,
but so, so worth the effort.

# John Otway

Otway subtitled his 1990 autobiography 'Rock and Roll's Greatest Failure'. He'd hit the charts in the punk era with 'Cor Baby That's Really Free' following a ball-crushing performance on the Old Grey Whistle Test (look it up!) but didn't manage another hit until 2002 when his fans banded together to get him a Top 10 record and a TOTP appearance for his 50th birthday. The Tavern show with Atilla The Stockbroker was Headbuts & Hallibuts and not, unfortunately, a performance of 'Cheryl A Rock Opera - an everyday tale of Satanism, Trainspotting, Drug Abuse and Unrequited Love.'!

Sand Palmer "I remember John Otway playing with Wild Willy. Who played a tree stump."

David Wright "Yes he did, while occasionally bursting into guitar solos at impromptu moments to the comical annoyance of John Otway. Their comic timing was perfect and I guess if more came to see them they would have played together as a twosome more often."

David Wright "The most ordinary off-stage musician I ever met whilst working on the door at the Tavern was John Otway - yet as soon as he hit that stage, he became the craziest, zaniest 'musician/clown act' I have ever seen. So, it was an easy mistake to make when I was working on the door for John Otway's first gig at the Tavern. A slightly balding thin bloke went to walk straight past me through the entrance into the gig and I put my arm across to stop him and said, 'It's two quid mate'. He looked at me with slight confusion in his eyes and said 'I'm Otway'. It took a moment to sink in because he never said 'I'm John Otway' just 'Otway'. I looked at the posters on the wall and saw to my embarrassment it was his picture and said 'Sorry John'. What else could I have said....?"

The Head Barman "After a John Otway gig one night I was drinking with John in the back room. He was admiring my bike which I used to leave in the pub after a few too many. He said he'd never been on a motorbike and couldn't ride. He said he would love to have a go on it. So he sat on it and I pushed him around the back room of the pub whilst he made motorbike noises and drank from a bottle of Jack Daniels. We were both slaughtered."

Mark Badgeman "Otway was always funny but Wild Willy impressed me with his... furniture! He makes amazing stuff carved from plywood and cleverly uses the laminated sheets to good effect!"

Mark Badgeman "There was confusion regarding who had booked Demented Are Go. It wasn't me, but as they were psychobilly and not a bunch of old pub circuit pros, I added them to my poster because I thought it'd help them sell tickets. But then I copped a load of grief after people started telling me they were Nazis. The story goes that they recorded with Skrewdriver's Ian Stewart as The Klansmen and made a couple of albums. I've tried looking this up and it's not clear whether they did or not. I didn't bother going to the gig though, just in case."

I HAVE NO EXPLANATION FOR THE AWFUL HANDWRITTEN FLYER ON THE OPPOSITE PAGE!

**market tavern**
comberton place kidderminster
tel: 0562 752590

| | GIGS IN MAY | |
|---|---|---|
| THU 2nd | DEMENTED ARE GO | £3.00/£3.50 |
| FRI 3rd | 25th MAY + CAKE INDIE NIGHT | £2.50 |
| FRI 10th | BLEACH INDIE NIGHT | £2/£2.50 |
| FRI 17th | SCORPIO RISING INDIE NIGHT | £2.00 |
| THU 23rd | U.K. SUBS | £3.50 £4.00 |
| FRI 24th | R E S Q U E INDIE NIGHT | £2.00 |
| FRI 31st | BLOW UP INDIE NIGHT | £2.00 |

1 MINUTE FROM THE RAILWAY STATION
LAST TRAINS - B'HAM 23:07 WORCS 23:49

**Poster 1 (left):**

# MARKET TAVERN
### Comberton Place, Kidderminster.
### Tel 0562 752590

Friday February 15th
**STOMP DISCO PRESENTS GIANT INTERNATIONAL**

Saturday February 16th
**UBX + WARNING**

Friday February 22nd
**THE 1000 + THE STAIRS**

Saturday February 23rd
**JACKNIFE DISCIPLES**

Wednesday February 27th
**HAYZ THREE**

Friday March 1st
**COUNTY HIGH**

Saturday March 2nd
**FATIMA MANSIONS**
KING WODERIK & THE YOGOTS

Friday March 8th
**KERNEL CLARKE**

Saturday March 9th
**GINHOUSE**

Thursday March 14th
**METAL MONKEY MACHINE**

Friday March 15th
**PROGRESSION**
LESTERS DISCO

Saturday March 16th
**AMBELIAN**
CAANAN ROSE

Friday March 22nd
**BAND OF GYPSIES**

Saturday March 23rd
**POWER**

Friday March 29th
**NEW INDIE NIGHT**

**KARAOKE EVERY SUNDAY**

**Poster 2 (middle top):**

# MARKET TAVERN
### COMBERTON PLACE, KIDDERMINSTER
### Tel - 0562 752590

Thurs March 28th
**OTHERSIDE** Free Adm

Fri March 29th
**INDIE DISCO**

Mon April 1st
**XMAS TREES STOMP**

Fri April 5th
**BEATRIDERS**

Thurs April 11th
**JOHN OTWAY & ATTILA THE STOCKBROKER**

Fri April 12th
**THE HAMSTERS**

Fri April 19th
**THE SANDMEN**

Fri April 26th
**NATURE THINGS**

Sat April 27th
**HAZE III**

Thurs May 2nd
**DEMENTED ARE GO**

Fri May 3rd
**25th MAY & CAKE**

Fri May 10th
**BLEACH**

Fri May 17th
**SCORPIO RISING**

Thurs 23rd
**UK SUBS**

Fri May 24th
**(INTERNATIONAL) RESQUE**

Fri May 31st
**BLOW UP**

**Poster 3 (top right):**

# market tavern
### comberton place, kidderminster
### tel 0562 752590

| Fri 20th Sept | Sat 21st Sept | Tues 24th Sept |
|---|---|---|
| POP AM GOOD + stop the world £2.00 | R.D.F. Radical Dance Faction TRIBE £2.50/£4 | CAKE (farewell gig) £1.50 |
| Fri 27th Sept SCORPIO RISING + Spiral Eye £2.50 | Sat 28th Sept CITIZEN FISH + support £3.50 | Thurs 3rd Oct TREVOR BURTON £3.50 |
| Fri 4th Oct VENUS BEADS + FRETBLANKET Teenage Mess £2.50 | Sat 5th Oct INDIAN ANGEL £2.00 | Thurs 10th Oct STEVE GIBBONS £3.50 |
| Fri 11th Oct DROP + Panic Beach Bathchair Suicide £2.50 | Fri 18th Oct FAMILY CAT + Elegy £3/£3.50 | Sat 19th Oct RED LEMON ELECTRIC BLUES BAND £3.50 |
| Thurs 24th Oct THE LURKERS + support £3.50 | Sat 26th Oct Bushfire (reggae) £3.50 | Sat 9th Nov Rythmn-ites + support £3.50 |

**1 MINUTE FROM THE RAILWAY STATION**
**LAST TRAINS - B'HAM 23:07 WORCS 23:49**

**Poster 4 (lower left):**

# market tavern
### comberton place, kidderminster
### tel: 0562 752590

**DECEMBER GIGS**

THURS 5th **TREVOR BURTON**
FRI 6th **ECHO & THE BUNNYMEN**
SAT 7th **WOLFSBANE**
WED 11th **JOHN OTWAY**
THUR 12th **U.K. SUBS**
SUN 15th **DANGEROUS** HEAVY METAL
WED 18th **THE SELECTER** 2-TONE CHRISTMAS PARTY!

**THE END OF TERM INDIE CHRISTMAS PARTY**
FRI 20th **CAKE / PANIC BEACH / FRETBLANKET**
SAT 21st **THE RIPPS**
MON 23rd **THE ROOSTERS**
TUES 24th **E-NUMBERS**

**TRAVEL:** ONLY 17 MILES FROM B'HAM
LOTS OF FREE CAR-PARKING
ONLY 200 YRDS FROM STATION
Last trains: B'ham 23.07
Worcs 23.49

**Sticker:**
POSTERS **1991** FLYERS & ADS

**Poster 5 (middle right):**

# market tavern
### comberton place, kidderminster
### tel: 0562 752590

| Tuesdays | Thursday (R+B night) | Fridays (Indie night) | Saturdays |
|---|---|---|---|
| RING 542 FOR DETAILS. (Discos, Parties, Gigs etc.) or hire | 10th OCT STEVE GIBBONS £4.00 | 11th OCT DROP & PANIC BEACH & BATHCHAIR SUICIDE £2.50 | 12th OCT CRUELLA DE VILLA £2.50 |
| | 17th OCT E NUMBERS £2.50 | 18th OCT FAMILY CAT & BILL PRITCHARD & ELEGY £3/£3.50 | 19th OCT RED LEMON ELECTRIC BLUES BAND £4.00 |
| | 24th OCT THE LURKERS & STOP THE WORLD £3.50/£4 | 25th OCT PRIVATE FUNCTION | 26th OCT BUSHFIRE (REGGIE) £3.00 |
| | 31st OCT T.B.C. | 1st NOV FLOWERDRUM (FROM CINDERFORD) £2.50 | 2nd NOV FOUR ON THE FLOOR £2.50 |

**1 MINUTE FROM THE RAILWAY STATION**
**LAST TRAINS - B'HAM 23:07 WORCS 23:49**

**Poster 6 (bottom middle):**

# MARKET TAVERN
### Comberton Place, Kidderminster.
### Tel 0562 752590

FRIDAY MAY 17TH
**SCORPIO RISING**

FRIDAY MAY 24TH
**RESQUE**

FRIDAY MAY 31ST
**BLOW UP**

FRIDAY JUNE 7TH
**HONEYTURTLES (TBC)**

TUESDAY JUNE 11TH
**WENCH**

FRIDAY JUNE 14TH
**DROP (TBC)**

FRIDAY JUNE 21ST
**HOPE SPRINGS ETERNAL**

**Poster 7 (bottom right):**

# market tavern
### Comberton Place, Kidderminster
### Tel 0562 752590

FRIDAY Nov 1st
**FLOWERDRUM**

FRIDAY Nov 8th
**INDIE DISCO**

SATURDAY Nov 9th
**RHYTHM-ITES**

FRIDAY Nov 15th
**BOB**

SATURDAY Nov 16th
**LEATHERFACE**

FRIDAY Nov 22nd
**THEE HYPNOTICS**

FRIDAY Nov 29th
**MIDWAY STILL**

FRIDAY Dec 6th
**ECHO & THE BUNNYMEN**

Wednesday Dec 18th
**THE SELECTER**

The Badgeman Promoting Empire was run from an office in my bedroom. I can't really explain why the first Carter poster was such a terrible hand drawn affair (even Spiny Dogfish posters had used Letraset!) but it was clear that I needed something better to make the promotional material. I eventually ended up with a combination of a black and white Mac Classic, bought from my old maths teachers who ran the Apple Centre on Lower Mill Street, a neat program called Bannermania and a hooky copy of QuarkXpress 3.1. Looking back, I must have pushed the 4mb of RAM to its limits with some of the designs! I also had a photocopier in my bedroom, unaware I was sleeping next to a machine relentlessly emitting ozone, and a steam driven secondhand fax machine that I thought made me the consummate professional.

ANNABEL IN BADGEMAN'S BEDROOM OFFICE

The early posters and flyers were all done on my bedroom copier but I eventually found a cheap printers in Brum who used to do A2 or A1 sized posters for a very reasonable price. I can't remember what they were called but I do remember that someone had graffitied the wall under their sign with 'PRINT THIS!' which I always thought was hysterical. I'd turn up with my floppy disk and go back a few days later to collect a pile of posters. Later, I got him to do the flyers as well, which saved me loads of effort by not having to cut them all out by hand.

Promoting the shows took up every minute of every day. My landline phone (no mobiles in those days) got hammered making endless calls to agents to chase decent acts, booking the support bands, corralling staff to help me out on the night, sorting out

which PA I was using, or calling other local promoters to catch up on the gossip and try to get a steer on who was paying what. If I wasn't on the phone, I'd be designing marketing material before distributing it around Kiddy, the little record shop in Stourport, Magpie in Worcester and the Birmingham outlets such as Oasis and the independent record shops. Most of those sold tickets for me too. Sometimes I'd use the Odeon to sell tickets for big shows because of the exposure you got by having it listed on the box office board.

The deals with agents were always a bit Arthur Daley. Their job is to get as much money as possible so touring bands don't have set fees, in the same way a wedding band might. If the agent thinks they can get £700 out of you, they'll try it. You might only want to pay £300. The trick to promoting is to figure out how many tickets you think you can sell based on the band's current appeal. At the Tavern, the most was 300 tickets (legal capacity was 99, oops!). You then need to offer enough money to tempt them to come to Kidderminster, but not too much that you'll never recoup it through ticket sales.

Rad Saunders (booking agent) "I think I tried to sell Badgeman loads of bands but he was too mean to pay a decent guarantee. I'd spend hours trying to talk him into something. Always fun, rarely productive, scarcely profitable for any of us."

To protect themselves from lower offers, agents negotiate a percentage of the profit on top of the guaranteed fee. When I first found out about this, I was utterly incredulous - what, you want a share of my profit? It's a bit complicated to understand when you come across it for the first time, but they normally want 70% or 80% of any money left after the costs had been paid. The promoter adds their desired profit into the costs, so I used to put £100 in for me and then any split would mean I've already made £100 and I'd be happy (under the circumstances) to get the extra 20% on top. These deals were called 'plus deals' and have

BADGEMAN & KIM IN A FIELD

by and large disappeared from the industry. They're now called 'versus deals' and don't allow the built-in profit. And I thought there was no money in it when I did it!

At the end of the night, the band's tour manager would inspect the costs to see if they could move the break point and make more money. If you didn't have a receipt for something, it could become an argument over whether to allow it as a cost. Absolutely no fun, standing there bickering over £15 for photocopied dayglo posters with some tight-arse who just won't let it drop. It could easily ruin an otherwise brilliant night.

Working with the local press was hugely important. Mark Langford at the Shuttle was my main target because there was a direct correlation between the size of the feature on the Spotlight page and the amount of tickets sold. But I dealt with at least five local papers, writing press releases, sending Walkerprints (artist-supplied black and white photos for reproduction in press articles) and offering tickets as prizes, because a competition normally guaranteed good editorial exposure.

What I needed more than anything, was a preview. A review was no use to me because the show had gone. That only benefitted the band, not the venue. We couldn't afford to place ads, and they didn't really work, so we relied on free editorial to get the word out. I think I used to fax my listings to about seven gig guides including the national music press. Everyone scoured the gig guides in those days! Incidentally, Mike Gayle was my gig guide contact at Whats On mag in Brum, the guy who went on to write the best seller, My Legendary Girlfriend.

If I didn't have a gig at the Tavern, I'd be out at night at someone else's gig and then flyering the crowd on the way out. The best way to find a punter for your gig is... at a gig! You could also get feedback from flyering because you'd hear people get excited about a particular act on the list. If there wasn't a gig on, I'd have a bucket full of wallpaper paste and I'd be on the prowl for boarded up buildings or subways to flypost, all over the local area. Kiddy had the poster rotundas in town that were legitimate flyposting sites but real estate was at a premium on them. The rule was that you didn't cover up a rival poster if the gig was still forthcoming. Unless it was Paradise, as theirs seemed fair game!

Lou "I remember seeing Mark sticking posters up in town during the evenings, when we were all budding 'crusties'. We used to follow him around and ask for freebies - my bedroom wall ended up full of Tavern gig posters!"

My fax machine used that thermo paper that fades if you don't photocopy it within a few days. It was attached to the phone line so if anyone wanted to send a fax, they needed to call first and I had to plug it in. People sent faxes like they might send an email now. I could probably sing that stupid 'handshake' noise they used to make even now, I heard it so many times. I used to

# He's Mr Music!

### By Entertainments Writer MARK LANGFORD

Within the last two-and-a-half years, Kidderminster's Market Tavern has established itself as a venue to be reckoned with for rising British bands.

Although hosting mainly 'independent', non-mainstream groups, visitors have also included some of the past and present stars of the national music scene.

They include Mike Peters of The Alarm, Carter USM and Dr Robert of the Blow Monkeys, and all have one thing in common.

The link is Mark Badgeman, the 24-year-old promoter who deals with the Indie bands for the Market Tavern.

Mark puts the Tavern's reputation today down to the successful first visit in autumn 1990 of Carter USM – at that time a promising yet little known London duo who have since gone on to national and international success.

Mark said: "I knew them slightly so I had that first inroad, although it still took three months of pestering to get them up here."

That initial reluctance was something Mark found himself ever up against in his early days.

"Bands hardly ever came here because Kidderminster wasn't the kind of place they came to. It just wasn't on the musical map," he said.

That first Carter gig was a success in more ways than one as the band actually enjoyed themselves and appreciated the hospitality of the crowd. So they began to recommend the Market Tavern as a venue to other bands as well as arranging a follow-up visit, which was a sell-out.

Mark said: "After Carter I had agents ringing me up asking about the venue and offering me bands.

"Now I think it's fairly true to say the place is pretty highly regarded on the small band circuit."

Known as Badgeman because of a penchant for brightly coloured badges, he was born Mark Dawson in Birmingham and moved to Kidderminster with his family when he was seven.

On leaving Wolverley High School at 16, he went to work for a printer but found it was not to his liking.

He dabbled with band management at 17 when he arranged gigs for the now defunct local band Spiny Dogfish, but it was with the arrival in 1990 of present Tavern landlord Andrew Price that Mark moved up a gear.

Mark said: "When he took over I heard he wanted to turn it into a venue, so I just went to see him."

The growth of the Indie and rave music scene in the Midlands saw him found the popular Straight Elephant magazine in 1991.

Sadly, cash flow problems led to the magazine being temporarily shelved, although there are hopes for a final issue later this year.

Mark admits not every band he books is a success, yet cannot see himself giving it all up for 'respectability'.

He said: "I much prefer the lifestyle of mixing with like-minded people rather than wearing a collar and tie."

● ABOVE: Impressive impresario Mark Badgeman, putting Kidderminster on the musical map.
● RIGHT: Carter USM, whose two visits gave Mark and the Tavern the initial jump on the bandwagon.

It took a while to live this one down! Cheesy local paper photo pose.

fax a hand drawn map of how to find the Tavern to the bands along with a schedule for the day that normally consisted of turning up at 4pm, finish soundchecking by 5:30pm, Andy serves the lasagne and then the doors open at 7:30pm with a couple of local bands. I was never a fan of touring supports because I viewed them as a wasted opportunity for the local bands so, whenever I could, I refused to take them.

I got sent loads of demo tapes. Every local band sent one. Agents would send CDs or tapes of acts they wanted you to book. The first CD I got sent was the Fatima Mansions album. Their agent, Emma Banks, called me to see what I thought, but I didn't even have a CD player at that point! To be honest, I didn't really care what a band sounded like as long as they were going to sell tickets. I was running a business and I needed to eat and pay the rent. I was pretty good at picking acts on the way up such as Radiohead or Terrorvision but I was equally good at misjudging and paying too much or booking a band no one cared about.

There was hardly any money in it. A good gig might make a couple of hundred but you could easily lose that the next week if you had a stinker. I was signing on because I couldn't guarantee making enough money to live on from the gigs. You'd get asked at the dole office if you'd done any work that fortnight or if you'd been looking for a job, then sign on the dotted line. Quite often, after I'd signed on, the job centre lad would ask me who was playing on Friday because he used to come to my gigs! I did wonder whether I should put him on a permanent guest list so that he didn't grass me up, but someone pointed out that he had a job so damn right he should pay for his ticket!

Eventually, I did a deal with Andy Price. He paid me £50 a week to book the bands and he took all the risk which meant I could go

BECCY, TOM AND DAN TESTING THE BAND'S FOOD. THIS ISN'T THE TAVERN - IT'S ANOTHER BADGEMAN GIG SOMEWHERE

Andy Price to Mark Badgeman "The one outstanding memory is that of yourself, because without you none of this would have happened. The first time we ever spoke was at 10.50pm on a very busy Friday night and a rather strange looking guy (it was a bikers pub, all denim and jeans) wearing brightly coloured clothes asked me if I could stop and chat about promoting bands. I am trying to serve customers as fast as I can so normally my reply is 'fuck off I am busy' but for some reason, I said hang on for 10 minutes. I never looked back!"

Duncan Bickley "Badgeman's gig promotion at the Tavern, back in the day, was an inspiration to me. I started putting on some gigs in Leeds at the turn of the millennium and it was great. I don't do it anymore as I seemed to fall out of touch with what was viable, but the good ones we did were great.

I don't know if I am right but what I took from those promotions was the idea that if what you want to see isn't on - stop whinging to your mates and put it on!"

legit and still get housing benefit to pay the rent. I also got on the (Starship) Enterprise Allowance Scheme which paid £40 a week. I'm a bit hazy here, but a precursor to that might have been a requirement to attend the Training and Business Factory on the Stourport Road, which was supposed to give you the skills to go out and get a job. They had a photocopier, so I used to do all my posters there to save my toner at home!

Gig days involved a swift trip around the ticket outlets in the morning to pick up the money and take them off sale. I presume I used to phone the outlets further afield and ask them to stop selling so I knew how many I had left to sell on the door, but I don't really remember. I might have had to go to the supermarket to buy some things for the dressing room but again, the memories are hazy. What I do remember is waiting for 3pm to turf out the last of the pissed up farmers and getting a broom to sweep the bloody straw out. All the tables had to go into the cafe, and if it was a decent headliner, the cafe would become their dressing room. I might fill any spare time waiting for the band to turn up by taking down the old posters and putting up new ones. I was a dab hand with the Blu-tac. You couldn't do this as a hobby. It was a proper full-time job that seemed compliant with the first law of thermodynamics - the more energy you put in, the more you got back out of it.

Kev Wheeler "We lived through an amazing time, and certainly a lot was down to Badgeman and his contacts for booking the bands over those years... So a massive thank you for what you did, it also gave a platform for local bands to promote themselves which is certainly lacking these days..."

# Wench & Mad Cow Disease

## Tue 11th Jun 1991

Wench are an all girl five-piece rock band from New York City, who have their roots firmly planted in the punk/foxcore movement of the early eighties. Combined with the influence of the early heavy metal bands, thrash, funk and blues, Wench offer a refreshingly new approach to the new wave of hard rock and heavy metal. Not unlike Prong and Soundgarden, Wench cannot be placed in any particular niche. Suffice to say, Wench are the female Jane's Addiction, and offer an original and raw approach to the hard rock genre of the 90's.

Their first demo, "Sumus Quod Sumus" was recorded shortly after the band's formation at the end of 1987. This first demo was warmly received by national and international publications, such as Kerrang!, Metal Forces, Metal Mania and Raw to mention a few. The band have just released their debut album, "A Tidy Sized Chunk" and are currently out on the road on their first European tour. The band have previously toured with Suicidal Tendencies, Wendy O'Williams and Candlemass in the States. The band can be seen locally at Kidderminster Market Tavern on June 11th and at Hereford Entertainer on June 13th.

Mark Badgeman "Wench are a long forgotten American female thrash band who'd supported some big names. In fact, I can't remember the performance but what I do remember is why they were a bit late on stage. Amongst my PA options was a cheap one run by Nick The Dick, his dad and his mate. We called him Nick The Dick because he was also a stripper and delighted in telling tales of his shows and handing out his glossy stripper promo photos. Clearly the temptation of an all-girl band was too much and when they were due on stage, Nick and the singer were nowhere to be seen but their van outside was rocking backwards and forwards. He totally denied shagging her!"

Andrew Wolfman "If Stan wasn't available. The Tavern's number two soundman was a part-time male stripper called Greased Lightnin.' He looked like a member of Skid Row and claimed to perform in the States as 'British Lion' in a troupe of pound shop Chippendales called the Centurions. He also claimed to have irreparably lost the skin on his knees when a stripping assignment went south on the artificial wicket of a local cricket pitch. Greased Lightnin' kept a thick stack of glossy 8 x 10s promoting his sexy sideline which he'd dish out to anyone who wanted one, and even if you didn't he'd ask that "you give it to yer Mum." In our little circle these photos were used almost exclusively as roach material. "Got any Lightnin?" kids would ask. "Sure, just a pec left". For one long glorious Summer everyone was smoking Lightnin'."

# Bleach & Cake

## Fri 10th May 1991

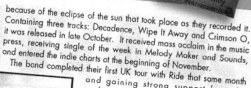

Russell Barker "Bleach arrived at the Tavern having just released their second EP, Snag. I thought their song 'Wipe It Away' was one of the best things around and Salli was a great frontwoman."

William Hyslop "I remember them commenting about the smell of the cattle."

## bleach

Indie popsters Bleach are nearing completion of the second part of their massive U.K. tour, and shortly after that will open the bill at the massive Mission/New Model Army gig at Finsbury Park on June 1st.

They were formed in the summer of 1989 and consist of brothers Neil and Nick Singleton on guitar and bass, Steve Scott on drums and Salli Carson on vocals and guitar. Their first gig was with two other prominent members of the grungy guitar scene, Swervedriver and Basti. Incredibly that gig was only eighteen months ago.

The band recorded their first demo at Purple Rain studios in Gorleston, containing four tracks: Fall, Paint My Face, the classic Wipe It Away and Burn. This secured them their first London gig at the Cube Club in Kentish Town during March 1990 after which the band signed to Way Cool Records.

Their first EP for Way Cool was recorded during the summer of last year, and called "Eclipse"

because of the eclipse of the sun that took place as they recorded it. Containing three tracks: Decadence, Wipe It Away and Crimson O, it was released in late October. It received mass acclaim in the music press, receiving single of the week in Melody Maker and Sounds, and entered the indie charts at the beginning of November. The band completed their first UK tour with Ride that same month

and gaining strong support from the audiences on the tour, John Peel and especially Everett True (!) they have built a name for themselves across the country. Their second EP, "Dipping", was released in February and again smashed into the indie charts and received rave reviews. The band's current tour has further strengthened their following and even their provincial dates have been attracting in excess of 300 people a night.

You can see the band play at Kidderminster Market Tavern on Friday May 10th, with Cake as support, and at Hereford Entertainer on Friday May 17th, with Elegy and the Flemgods supporting. Both gigs are at the bargain price of ú2.50 and should not be missed. For further information on these gigs ring Kidderminster 0562-752590 and Hereford 0432-276529.

# CAKE

### BAND FILE

## AN ABSURD UNDERAGE RIOT!

**Name of the band?**
Cake. This was later changed to Cake (UK) to fend off legal action from the more conventionally popular American band of the same name.

**Which town were you based in?**
Cake were from Kidderminster. Or KidderMADster as they unsuccessfully tried to re-style it on their 1991 'John Day' EP.

**What years were you active?**
1990 - 1992

**Who was in the band? (Around the time you played the Tavern)**
David Watkins played lead guitar and looked fantastic in a dress. Nick Dutton added rhythm guitar and had pop star good looks (unfortunately, it was the pop star Chesney Hawkes, but still.) Bassist James Mitchell wore his axe like a bowtie, a decade before The Strokes made it popular, while his (just about) teenage brother Andy 'thumped' the 'tubs'. According to Straight Elephant magazine, front-man Andrew Wagstaff, "jumped about like an idiot".

Of course, in the early nineties, no band in their right mind would take to the stage without a Bez styled freaky dancer or a Flava Flav-esque hype-man. Cake had both: Stan and Al. Stan would wander on between songs as Polish coal miner Buckley Stofe and drain pints of mild while the band vamped and fans chanted a song about regional trunk road the A38 (it goes through Droitwich). Al, meanwhile, dressed as a giant sausage roll, his pink head and feet poking out of a pastry coloured mattress that was gaffer taped around his middle. He danced through shows enthusiastically (and sweatily) only stopping to perform sense-defying acts of silliness: gherkin wrestling, human daffodil, that sort of thing.

Sarah Fawsitt "Stan and Al were our friends from King Edwards in Stourbridge, who we all loved dearly for their Vic and Bob type humour."

For headline gigs, the band were joined by Ben the Tavern doorman (dressed as Princess Leia, because, why not?) who had acquired a mini-trampoline and herded wave after wave of feral teens through a non-stop orgy of spring-assisted, high complexity stagediving. If the band's 'hits' (Ariel, Metal, Excellent - lots of other songs with enigmatically vague one-word titles) failed to make an impact on an audience, getting squished by a seventeen stone high-flying man-pastry generally did the job.

### What kind of music did you play?
Sarcastic indie rock? Ironic youth? Sonic flower grunge? Borderline baggy metal?

### Who were the influences?
Dave was a devotee of the sixties garage racket you'd find on Pebbles compilations, Andrew and Nick grew up on a diet of Dinosaur Jr and Dave Lee Roth. James claimed he was into techno and Prince, while his brother Andy, who was ostensibly still a child at this stage, presumably just liked LEGO. Everybody thought Mudhoney were great.

Stan and Al's influences were more classical. The clownish wisdom of Shakespeare's Rude Mechanicals, Jacques Tati's ambivalence to the absurdities of modernity, a Dadaist rejection of the logic, reason and aestheticism of modern capitalist society. Oh no, sorry, they liked Frank Sidebottom, Ween and pints of mild.

### What level of success did you achieve?
Cake (UK) were an entirely Market Tavern phenomenon. An absurd underage riot that could only breathe in the venue's heady bovine air. Kids loved it, bikers thought it was sort-of-funny, grown-up bands like Radiohead had absolutely zero interest in going on before it (humiliating) or after it (suicide). A stint on baggy chancers Top's 'Marathon' tour ended abruptly at the Hereford Entertainer with a skinhead stage-invasion, record takings at the venue's outside bar and the realisation that sausage rolls may have a limited shelf life.

### What do you remember about playing at the Tavern?
The Market Tavern was more important than Mark Badgeman (who probably hasn't bothered to copy edit this bit) even thinks it was. In a time before the world became connected and the history of music became available to everyone, everywhere, all-of-the-time, Mark brought bands you could only read about in the music papers right to your front door (or at least to the back room of a flat roofed pub with actual cows in it quite near your front door).

Badgeman would help you form a band, get a gig, give you a job around the place. He'd bring in bands from Europe and the States that let you know there were like-minded kids out there, miles beyond the end of your road. When you played at the Tavern, you were more than just a local band playing a shit show to your daft mates, you were part of something bigger; distantly but definitely connected to an international underground of incredible music and alternative art. Mark didn't just promote gigs, he built a community.

Other things I remember about the Tavern: veggie lasagne, Red Stripe, stripy tights.

### Any memories of the other bands you played with at the Tavern?
Cake (UK) were very lucky. We badgered our way into a support with gobby Scouse rappers the 25th of May, the self-proclaimed "white Public Enemy" (can you imagine?). The band had courted controversy with the song "Fuck the Right to Vote" and extolled the virtues of shoplifting on their single, "It's All Right." Unfortunately, it turns out it wasn't entirely alright with the Merseyside Police, who nicked the band the night before the gig. With no time to book a replacement Cake (UK) got bumped up the bill and somehow packed the place with punters.

After that we were pretty much trusted to pick who we wanted to play with, so, obviously, we chose all our great mates:

Stroke Bagpuss: If pushed, my favourite type of music is probably scratchy outsider art-folk made by kick-ass punk rock women desperately trying to annoy Mark Badgeman. Hellen and Beth's band Stroke Bagpuss were the best the genre would ever produce, and, therefore, the best band there has ever been.

Freek: Or possibly Freeek. I've never known how many 'e's were in Freek. (Hey, it was the nineties, if you could remember how many e's anyone had, you weren't really there, man.) Like Cake, Fre(e)ek started out as a bedroom band, home taping hits and hilarious skits for their next-to-no-mates. Seemingly overnight they transformed into the sort of serious-business thrash metal band that should be headlining Brazilian football stadiums every weekend. Annoyingly, this occurred just as the world decided that, actually, it preferred scrappy four-track joke bands, thanks very much. A too-late pivot to becoming Franche's answer to Faith No More with the funk-metal "Flu Boost" wasn't enough to prevent the incoming grunge revolution from claiming another victim.

Lee Biggs (Dive / Love Buzz) "We played with Cake there. Then I played for them at the last minute. (AW: you were amazing. Two snares, hair, blood everywhere) It was mental really, but full beans was my motto."

There were other bands too, it wasn't all brilliant: These were usually feeble shoe-gaze affairs called things like Spiral, Rise, Trip, Drop, Drip or something. I don't count Dive in this, they were excellent. Astral, Shine, Hypnotize, and Jennifer's Flower Kitchen? Not so much. These hopeless creatures would snuffle about under their fringes, fussing over guitar pedals, and putting on fake Oxford accents like they were extras in Inspector Morse. We would generally lend them a strobe light, then go and wait it out in The King and Castle until it was all over.

Thinking about it, if I did have any regrets about my time as the spunky young frontman in a white-hot West Midlands rock band, it would probably be the baffling amount of time we spent sulking about it in an old man's pub fifty yards away from where the best party in the postcode was being thrown. In the early days of the Badgeman era, gigs would be packed with winningly mixed crowds of creative, switched-on, hilarious young people: girls, boys, goths, grebos, crusties, punks and ravers. We sat out half of that in a train station boozer deliberately done out to look like the Second World War. What a bunch of dicks.

David Watkins "The feeling at Cake's last gig. It was Christmas '91, and it was rammed. I ended up in the audience after the first song. Wham's 'Last Christmas'. Wag too, I think."

How did the band end?
Yes, about that…

Did anyone go on to further success or have a career in the music industry?
Dave went on form the band Canute, before hooking up with former Hefner frontman Darren Hayman in the Secondary Modern and Hayman, Watkins, Trout and Lee. He has worked with a host of big names names producing music books for Faber and Faber and Reaktion.

Andrew parlayed an unsuccessful music career into an even less successful one as a music journalist for the NME. He was sacked twice before returning to live performance and finding unlikely chart success in Slovakia with The Winter Olympics. He currently records with his band West Midlands.

Nick played with Canute, The Winter Olympics, Kape Kanaveral and an early incarnation of North London cow-pokes, Scott 4.

James played keyboards on the Winter Olympics' album Profit and Loss and is an award-winning euphonium player.

In 2007 Cake performed a one-off reunion show to mark 15 years since their final Tavern appearance. Al dressed as a lamp.

In 2016 the band's long assumed lost recordings were remixed, remastered and released on the Grave Tapes label as 'Cake Tape Twenty Five.' I haven't checked, but I assume that it's probably still in the charts.

Julie Marshall "I really liked the Cake band. They had a great frontman. He had a great mop. So very charismatic."

What else do we need to know about the band?
After our particularly exuberant 1991 Christmas show I woke up half-out of a bottle green catsuit, caked in blood and with two-thirds of a pint glass sticking out of my spine. This was chalked up to 'stagecraft'.

Stan the PA Man was always brilliant to us, trying to encourage the band with the promise of his little black book of industry contacts. This, he claimed, was an artefact as miraculous and powerful as the Ark of the Covenant. "Let me know when you want to go pro lads, just say the word and I'll open the book. I've got 'em all in here." But with great power came great responsibility, "Just so you know, once it's open, it's open. There's no going back. You'd better start acting like a proper band. No more of this silly bollocks."

If that didn't work Stan would just doctor the band mid-set. If he felt someone was under performing he'd mute your channel and give you a thumbs-up. If the whole band had succeeded in pissing him off enough (usually with stage divers, drinks / blood / pastry in his monitors) he'd mute the whole band mid-song and stick Motorhead through the front of house at full volume. This would usually backfire as people REALLY like Motorhead, and people who really like Motorhead often also enjoy smashing things up.

# CITIZEN FISH

(Face 0$)
{Cond 3}          (Kiddy)
{U.C.E.
Language
Break/Rain
Flesh & Blood
Starving
Sink
1st Imp.
Supermite
Charity
Chili Pain }
Home
CNS
Talk is Cheap
Beethoven
------------
Phone, SSW

I can account for at least 6 Citizen Fish gigs at the Tavern and there may be more, although the band only formed in 1989 so they definitely played some of their earliest gigs in Kiddy. Their socially aware crusty ska punk made them a perfect Market Tavern band. Dick is also in the Subhumans and also plays in Culture Shock with Jasper. All three bands still play.

● Aside from a fiery brand of punk/reggae/veggie crossover, Citizen Fish will also bring a rather unusual claim to fame with them when they arrive at Kidderminster's Market Tavern tonight, April 2.

Dick, the band's lead singer, claims his troupe, formed from the ashes of Crusty forefathers 'Culture Shock' were the inspiration behind 'Citizen Dick' — Matt Dillon's band in his new film 'Singles' about an American grunge band. Decide for yourself.

American Riot Grrrls 'Spitboy', part of the original pro-feminist movement which is currently flavour of the month with the music press, will be supporting. Opening the show are Kidderminster's 'Preacher.' Admission is priced at £3.50.

Benny Tovey "Remember watching Citizen Fish and they pulled me up on stage. I must have only been 16ish. I still have the set list that the band signed for me."

THE GRUPS

10th DEC
MARKET TAVERN

kidderminster market tavern
thurs 13 Dec 90
+ kitchen police

CITIZEN FISH
TELEPHONE
FLINCH

CITIZEN FISH
Disposable Dream
Flesh and Blood II

CITIZEN FISH
tv dinner
half way there

Mark Badgeman "Dick always made a point of dedicating a song to the cows."

By John
Peutherer

**Which town were you based in?** Kidderminster

**What years were you active?** 1989-1992 (I think!)

**Who was in the band?**

Ian Calder (Pud) bass
Greg Cooper Lead guitar
John Peutherer drums
Dave Cooper vox & guitar
Dave replaced Matthew Morris (Mop)
who unfortunately died not long after leaving the band

**What kind of music did you play?**
A kind of punk ska mix

**Who were the influences?**
Mainly The Clash

**What level of success did you achieve?**
None whatsoever!

**What do you remember about playing at the Tavern?**
We were all regulars at the Tavern from day one & had played gigs there before Andy took over when we could hire the room & promote our own gigs. It was basically our home base. We even played a couple of Christmas Day lunchtime gigs.

**Any memories of the other bands you played with at the Tavern?**
I recall playing with the UK Subs & The Selecter especially. The Frank Boff Big Band, I had a hand in getting over as my friend played trombone with them. I think we played with them a couple of times.

**How did the band end?**
We just got fed up with getting nowhere. We were a little bit out of kilter with the scene at the time, we were Clash wannabes in a world of shoe gazing & baggy... we were too niche. Maybe a few years later we would have been something but wrong time for us. Shame, we had a lot of good songs.

**Did anyone go on to further success or have a career in the music industry?**
Only in so much as Dave became a big wig at Klark Teknik. A regular behind the mixing desk at major stadium gigs. We once went on a jaunt in the company Jag to see Rod Stewart at the Villa on a freebie!
Myself & Pud went on to play with the Bullfrogs with John Parmenter.
I continue to play now & have been lucky enough to play with Rob Plant a couple of times locally and Mick Jones of The Clash played a guest slot with a Clash appreciation band I play in.
I also played with The Ripps on the Planty benefit night.
Steve Bray & Jeff Bennett from the Boffs were also in Dr Bullfrog, who later became The Bullfrogs.

# BAND FILE

# STOP THE WORLD

I have good news for diehard fans of local bands Adrenalin Kick and Stop The World concerning forthcoming out-of-town gigs.

Both bands have laid on transport, Adrenalin Kick for Wolverhampton and Stop The World for London.

Stop The World are first, supporting current Melody Maker darlings Suede at the Chequered Flag in Wembley on May 8 (vocalist Dave nearly gave me heart-failure when he rang and told me they were playing at Wembley before pointing out the venue wasn't the stadium!)

The meeting time is 5pm at the Market Tavern in Comberton Place. Tickets are £11, although don't worry if this sounds a little pricey as it includes the admission cost as well.

As for Adrenalin Kick, they play at Tivoli's in Wolverhampton on May 15. Again, meet at the Market Tavern for transport which leaves at 9pm. It costs £2, and £2.50 to get in for the gig.

● ABOVE: Rockers Adrenalin Kick, at Tivoli's in Wolverhampton. LEFT: Stop The World, Wembley-bound on May 8.

# Local lads back at Tavern

It will shortly be the turn of the local lads to lay on the music at the Market Tavern with a slot by Kidderminster band Stop The World (above).

Consisting of Feller and Greg Cooper on vocals and guitars, Pudding on bass and John on drums, they present their brand of punk/ska on March 21.

The band have been beavering away for 12 months, and some of you may have seen them support The Lurkers at the Tavern a few months ago.

If you miss them on the 21st, then worry not as Feller told me they are due to support The Selector at a return gig at the Tavern on May 1.

Tickets for their gig are available from the Market Tavern and Sounds Around.

Two days on from March 21 sees the return of a band who last played here more than 12 months ago.

The band is Citizen Fish, hitting the road to promote their second album *Wider Than A Postcard*.

Best described as mutant ska punk with tinges of reggae, Citizen Fish have been out supporting the album with a mammoth 200-date tour, which apart from the UK has taken in America, Yugoslavia, Denmark and Spain.

Again, tickets are available from the Tavern or Sounds Around.

47

# PUNK AT THE TAVERN

## UK SUBS

## The LURKERS

## the Vibrators

THE NEW ALBUM
VOLUME TEN
OUT NOW

WITH ANOTHER FINE MESS.
THE SEX TENTACLES
THURS. 27th JUNE TICKETS AT THE BAR £3.50

These three original punk bands all formed in 1976 and each played the Tavern multiple times. It seems strange now that only 15 years later, we viewed them as a bunch of has-beens. All three bands are still going. If the Tavern was still going, I'd stick them on the same bill!

Mark Badgeman "I'm not sure who booked the UK Subs, probably Martin. But I can't help wondering if the fact that Alvin Gibbs had played with Cheap n Nasty in that weird under-the-radar gig had anything to do with the Subs wanting to play."

Mark Badgeman "We all thought Charlie Harper was really old but actually he was considerably younger at the time than I am now!"

Stig "UK Subs were great. Very sweaty. Stop The World supported them. Remember chatting for what seemed like hours after to Charlie Harper. Top chap, loved what he did."

Andy Stooksbury "Saw the Lurkers there twice. First time saw them soundcheck and had a chat with Arturo Bassick the bass player. Second time saw him walking down Comberton Hill walking his dog. Spoke to him again and I think he remembered me from the previous time. Lovely bloke, great band but remember feeling sad for them as there were very few of us there. I did wonder how they could have made any money."

Kev Barker "Supported UK Subs once when I was fronting Fever Dream, it wasn't packed, the crowd weren't there to see us, but was still a great night."

the Vibrators
+
ANOTHER Fine MESS
AT
MARKET TAVERN
KIDDERMINSTER
THURSDAY
27th JUNE
£ 3.50 ON DOOR

U.K. SUBS

PUNK

# The Primitives

Andrew Wolfman "Is 'Crash' by The Primitives the biggest hit single ever played at the Tavern? It must be 'Crash', or 'Creep', or The Selecter's 'On My Radio'? Hold on (checks notes). No, it was 'Spirit in the Sky' by Dr and The Medics. It still might be the best single, though."

The Primitives made the successful transition from indie to mainstream courtesy of the perfect pop song - 'Crash'. They couldn't repeat the success and disbanded not long after the Tavern gig. They've recently reformed. The support was advertised as Bell Tower but ended up being Emma Gibbs Loves Badges from Tamworth.

Neil (The Primitives) "It was rammed. Having chart success three years before with Crash in '88 enabled that. I remember the band who were supposed to support, The BellTower. They were from the States with an English bass player. Unfortunately they didn't make all the gigs as they either had trouble getting into the country or they were still recording at The Manor."

Mark Badgeman "You can't go too wrong when you get offered an act like The Primitives as long as you realise that their glory days are behind them and that, even though there's a cachet that comes with having an evergreen pop hit, it's not a guaranteed sell out. I haven't got any records of the gig but I don't think it sold out, although it did really well. We'd only been putting big bands on for just over 6 months so this was a massive coup for Kiddy."

## KIDDERMINSTER MARKET TAVERN
COMBERTON PLACE TEL:0562 752590

**FRIDAY 28TH JUNE**
## THE PRIMITIVES
+ BELL TOWER

£3.00 ADV       NO: 150

Mike Moore (DJ) "Paul the guitarist wanted to come on to 'Message To You Rudy' by the Specials. Unfortunately, I was pissed up and let the LP carry on playing for the first 2 or 3 tunes of their set and you could clearly hear the Specials under the Primitives, cue abuse from the stage..."

# Korova Milkbar

Tue 11th Jun 1991

Mark Badgeman "I used to like the Surf Drums in the early 80s and I went to a few of their gigs. I still have one of their records which came out on Joe Foster's label before he started Creation with Alan McGee. They split and re-emerged as Korova Milkbar. They'd had a couple of records out on Chapter 22 but this was towards the end. Might even have been their last gig. I don't think we had many in."

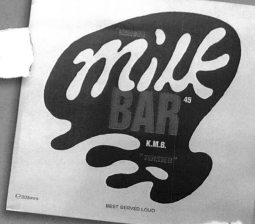

David Myers (Box 'Em Domies) "It was a night of cider and shaving the crowd's heads, Dave cut this lad's head and took a mole off, he was dripping blood all night, he didn't seem to mind hehe."

Dave Travis (Click Club promoter) "I shaved members of the audience's heads while Box 'Em Domies played. There was blood everywhere apparently, in fact there usually was when I did the haircuts as I never put a guard on and was pissed!"

# PANIC BEACH

By Mat

**Which town were you based in?** Wolverhampton & Dudley

**What years were you active?** 1990 – 1994

**Who was in the band?**
Rich Leach vocals rhythm guitar
Andy Gray lead guitar backing vocals
Darren Dickens bass guitar
Mat Power Drums

**What kind of music did you play?**
Heavy indie rock

**Who were the influences?**
Dinosaur Jr, Mudhoney, Led Zep all the classics really

**What level of success did you achieve?**
Released our EP King Normal in 1992 on Chapter 22. Supported Ned's Atomic Dustbin. Toured with PWEI as were label mates. Supported Midway Still a fair few times.

**What do you remember about playing at the Tavern?**
Always had good times at the Tavern. Good crowds... irate farmers, smell of cows, alcohol and cockles...

**How did the band end?**
Called it a day in 94 after recording some great songs...time to move on. We've never been altogether in the same room since...just circumstance not through pure hatred of each other..I think...

**What else do we need to know about the band?**
We were named after the Maria McKee song... no idea why. I think Andy fancied her.

22

**BAND FILE**

# PANIC BEACH

Panic Beach are doing everything they possibly can do to avoid being tagged as part of the Stourbridge scene. They've produced t-shirts bearing the legend 'Never Been To Stourbridge' and are at pains to point out that none of them actually live there. However, geography never mattered much to Scorpio Rising, the only Stourbridge band to come from Liverpool(!), so with Panic Beach originating from Dudley - home of legendary 'Stourbridge' venue, JB's - they're going to have their work cut out convincing people.

Their trump card in this battle is going to be their music and no, it's nothing like the Wonderstuff. Heavily influenced by the Seattle Sub-Pop scene and with an ear for a good tune, they're closer to the likes of Nirvana and Dinosaur Jr. "A melodic noise band" as Matt the drummer observes.

Vocalist Rich and guitarist Andy, started the band last February with the dubious moniker of 'Scream'. They eventually acquired Matt and his cousin Darren on bass and filched the name Panic Beach from a Maria McKee song. They're currently the proud owners of a fanatical local following and the buzz surrounding the band hasn't been this strong locally since the Neds broke out of Stourbridge.

A support slot with the Binmen at Kilburn National, whilst doing little to distance them from the shackles of the St**rbr**ge tag, did wonders for their confidence.

What about before you went on though? Nervous?

"A bit at first" remembers Andy, "...but then it turned to adrenalin and we ended up going down really well."

"About a minute before we were due on stage," continues Rich, the 100 words a second frontman, "we realised that we didn't have any setlists so I just wrote one out in bright green ink as that was all I could find. When we got on stage under the lights, you couldn't read it - it was just a blank piece of paper so I had to introduce each song for the benefit of the rest of the band. Very unprofessional!". Well, the crowd didn't seem to think so and subsequently snapped up all the bands t-shirts.

They've had the usual handful of majors sniffing around but the boys aren't about to leap head first into a deal for the sake of it. They plan on doing it the old fashioned way of working slowly towards the top and are looking for a label prepared to offer them help rather than one who'll just throw money at the band. Rich: "You see all these bands who blow their advances on nice gear but I'd rather it was spent on promotion. We're not after big houses and flash cars, we just want to build it up steadily." "It would be nice to be in the charts doing what Nirvana are doing." adds Andy. And with the state of the charts in recent years, it would be nice to see them there. You can write to the band for details on merchandise and general info at 10a Waverley Street, Dudley, West Midlands, DY2 0YE.

STOP PRESS... Panic Beach will be releasing a single on our favourite label, Chapter 22, in the near future.

## PANIC BEACH
## FOAM
### LONDON ISLINGTON POWERHAUS

On a more cheerful note, Panic Beach proffer the kind of manic, post-Fraggle, shake-yer-hair-until-your-brain-implodes noise which sends Verve fans screaming for the Fash Police. With a frontman who's a lively dead ringer for Joey Ramone (give or take the odd ten stone) it's hardly surprising that a fair chunk of their set relies on whamalamalong sing-song blasts. With loads of hair-shaking.

Equally, given their West Midlands birthplace, the quartet's mish-mash of cheerful thrash rumbles and furry freakouts doesn't exactly register alarmingly high on the amazement scale. Like a huge number of their contemporaries, Panic Beach are providing already-made music for — judging by the accompanying mini-fan club — a ready-made audience.

Intellectual stimulation doesn't enter into it. This, after all, is a comic caper with all the mental sophistication of a dead sloth, which means that it's fun, frivolous and destined to f— off people who — oddly enough — choose not to wander around in extremely short trousers.

Panic Beach? Man those coastal machine guns, if you dare.

**Simon Williams**

Panic Beach
Fri 5th June
MARKET TAVERN
Kidderminster

PANIC BEACH at the Tavern

King Normal

# Scorpio Rising

Andrew Wolfman "Armed with snotty grebo attitude, baggy beats and a boot full of crap oversized watermelon t-shirts, Birkenhead's Scorpio Rising were pretty much the perfect Tavern band. They played everywhere in 1991 and 1992, supporting everyone from the Ned's and PWEI to The Smashing Pumpkins. Their Kenneth Anger inspired name becoming as common at the bottom of gig posters as 'Doors - 7pm' and, dear Lord, didn't they think they were The Doors?

All the band's best stuff was on local label Chapter 22. 'Saturnalia' and 'Silver Surfing' had stirring psych guitars, end-of-the-decade Chemicrazy drums and just enough of a tune to attract the attention of Sire Records, whose legendary boss Seymour Stein (The Ramones, Madonna, Talking Heads) personally picked-up the band.

Hits proved stubbornly hard to come by, however, and the label failed to support their full-length debut 'Pig Symphony' before passing completely on its follow-up, the 'welcome-to-our-new-direction' dance effort 'Brutal Deluxe'.

For a brief window, though, Scorpio Rising were a great night out. A gobby woollyback mishmash of The Stone Roses, The Wonder Stuff and something darker. One proper pop tune away from something special. A guaranteed Market Tavern good time."

Stan The PA Man "As a small local PA company, the gear we had was not always of the highest spec, and at times was a little temperamental. I was standing side of stage on one occasion with, I think, Scorpio Rising soundchecking, when the drummer called to me that the drum fill was on fire. Thinking that he meant it was blown, I went over to find that indeed it was on fire and there was a 2 foot flame licking up the front of the cabinet. I unplugged it, carried it outside and emptied an extinguisher into it whilst the band just carried on regardless."

Lou "I'll never forget this gig (10th July 92) because I interviewed the band! Mark used to produce a fanzine and I ended up being invited to join the girl interviewing them, and wrote up my own version for my media studies coursework. They were a really fun group of guys and the gig went down a storm. It was pretty busy from what I remember with a very energetic crowd."

# Rising stars of Tavern return

News of two bands coming to the Market Tavern who are making waves.

First off are Scorpio Rising, no strangers to Kidderminster having played here last year and who return on February 7.

A chat with lead singer Mickey revealed he has his own personal memories of the Tavern.

He said: "It was a good gig last time, it had a good atmosphere, but it took me a while to get used to the cow s**t round the back!"

This is the band's second solo tour and flogs the launch of the LP If... which was released last week.

Mickey said: "With an EP, you have to cram it all in and blast it out. This is a bit deeper, a bit more ourselves. You could say we explore the dark side of our psyche on this one."

Liverpool-based, Scorpio Rising consist of Mickey, drummer Colin, bassist Steve and guitarists Sploote and Martin.

They took the moniker from the Kenneth Anger film of the same name, and proceeded to make it known nationally with a tour supporting Ned's Atomic Dustbin, a band they are often compared with.

Not so, says Mickey. "We're closer to people like the Boo Radleys, I'd say. We don't use synthesisers or anything like that. We try and keep the live feel, and hopefully this is the year for it."

All sounds good, and worth a look. Ticket details are available from the Market Tavern on Kidderminster 752590.

● Now the second band making waves, or should I say a buzz, are Daisy Chainsaw, who made the Top 40 last week with the quirksome *Love Your Money*.

Coming straight from nowhere, they have already made Number One in the Indie charts and are one of the current faves with Radio One.

They play the Tavern on March 31 with a show that guarantees to be just a little bit different.

The band have decided to do away with the traditional format of support/main act.

Instead, what you will get is Daisy Chainsaw plus two other acts, all alternating on stage at the same time.

The aim is to combine the bands, theatrics, lights and DJ all into one coherent unit with a showtime of two or three hours – which should make for one interesting show.

Tickets are £3.50 and go on sale in next week.

● Mickey in full flight for Scorpio Rising

# REGGAE AT THE TAVERN

Dennis singing with Rhythmites

The crusties, the punks and the dope smokers all loved a bit of reggae. Bushfire, Progression and The Rhythmites were the three main bands who played multiple Tavern shows.

Bushfire were from the 'Thames Delta' if that makes Southend sound a bit better. Formed in 1988, they came armed with their own PA and, as far as I know, used to hire the room themselves. Eventually they acquired their own travelling festival stage, courtesy of Wango Riley. They recently reformed and you'll find an excellent selection of their music if you search YouTube for 'The Bushfire Story'.

Progression were a 5 piece roots and dub band from Wolverhampton featuring DJ Dread Lester. They supported Eek-a-mouse, Aswad, Black Roots, Misty in Roots, Ariwa Posse, Maxi Priest, Billy Bragg and more. Their singer, Dennis, joined The Rhythmites in the mid 90s. If you want to hear them, there's 3 songs on Reverbnation if you search for Progressionband or you could see a reformed version who are still playing, although Lester sadly passed away in 2009.

The Rhythmites formed in the late eighties as a three piece. By 1990 they had grown into a 7 piece. Following the first album 'Integration' they played sell out tours and festivals all over the UK and Europe.

We did at least 5 Tavern shows and they were the most popular of the reggae acts, possibly because they were also regulars on the festival circuit. A brave attempt at musical cross pollination saw Credit To The Nation supporting on one of them.

The band split in 2000 but reformed in 2010 and recorded 'Stand Strong'. The album got great reviews and saw the band back out on the road and back on the festival circuit. In 2015 the Rhythmites went back to the original line up and remixed the first album 'Integration' (it's on Bandcamp as well as on CD). At the time of writing, a brand new album is in the pipeline.

The Rhythmites

DOWNLOAD
ALL 6
ISSUES
FOR FREE
ON
LULU.COM

54

# STRAIGHT ELEPHANT

Fairly early on in my tenure at the Tavern, I got a call from Conal Dodds who was booking shows into Hereford. We teamed up to offer agents the easy option of Kiddy on a Friday night and Hereford on the Saturday night. After a couple of weeks of talking and trading shows, Conal announced he had an idea for a fanzine that was going to be called Straight Elephant and did I want to do it with him. As I used to be a printer and knew all about old fashioned cut and paste, I took on the job of laying it out as well as being the co-editor.

If we'd written down our aims for the fanzine, they'd be; get more free records, get on guest lists, promote our own shows by writing about the bands. Possibly in that order! I enlisted the help of my Dutch friends, Annabel, Martyn and Maartje and we got other people to write articles and reviews. Conal photocopied it at work and then we smashed up copies of Langfield Crane's single for our front cover gag of 'Free record... when you buy 500 copies'. Langfield Crane's manager found out and wasn't very happy. We thought it was hysterical.

The first one sold really well and whilst we were flogging it in Worcester outside a gig, we were approached by Kevin Savage, who ran a graphic design company called ImageSet. He liked it and wanted to offer his services to do the design. We were impressed because he was young, had a flash car and his posh offices were in an old half-timbered building in Worcester. The deal was that he'd lock us in the office at night, we'd type our content onto his Apple Macs and then he'd let us out in the morning and do the page layout the next day. He also copied the second one for us because Conal was now doing gigs full-time and didn't have access to a work photocopier. It looked really good and we sold all 1000 copies.

By the time of issue 3, we were getting it properly printed and stapled. It was probably the best laid out fanzine in the country as desktop publishing was still pretty new and it was really hard to buy Apple computers because they weren't available in shops. Kev's design went from strength to strength, we still pissed ourselves all night, locked in his office, coming up with childish slag offs or typing in contributions ready for the page layout process.

Every issue sold out of its 1000 print run, mostly because we'd engage in all sorts of tactics like putting a band on the cover because we knew they were going on tour and then flogging it to the queues on the way in. We started to slow down by issue 6 and we were a bit slow to put it out, possibly losing a bit of momentum. It's a shame because issue 6 was the best one - it had Nirvana on the cover and an interview inside, Hellen had been kidnapped by Courtney Love and wrote about sharing a bed with her, I'd done an interview with Siouxsie's Banshees in Holland (she doesn't speak before gigs apparently) and we'd crammed in all the usual suspects.

The big coup was something we couldn't use. Courtney had shown Hellen how she'd smuggled smack into the country for Kurt Cobain (still called Kurdt at the time) in a secret compartment of her make up compact. Kurt was smacked out in the tour van when Conal did the interview. We were friends with their press officer and there'd been nothing in the music press about his drug use. We really wanted to print it but we thought we'd end up falling out with too many people so we just hinted at it in the article. You can see it a lot easier now, reading it with hindsight. We just knew it wasn't going to end well.

I think we ended up with boxes of issue 6 under our beds so we never did another one. I did a new fanzine called Back To Front (which was brilliant!) but it only lasted for one issue. I did get involved with a couple of other people's fanzines such as printing up Chesh and Katie's Radio Elixir. Conal went off and became the promoter for some band called Oasis amongst others.

Conal "I remember the time we went to Cambridge - we had EMF on the cover - we got the date wrong and were there a day early, we went to the cinema and pub I think and then slept in Badgeman's Bedford Rascal!"

Conal "I think the story at the time was that Kurt had narcolepsy which was given as the excuse for him falling asleep randomly."

55

# BOB & The Liberty Thieves

Arthur Tapp (Liberty Thieves) "The Market Tavern was always one of those venues you had heard of, it was on every band's gig list in the music papers and so, being Birmingham based, it was always an aspiration to play there.

The Liberty Thieves got their chance in Nov 1991, supporting one of our favourite bands BOB.

BOB were great to us, giving us support slots and eventually they were part of the reason for me becoming a gig promoter for the past 30 years (notably the Jug of Ale 1992 - 2006, Birmingham O2 Academy 2000 - present and various others!)

Somehow it seemed easier to get the bands I loved to come to me rather than following them round the country. Mark was always hugely supportive and I recall many happy chats on the phone discussing indie music and sharing our thoughts.

Things came full circle when BOB reformed around 25 years later in the 2010s and I was roped in to play bass guitar on tours. I wonder what that teenage fan would think of this strange life. I think he'd be pleased somehow."

THE LIBERTY THIEVES

ORIGINAL BADGEMAN ARTEFACT
A HANDWRITTEN PRESS RELEASE!

# Top Fri 6th Sept 1991

TOP - KIDDERMINSTER MARKET TAVERN - 06.09.91
This was the sort of gem we used to get at the Tavern on a fairly regular basis thanks to the Badgeman. Top flew just enough below the radar to enable us to get to see them at the Tavern. I'll never truly understand why some bands don't get fame, or at least critical adulation. Top were well placed to receive both. Emotion Lotion is an excellent album, full of top pop tunes. Yet whatever it was, bad timing, lack of record company push, it never happened. They were a decent live band too.
Prior to their set, we had watched Cake again. Either there were no other local acts at the time or they had something over Badgeman. This can be the only way to account for them always being the support band.

FROM LUNCHTIME FOR THE WILD YOUTH

TOP'S No 1 DOMINATOR SINGLE GOT TO No 67 IN THE CHARTS!

CRAZYHEAD PLAYED TWICE IN 1991 & 1992

£3.00 advance
£3.50 on door

kidderminster Market Tavern Fri 16th August '91

Traci Templer" Ooh...I went to the Crazyhead gig...I remember it being good even tho' there was a distinct lack of Porkbeast if my memory serves me right..." (Porkbeast was the bassist)

# ROBERT PLANT
## Benefit Gig - 1991, date unknown

John Peutherer "I was playing for local r'n'b/ part-comedy part-funk band The Ripps. Previously known as the Incomparable Kernel Clarke. I'd taken over drums from Garry Hawkes who was concentrating on UXB with John Parmenter. The previous drummer had been Jason Bonham. The lineup when I played was:

John Peutherer: drums
Bunter Clarke: vocals
Darren Norgrove: percussion
Andy Hipkins: bass
Chris Jones: guitar (also with The Stubble Brothers)
John Taylor: Harmonica

Robert Plant had got up and played with the band at times before I joined.

Anyway we were shattered when Darren was killed in an accident at work on a building site on New Rd. There was a pretty bad recession on at the time and work was scarce. Darren was self-employed and uninsured. This left his wife Katrina and young son Jack in a terrible crisis in every way.

We decided to do a memorial gig to remember Darren and to raise some money for the family. Planty put a band together with Chris Jones, Ian 'Tat' Hatton, Jason Bonham and a bass player I can picture but never knew. They played second, basically as our support band, the set was r'n'b standards like 'Baby Please Don't Go' and Roy Head's 'Treat Her Right'.

The Stubble Brothers played first I think. There was also a performance duo juggling on unicycles etc. The whole set was relayed via tv into the bar.

I was a bit of a punk and not overly impressed by this Led Zep crowd and Jason not bringing his own sticks to play my kit... so I took mine away after soundcheck. I remember him yelling at me for sticks! I gave in and he gave me some cymbals later in return... good deal!! I've met him in more recent times and he's a very different person now and all the better for it.

I have played with Planty since and he really is one of the greatest people you could ever meet. So knowledgeable, very humble. Really great guy."

Stan The PA Man "Probably one of the craziest nights was the night that Robert Plant played, it was a benefit gig for a guy who had been in bands and Robert knew. I have no idea how many were in but I have never seen so many people in one place. All I can remember is people standing on every surface or table or chair or each other. I hate to think how far over capacity we were."

# Rockin' Robert!

Rock stars Robert Plant and Jason Bonham were on the bill at a fundraising concert for the family of a Kidderminster musician who died.

Together with local bands The Ripps and Billy Bowel and The Movements, they raised £3,000 in front of a capacity crowd at the Market Tavern in Kidderminster on Friday night.

The ex-Led Zeppelin lead singer sang six songs – Born Under A Bad Sign, Love Potion Number 9, Money, Blues, Baby Please Don't Go and Treat Her Right.

The money was for the family of Darren Norgrove, percussionist with Kidderminster band Kernal Klarke which was forerunner to The Ripps.

He died earlier this year after a fall at work, leaving a wife and three children.

A spokesman for the Market Tavern said: "Robert Plant knows Kernal Klarke, he's jumped up on stage with them in the past, so when they approached him and said they were doing this he didn't hesitate to agree."

● Rock legend Robert Plant, hekping the fundraising in Kidderminster last week.

Players

# Big break blow hits local R'n'B hopefuls

Wyre Forest rhythm 'n' blues band The Ripps are fretting because they have lost their lead guitarist for an R&B contest that could give them their big break.

Guitarist Chris will be working abroad when the band join the annual Musicians Against Cancer/Banks' Brewery National Blues Contest at the Stewponey Hotel, Stourton, near Stourbridge, on Friday, April 24.

They were overjoyed when they were told they had qualified for the last 100 bands in the contest, but dismayed when they realised Chris would be unavailable.

So the others - bassist Andy, vocalist Bunter, harmonica player J.T. and drummer John - urgently need a stand-in for the night.

Any guitarist who can help is urged to telephone Bunter on Kidderminster 823261.

Pictured around Chris's vacant guitar, from left to right, are J.T., Andy, Bunter and John.

You can read about The Ripps / Kernal Clarke in John Combe's Get Your Kicks On The A456, the classic text on the Kidderminster music scene, so I won't repeat it here (get it from the library if you don't have a copy!). If they weren't headlining or playing with Robert Plant, you might have seen them supporting Steve Gibbons or Trevor Burton either at the Tavern or elsewhere on the Midland's pub circuit. The picture in the cutting below was taken at the Market Tavern.

---

**MARKET TAVERN**
COMBERTON PLACE KIDDERMINSTER

A benefit gig for the children of Richard Norton

D. Block          **Bob's Last Band**
The Ripps

Saturday 4th April 1992

Evening 7.30

UNRESERVED

£3.00   Advance

No. 0113

Retain This Portion   Conditions Overleaf

---

# This Kernel's going nuts for more live gigs

Introducing the Incomparable Kernel Klarke, who will be gracing the hallowed stage of the Market Tavern this weekend.

This is the latest band I'm putting in the Spotlight following my brainwave of occasionally featuring local groups and letting you know who they are.

IKK are all local lads, and here's who they are. On bass is Andy Hipkins, Chris Jones is on lead guitar, Jim Clarke is vocals, John Taylor on bass, John Peutherer on drums, Jim Ganderton on keyboards and Darren Norgrove on congas.

Apart from new addition John Peutherer on drums, the lads have been going as they are for the last five years.

They play a mixture of R'n'B and funk, and are working at laying down their first demo.

You can see them at the Tavern this Saturday night, ring the pub on Kidderminster 752590 for details. Support is the Madison Blues Band.

P.S. If you like what you see on the night and want to book them, ring John Clarke on Kidderminster 823261.

● RIGHT: An incomplete but Incomparable Kernel Klarke — Chris Jones (top left), Andy Hipkins, John Peutherer, Darren Norgrove, John Clarke and John taylor. Missing is Jim Ganderton.

---

Stan The PA Man "I soundchecked Steve Gibbons Band and the guitar was ear splittingly loud. Despite my requests to turn it down, he refused so I waited until they had finished and thought I would turn it down myself. I now know I was not the first engineer to try this as I found the volume knob glued in place."

Su Taylor "Off my beaten track, but I remember seeing Steve Gibbons there. Probably others too but my memory is poor these days. Seem to remember the atmosphere was a bit intimidating."

# BIKERS & REGULARS

The Head Barman "Pete from Chaos MC was hitching a lift from the Loom & Shuttle on the Stourport Rd. He was picked up by Andy Price on his way up from Bath to take over the Tavern. Pete said Chaos were looking for somewhere new to drink so Andy invited them to use the Tavern. The bikers who used the Tavern were Chaos, a few of the Outlaws and after about '95, the Unforgiven."

Pete

Angela Thould "I was working the bar (as a favour as the afternoon shift hadn't appeared) when the Hells Angels came down and attacked the Outlaws."

The Head Barman "The Hells Angels turned up one day looking for three particular bikers. It was a Saturday lunchtime and people were eating. The Angels arrived in five cars and made a pincer movement on the pub, coming in through all the doors and windows at the same time. They told anyone who didn't want to get involved to go in the back room and they locked the women and children in the toilets. It was carnage - there were machetes and guns involved. When we cleaned up afterwards, it looked like an abattoir. The police were sat at the bottom of the road waiting for it to finish because they didn't want to get involved."

John Gorman, Angela Thould, Dawn Hill, Dave Stone and Shooie

Marcus Jones "I remember once seeing a load of blokes turning up with hammers, smashing up all the bikes outside and then going inside, presumably to do the same to the bikes' owners - me and my mates legged it into the Farmer's! Probably about 1996."

Jimbob, Andy Farley & Shoob

Neil Phillips "I saw Pulkas play there and I think that may have been the gig when a load of Essex Hells Angels burst in and put an axe in someone's head. I remember them holding his head together whilst they mopped the blood up around him. Me and my mate were interviewed by Central News outside afterwards."

The Head Barman "One afternoon, Pete the Piss was throwing knives at me which were sticking in the wood behind the optics. He eventually passed out so I drew panda eyes on him with a permanent marker and wrote TWAT on his forehead in mirror writing. He came round and went down town where he noticed what I'd done. When he came back, he spiked everyone's drinks with LSD and then smashed the pub up with a pool cue. Andy was just rolling around on the floor laughing."

Andy Price "I would like to point out that the acid in the 90s was nothing like the acid of the 70s, I called it baby acid."

# Radical Dance Faction

Sat 21st Dec 1991
w / Tribe

Fri 19th Mar 1993
Ancient Ones, Jerk Frenzy

Fri 15th Dec 1995
w / Rhythm Killers

Chris Bowsher's Radical Dance Faction (RDF) was surely the blueprint for Sleaford Mods? Socially conscious and politically aware spoken lyrics over dub beats and bassline. They were the ultimate crusty band and a great Tavern booking, although they were consistently only worth just under 200 tickets, whereas the likes of Back To The Planet could sell out.

Lou "I hadn't heard of RDF before, but it was a great night - I bought an LP and still have it today, nearly 20 years later!"

Aidan Cope "I remember the guy out of Radical Dance Faction being a TOTAL prima donna. Not very crusty."

ANOTHER TRULY TERRIBLE HAND DRAWN POSTER!

Andrew Wolfman "I think RDF got banned from going near the kitchen because they were too unhygienic. Or was it something more sinister than that?"

# TAVERN MEMORIES

Rich Morley (Pale Kings) "The Tavern had a unique vibe, it was just the place where all the right people got together and made things happen. It often felt more of an accident than design. We didn't realise that we were living in times that would be looked back on so fondly and that we were getting involved in something that was so special. I remember badgering Badgeman a few times to get us some good support slots and to be fair, he really had his finger on the pulse and got us and the venue so many memorable nights - all of a sudden Kidderminster was on the map! The Tavern was open to any creative ideas and I even remember us putting on an Industrial Techno night. It was so sad when it closed, there was nothing to fill the void it left until Sid and Sand Palmer took on the Boar's Head, but that didn't last for long."

Janine Calder "The whole vibe was incredible . I used to have people from all over that attended the gigs camp out at mine, inside and outside in live-in vehicles. We would then troop down Lorne Street in colourful clothes and with expressive hair styles, heading to The Tavern for a gig. One big happy Tribe. I had a couple of Uk Subs stay at mine. Citizen Fish and a few others."

The Head Barman "At one of the busy gigs, maybe RDF, somebody let the cows out. One went all the way down Comberton Hill. The police came and shot it!"

Birdie "I remember straw in the toilets, Chumbawamba's Dan But No Bacon putting us on the guest list when we arrived from Wales only to find it sold out, parking the trucks on the car park outside and drunken after-parties, the last couple of gigs I went to it was feeling 'edgy' because the bikers had taken over. Mark on the door was a sound fella. Johnny Vinyl kicked the back door open for us on the odd occasion!"

Andy Price "They were very special days, the correct mixture of everyone, we all bounced off each other."

# JOHNNY VINYL
## THE BROMSGROVE MASSIVE

"Kiddy Tavern - for the scene/lifestyle that my friends and I were into: crusty/punky/new age travelling, dub lovers... it was the closest thing to being at a (free) festival (not 'free', apart from the occasional... snook in... sorry!) that we could find in our locality. Half of us (the Bromsgrove Massive) actually held down full-time jobs. Though some were, went on to become and still are, 'proper' New Age Travellers. The scourge of the Daily Mail, amongst others.

The Tavern kept us going, in between days spent lying in muddy fields, or dancing in the rain to RDF, Back To The Planet, Rhythm-ites, Credit To The Nation, Senser et al and long trips anywhere, to meet up with kindred spirits in pubs, clubs, bars and homes. London, Bristol, Birmingham, Redditch, Northampton and Peterboro! (Yes, they all had a free festival, at some point).

Everybody loved Kiddy Tavern! Meeting up on the car park (why go anywhere else before the Tavern?). A fine selection of vans, trucks and... my 2CV! Bringing crusties, booze and copious amounts of narcotics to our favourite haunt. And in a town where the only other reason to visit, was Mr Tee's!!

The approach to the front door was tinted with caution due to having to run the gauntlet of the bikers who would be commandeering the pool tables and offering up quizzical looks in the front bar. We didn't look back and they generally ignored us. The only time we loitered was to get a beer in that front bar, having seen the queue to get in to the gig. It was never more than five minutes to get in, but five minutes is an eternity without alcohol in hand! Sometimes there was no queue and sometimes it had long gone, as we were hanging around in the corridor to the loos... having just met up with someone who was last seen, flailing around to the Ozrics at the One World festival, in... Frome! Then the speed kicked in and and the strains of the support band could be heard and off we went into the room for beer... and to dance.

As dogs on ropes weren't allowed in, crusties kept up some of their image by spilling gallons of cider onto the floor. One dub-step outta place and down you went. Everyone smoked and that

resulted in getting pretty messy. A badge of pride. The Tavern WAS a minor mecca for the New Age underground. Beats, bongs and poetry. RDF (best band on the planet), AOS3, Credit To The Nation, Back To The Planet, Citizen Fish, The Rhythm-ites... they were all our 'kin'. Amazing 'finds'.

To miss RDF or The Rhythm-ites, or Chumbawamba...was bordering on sacrilegious and for those who didn't make it to the Tavern... there was NO excuse, bar death! RDF by far had the best songs and 'Surplus People' was an anthem of the age... We all learnt about poetry thanks to RDF (and LKJ...who did not play the Tavern).

It was a great place to meet friends and acquaintances before you saw them again... two weeks later, lying in another field. One foot tapping away to the not so great Blaggers ITA. Missed them at Tavern, if they played? The Rhythm-ites were fantastic. Full of love and dub and sweet sounds and great connection with the audience. After releasing a cassette (bought and lost at the gig) they released 'Integration', one of the best British reggae albums EVER.... A fairly unknown LP... even now.

There was rarely any trouble at the gigs... we were after all, not just nutters from Bromsgrove but peace loving, fun loving dopers and pissheads... out for a great time and in a great place. One thing that annoyed me was the smashing of glasses and free abandon pissing out the back. Our rule was: don't fuck up a place that serves you so well!

I could ramble on all day but ..RDF, Rhythm-Ites, Fun-Da-Mental, Credit to the Nation and BOFF..unmissable! Great times. All hail Dick and Citizen Fish... All hail the Tavern!"

# Midway Still

Andrew Wolfman "There was much more to Midway Still than met the eye. At first glance, they were all matted-hair and mouldy Converse, hard-gigging, Transit-van road-dogs. They seemed to turn up at the Tavern on any day that had a 'y' in it, plying t-shirt shifting punk-pop like a less silly Snuff, or a slightly less successful Mega City Four.

This does them a disservice though. The 'hits' (as much as there were hits) like 'I Won't Try' displayed a surprisingly affecting emotional heft on top of the hurtling rhythms. Later songs like Summercide had legitimately bruising guitars, and, at their best, the band recalled a heartfelt Home-Counties Husker Du (I told you they were Mould-y) at a time when most bands were still praying to Jesus Jones.

Much more than many of their peers, Midway Still's back-catalogue stands up to a reappraisal. After a long hiatus, the band emerge from time-to-time: never showy, always under-rated and, arguably, better than before. (That's the name of one of their songs, by the way. Honestly, I'm not just phoning this stuff in)."

HOLOGRAM PRESENTS:-
The **BOLLWEEVILS** + **FRETBLANKET** + MERCENARY TREE FREAKS
Fri 22nd Nov £2.50

HOLOGRAM PRESENTS:-
**MIDWAY STILL** + **PANIC BEACH** + **SLOTH**
Fri 29th Nov £3.00

**MARKET TAVERN**
**KIDDERMINSTER**
Last Trains - B'ham 23.07, Worcs 23.50 (1 Minute...)

THE RETURN OF...
**MIDWAY STILL**
+ The Berts
+ Genius Freak
**Friday 4th February**
**MARKET TAVERN**
KIDDERMINSTER
£3.00 Advance
7.30 - 11.00

**MIDWAY STILL**

**BETTER THAN BEFORE**

## Welcome break

In the wake of the upsurge in popularity of all things American, Midway Still provide a rather welcoming break.
The British answer to Buffalo Tom and Husker Du have been out of the spotlight since the release of the excellent 'Dial Square' album which coincided with their tour with Mega City Four. But they return to the scene with a gig at Kidderminster's Market Tavern tomorrow night May 14 supported by the new look Panic Beach whose change in direction has earned them the title of the 'British Metallica.'
The bill is opened by Elizabeth Jane and admission is £3.

**MIDWAY STILL - DIAL SQUARE**

NECK CD LP 8     081-806 9922

SIDE B
Make A Start
What You Said
Wish
Brand New
Sweat
Heaven

SIDE A
Found
Better Than Before
Me In You
Gun
Making Time
Killing Time
Come Down

ROUGHNECK RECORDING CO.

## MIDWAY STILL, THE BERTS AND GENIUS FREAK

Midway Still last graced the Tavern stage at the now legendary Kidderminster Free Festival back in the summer. They were one of the top bands who have enjoyed playing Kidderminster so much in the past that they came up and did it for nothing.
This time they're back with a new set ready for the new album although they plan to romp through all the old crowd pleasers like Better Than Before and I Won't Try.
The Berts are one of Worcester's best bands, their punk inspired pop songs won them the Three Counties Battle of the Bands at the Northwick recently and they currently have a bit of label interest.
Genius Freak is just one man these days. Leeson O'Keefe, his guitar and his tape player may sound like a cabaret act but you'll be in for a pleasant surprise. He spent the summer playing guitar for ex Pogue Shane Magowen's new band which culminated in a huge festival in Ireland attended by 40,000, but his own music is firmly in the tradition of The Senseless Things and Leatherface. He's supported Carter and Mega City Four and despite the unusual line up has always gone down a storm. Get there early to make sure you see him.
Admission £3.00 Advance

PRESS RELEASE

# FRETBLANKET

### By Andrew Wolfman

I was at a party with Fretblanket the night that Kurt Cobain died. I doubt, at the time, we appreciated what a significant evening this would be for our musical ambitions, or what a niche nineties name-drop this might eventually become.

We found out the tragic, but not entirely unexpected, news from Ceefax (ask your Nan) in between games of Sonic The Hedgehog (the third one was just out) and cans of Colt 45. There is, perhaps, a reason why Prince partied like it was 1999 and not 1994.

It was a bad scene. Kids were crying, Simon Bell locked himself in the cellar with the CD single of 'Sliver' (which I always thought was a bit overdramatic) and one wag walked up to Will Copley, Fretblanket's gravel-voiced front man, and said, "Looks like there's a job going. Are you going to apply?"

"Mate," Will twinkled, "that's in pretty poor taste. And anyway, why would I want to join Nirvana? I'm the singer in Fretblanket."

He had a point. You'd be forgiven for not knowing it now, but Fretblanket were kind of a big deal. These days, there's depressingly little left of them online. You won't find their songs on streaming services, there's no deluxe box set of their classic albums.

And yet, they accomplished more than most bands could ever dream of. There was an NME single of the week, a major label record deal, an MTV video hit, and, perhaps more Market Tavern appearances than any other band. They made a pretty-bloody-good stab at 'breaking the States' with major festival slots and dates with Radiohead, Weezer and

Hole, but their big achievements seem to have fallen on the wrong side of both the dot com boom and the Atlantic to be properly celebrated back home.

In April 1994, though, not only was it not absurd that Will might get a phone call from Dave Grohl, it seemed only a matter of time until his band broke internationally. Fretblanket were confident, good-looking and very young, a precocious power pop band, built on big guitar lines and a passionate throaty vocal. They had, in the words of chief songwriter Clive Powell, "lyrics that people wanted to listen to and a voice that people wanted to hear. We had a belief in what we were doing which came through as intensity and power. And we rocked, hard."

That they did, and, unusually, for Stourbridge's 'next big band' their music had more in common with the muscular Mid-West melodies of, say, Bob Mould's Sugar than the sampleadelic smart-arsery and umpteen bass players of their DY8 forbears. The breakthrough songs: Twisted, Curtainsville, Now We're 30 (remember when 30 was the most ancient age you could possibly imagine?) are deceptively simple direct hits: teenage love songs played by a lion lunged Buzzcocks with a decidedly American fuzz box. They were properly good.

Of all the bands that regularly frequented the Market Tavern, Fretblanket seemed to be the most fully-realised and mature, which was weird, because they really were just boys when this was all happening.

Bass player Dave Allsopp remembers that when the band signed its record deal with Polygram/Polydor, "We had to fly Will's mum to New York with us, because at age 17, he wasn't legally old enough to sign the contract on his own."

By this stage, the band had already been together for years, having originally met 'in utero' (could this story be any more grunge?)

"My Mum met Will's Mum at a new mothers' group - I was a baby and Will's Mum was still expecting," says Dave. Drummer Matt Carey didn't sign on until he was 7, and guitarist Clive was a practically geriatric 11 before meeting the rest of the band. Mrs Copley would provide a rehearsal space for the fledgling Fretblanket (and, it needs be noted, made spectacular chutney).

"Being so young, we had A LOT of time on our hands," Dave recalls, "our practice space was the cellar at Will's house, and we were

quite fanatical about going there after school and on weekends to hang out and rehearse. There was this very accelerated timeframe where we were playing constantly, listening to other people's music and learning how to construct songs."

Will confirms that, sort of. "Originally, we listened to a lot of Anthrax and did a thrash metal version of 'The Only Way is Up' by Yazz," he laughs, "before Clive turned up and told us about The Stone Roses and Ride."

Powell quickly started bringing complete songs to the band, "He came into his own as a songwriter very quickly," notes Dave, "it became apparent almost immediately that he had the real songwriting talent. And he would write A LOT."

As Clive saw it, "At 16, we hit a point where our emotional life was charged (or mine was), so the songs were real. We had a bit of spare cash to buy better kit... And of course, we were all young and devastatingly attractive..."

This certainly helped, and the band started gigging, graduating from a lunchtime slot in the Redhill School hall, "it was raining so most of the school showed up," boasts Dave, to, "fly-posting Stourbridge high street with a couple of hundred posters in preparation for a gig at the Mitre."

With a hundred quid in pocket from the sold-out Stourbridge show, The Market Tavern played a big part in their development. "Our first supporting gig at the Tavern was a big deal," Dave remembers, "not only was it a 'proper gig' in a faraway town (it's literally seven miles away - AW) but we had to impress the legendary Badgeman to get it".

"Eventually, we took Badgeman for granted," Will suggests, "but I remember being impressed by him counting money in the foul smelling back room of the Tavern, then the next thing you know he's driving us around in the Badgevan to support big bands".

Clive, rightly, points out that, not only did Kidderminster have an excellent venue, but, "a great guitar shop (Crotchet Quaver) where we could spend Saturdays perving over shiny new gear, and a splendid chip shop (Captain Cod's) which (junk) fuelled pretty much all of our Tavern adventures."

(NB: Junkfuel was the name of Fretblanket's blistering major label debut

Ben Anderson "Well I only ever managed a couple of visits to the Tav, it's not easy when you live 15 miles away and you're 15, but can still remember seeing one of my all time fav's Fretblanket live, awesome, although the wheels fell off towards the end of the night, too much of the good old JR Severn Bore!!!"

Sarah Fawsitt "I would tend to drive a couple of the Frets, Will, Chris and co plus equipment to the gig in my Fiesta, watch the bands then drive them home, drink tea and listen to all the stories of the night until the early hours."

**fretblanket**

Photo Credit: Karen Mason

single of the week under their belt, the journalist / DJ / human gig-machine Steve Lamacq declared them, "too young to drink, but old enough to smoke like bastards" before the band guest-starred on the Channel Four reality series "The Next Big Thing" swiftly making the show's supposed stars FMB look like the hopeless half-arsed anti-talents they so obviously were.

And then Kurt Cobain died.

The bottom fell out of grunge almost immediately in the UK. Long-haired lumberjack guitar bands were swiftly usurped in the hearts of the record buying public by the flag-waving oompah and full-English Brexit of Britpop.

album. Clive didn't technically say that anything had been junk-fuelled by Captain Cod. I added that bit, and it is pure fan speculation, that the album took its name from trips to the Comberton Hill eatery - AW)

Success came quickly. Early, fringe-swingers like 'Diesel' gave way to radio-friendly buzzsaw bangers like 'Twisted' from the 'Better Than Swimming EP' and, in spite of a seasonal show with Cake and Panic Beach where they performed a days-long distorted version of the twelve days of Christmas, changing 'a partridge in a pear tree' to 'a fart in an astronaut suit' (which is why Clive, rather than Will, wrote the rest of their lyrics) the band were taken on by The Wonder Stuff's manager Dave Alldridge. By next Christmas they would be playing with Pulp, and the four school friends were by far the bigger draw.

Big gigs followed. The band played to 2,000 at the Chester Northgate Arena with Ned's while still at sixth form. They rammed the second stage of the 45,000 capacity Phoenix Festival, with a much-talked-about first on, before recording their debut album at Ridge Farm with Tim Palmer (the producer of Pearl Jam's 'Ten'). Already with an NME

"Any sensible band would've gone to Camden and caused some trouble." reckons Will. "That's what the UK press wanted." All eyes were on London, and the heads of the music industry were being turned by any number of Dickensian street-urchins with Union Jack guitars, but Fretblanket, "stayed in The Bell in Stourbridge having girlfriends and playing pool, not wearing daring outfits or doing anything interesting with our hair," Will shrugs.

"Our style of music was much more suited to an American audience than a British one at the time" notes Dave, "so most of our business was done over there."

WILL WITH MEAL TICKET
AT PHOENIX FESTIVAL

brilliantly loopy espionage-themed video for lead single 'Into the Ocean,' complete with underwater cars, jet-packs and judo.

It was star-making stuff, like The Beastie Boys being let loose on Thunderbirds' Tracy Island, and the video made a fittingly big splash on MTV's 'Twelve Angry Viewers' before going into rotation on the station. Somehow, though, the album campaign stalled. The band never quite shifting enough units to appease their label, and with some reviews lazily lumping the band in with Gavin Rossdale's, infinitely inferior band, Bush, as a pretty boy Brits-abroad grunge band.

This was criminal. Ten years, and a little eyeliner later, Home Truths could be filed under emo, and The Get Up Kids and Jimmy Eat World would fill swimming pools with champagne thanks to the money they made from this kind of high-class, heartfelt pop. These though, were the Clinton years. The US had just got rid of one Bush and couldn't really risk another one. Not for a couple more years at least.

Dave Allsopp is refreshingly, open about the band's time in the US.

"We were a bit naive about the music industry (as it was then). We really had no clue what we were doing and mostly went along with whatever people asked us to do. We were indie kids in the early '90s, so we found most of the major-label business stuff - particularly as British kids dealing with Americans - to be distasteful and weird."

The band were a staple of college radio in the US, and toured hard there in support of Junkfuel, before recording their second effort 'Home Truths From Abroad' with Tim Patalan and a respectable budget. The album documented the band's transatlantic displacement and boasted beefed-up guitars, and significantly more complex songwriting. Ironically, perhaps, given the perception of the band as being slightly too American for the Britpop palate there was a little of Oasis' 'Acquiesce' in the swaggering vocal and trademark high harmony of the album's standout track 'Hammer and Tongues'.

The record was mixed at Nirvana producer Butch Vig's studios, "while Vig was next door mixing U2 songs and writing stuff for Garbage's first record," recalls Dave. The band were in lofty company, and soon headed to Hollywood to shoot the

## SINGLE OF THE WEEK 2

**FRET BLANKET: Twisted**
*(Neck Mohican/Atlas)*
*Arrh, this should cheer the miserable cynics who moan music is dead. Four 17-year-old lads from Stourbridge who, despite the recent vibrant musical history of that area, have still managed to make a record that's individual and current. This, their debut single, is marvellously uplifting in the manner of Hüsker Dü. It's a love song, sour in emotion and drenched in sincerity.*
B: "Brilliant! The perfect pop song. 'Take off my clothes and drag me to the sea' – what a line, man. I know what that feels like. I'm absolutely blown away, I wasn't expecting that at all. It sends shivers down my spine. I

wanna hear that again and then steal the tape."
C: "Yep, that's really cool. They communicate really well. I did get a feeling off that and that's what bands are meant to do. Obviously guitar bands say something to me, it's all I've ever listened to so I'm gonna understand them a lot better than someone like Einsturzende Neubauten. And another thing, they're obviously not pandering to the radio market either, because they say 'f—' on it. Has to be a Single Of The Week."
B: "Oh yeah, it was brilliant. It really moved me, I thought it was so well-written and . . ."
C: "You are very easily moved though. Elevator music moves this guy."

Will agrees, "In America we spent most of the time in our bus playing cards on our own, making fun of things. I think we thought that because The Beatles were incredibly charming all the time, people would think we were too, but we thought they were strange, and they thought we were rude."

Winningly, the band seem to have few regrets. Will suggests that "maybe, we didn't need to always order the most expensive thing on the menu. 45 bucks for some meatloaf!" Dave thinks, "Maybe we missed some opportunities in terms of how the band was promoted which could have taken us to another level. But, at the same time, I think our youth and inexperience was key to how wildly enthusiastic we were about our music and how we bonded as a band, and I wouldn't want to go back and change that".

A third Fretblanket record was recorded, but never released. It's slightly slower, older and wiser. A great grown-up album, by a band still five years away from thirty. Like everything they did, it was a class act. Powerful, passionate and cripplingly underrated. In 'Digging Your Scene' it features one of the band's best songs.

There was no big break-up, no real falling out. Drummer Matt didn't suddenly turn into Mariah Carey and throw a diva strop, "it all just went a bit poo," he says, "we sort of drifted off and did other things. There are no dramatic onstage bust ups to report on, the rhythm section just moved to America."

And so, this incredibly tight-knit group found themselves split up. They always seemed an island of their own, 'too American' for Britpop, but too brash and British for the States. They were miles ahead of their peers, but slightly out of step with the whims of the music industry.

T-SHIRT MODEL'S OWN

A brilliant band that never quite found a home on either side of the ocean ended up on both.

Going back to that party in 1994, Nirvana never did call, but The Foo Fighters were definitely making notes as they became the biggest band on the planet with a decidedly Fretblanket formula. If what the world wants is hooky, two-footed grunge-pop belted out by a good-bloke who sings like a friendly bear who stood on an upturned plug, you can keep your Dave Grohl, Will Copley and Fretblanket are my guys every single time.

PHOTO BY JOHN HULME

By Chris Perks

**Which town were you based in?** Stourbridge

**What years were you active?** We started at secondary school around 1989, but didn't settle into our final 3-piece line-up and start gigging properly until late 1990 or early 1991. We continued playing until 1993.

**Who was in the band?**
Dan McEwen (Lead Vocals and Bass), Lee Biggs (Drums), Chris Perks (Guitar and Backing Vocals)

**What kind of music did you play?**
Indie-rock – our demo tapes sound a lot more 'shoe gazey' than our live shows, which were pretty loud.

**Who were the influences?**
Different for each band member, but including Ride, The Wonderstuff, Pearl Jam (we covered their 'Elderly Woman Behind the Counter in a Small Town' a couple of times), the Cure, Pixies, Dinosaur Jnr., Buffalo Tom, James, Led Zeppelin, The Wedding Present.

**What level of success did you achieve?**
Our highlight was getting into the final of the Express & Star Battle of the Bands in December 1992 and playing at the Wulfrun Hall in Wolverhampton in front of a big crowd with a massive PA and lighting rig... Some huge acts have played at the Civic and Wulfrun Halls (Chris saw Ice-T at the Civic), so it was amazing to get the chance to gig in the same place. Fretblanket lent us all their amps and kit and some of them roadied for us. The amazing Vicky from Fuzzbox and Jonn Penney from Ned's Atomic Dustbin were two of the judges... we didn't win. We also got a call from Sony Records once, asking us to send in a demo tape. We never heard back, despite chasing.

**What do you remember about playing at the Tavern?**
Making good friends, a lot of laughing, and very good times. Newcastle Brown Ale in fullsize bottles. Bechy's amazing vegetable lasagne. Cramming amps and drums into our friend Sarah's tiny car, and her volunteering to drive back and forth to Stourbridge to take our kit and us home. Running like crazy to catch the last train back to Stourbridge just after 11... In fact, we had a song called 'Last Train Home' which was inspired by this incredible rite-of-passage which many punters (and some band members) went through after each gig. The overwhelming smell of cattle in the toilets. Mosh pits. Swinging from the lighting rigs to be told to get off, as it wasn't designed for the weight of a human. Smoking on the metal staircase

**Any memories of the other bands you played with at the Tavern?**
We played with Fretblanket, Cake and Scrash, who were mates of ours (there was an annual Stourbridge bands and fans vs Kidderminster bands and fans football game for a while). I remember finding and buying Korova Milkbar's album in a record shop after we played at the Tavern with them. It was so exciting to walk through the Stourbridge ring road underpass and see a poster for a Tavern gig, and even better if it had your band and photo on it.

**How did the band end?**
We were really only ever in it to have fun with friends, and the band and our mates all drifted off in different directions to jobs and college, so it just wasn't possible to keep the band going.

**Did anyone go on to further success or have a career in the music industry?**
Unfortunately not, although Lee has drummed for a few bands over the years and had a real talent.

**What else do we need to know about the band?**
We went through several combinations of people and instruments (including attempting AC/DC's 'Whole lotta Rosie' as a 5-piece band named Shotgun Wedding) before we became indie trio Dive. We're pretty confident we hold the record for 'most fans upstairs at The Mitre in Stourbridge', getting in over 100 people to one of the smallest venues you've ever seen. Our fans were amazing; band practice in a smoke filled cellar was always attended by a really supportive group of friends.

DIVE

DIVE...

I CAUGHT YOUR FALL, BUT MISSED MY OWN, NOW I MISS YOU TOO, AS IM HERE ALONE. all lyrics and music by DIVE

THE DRUMS

DO IT AGAIN

ENOUGH OF YOU

AGAIN AND AGAIN

VOCALS BASS BACK

I CAUGHT YOUR FALL, BUT MISSED MY OWN, NOW I MISS YOU TOO, AS IM HERE ALONE. all lyrics and music by DIVE

ENOUGH OF YOU

FOR BAND    GS PHONE
DAN    (0384)    775
CHRIS    39.3

By Dave Morgan

**Which town were you based in?**

Kidderminster

**What years were you active?**

1992 - 1995

**Who was in the band?**

Dave Morgan - Vocals / Guitar (ex Spiny Dogfish)
Steve Kelly - Guitar (ex Spiny Dogfish)
Jason Turvey - Bass (ex Secret Garden)
Stuart Rose - Drums (ex Secret Garden)

**What kind of music did you play?**

Indie Rock!

**Who were the influences?**

Bunnymen, PJ Harvey, Julian Cope, Pixies

**What level of success did you achieve?**

Zero success. One 12" single - 'August EP' 1994 on own label 'Auto Motel Recordings'

**What do you remember about playing at the Tavern?**

Not supporting Radiohead when they postponed the gig due to illness. They brought their own support for the rescheduled gig. The original gig went ahead anyway with us and Fretblanket. I can still remember seeing the silhouette of Clint Mansell's pineapple hairdo at the bar while we were playing.

**Any memories of the other bands you played with at the Tavern?**

Funnily enough we didn't play that often at the Tavern. Kidderminster bands rarely pulled a Kidderminster crowd so we weren't much of a banker for the promoter. All we wanted was gigs in Birmingham and JB's etc. Get out of kiddy.

**How did the band end?**

It just fizzled away to nothing.

**Did anyone go on to further success or have a career in the music industry?**

Not at all. Dave Morgan is currently playing guitar for Dimitry Datus in Cork and is also working on a project with Glen Galvin called Sonflowers. Musical endeavours by other members are currently unknown

**What else do we need to know about the band?**

They were never as good as Spiny Dogfish.

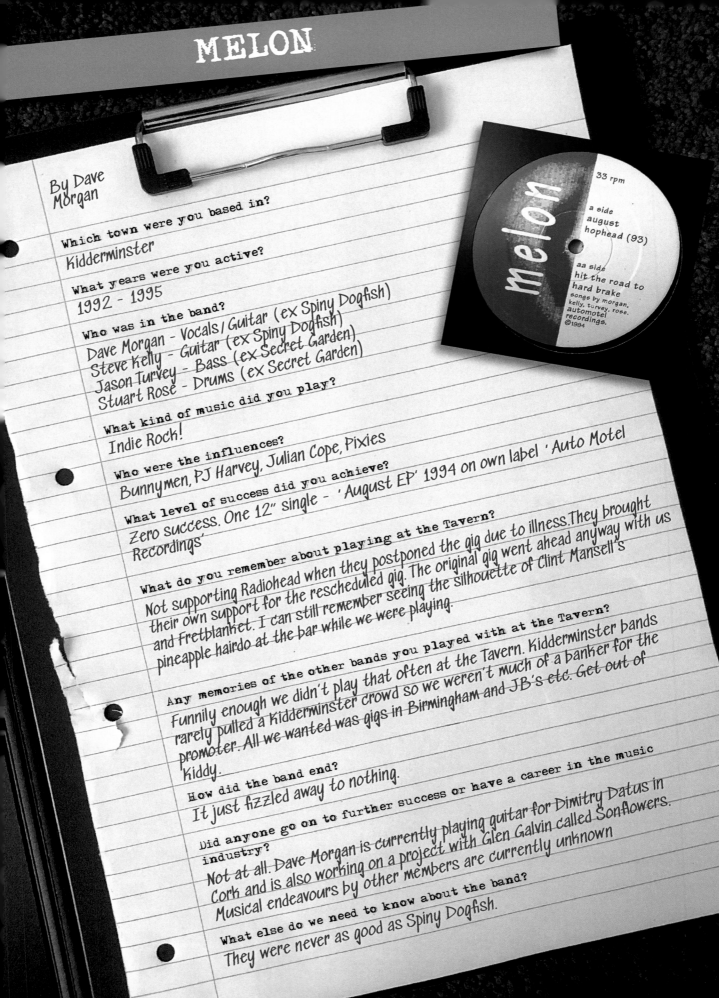

melon

33 rpm

a side
august
hophead (93)

aa side
hit the road to
hard brake
songs by morgan.
kelly. turvey. rose.
automotel
recordings.
©1994.

# Echo & The Bunnymen

I'd seen the Bunnymen in the mid 80's at Brum Odeon a couple of times, so whilst this might look good from a distance, it was a version of Echo & The Bunnymen without the singer, Ian McCulloch. Had he been in the band, there's no way they'd have played the Tavern. As it was, I was trading on the name and hoping there'd be enough interest. We were busy but not sold out. I didn't pay them anywhere near what they were originally asking and managed to make a profit.

Martin Wharton "I remember getting 'Chinese eyes' with The Bunnymen backstage. Good times"

Andrew Wolfman "Why on earth were Echo and The Bunnymen playing to just 247 people in Kidderminster two weeks before Christmas in 1991? Scratch that, I just checked, and it looks like the drummer had sadly died, the singer had left, and they played the entirety of their crap new album, zero hits and some Stones covers. That would probably explain it."

Steve Barker "I remember seeing Echo and the Bunnymen, I was right at the front, it was absolutely brilliant but bloody hell I ached the day after!"

FREAKS DWELL
FALSE GOODBYES
CUT + DRIED
DEVILMENT
WIGGED OUT WORLD
GO BLIND
SENSELESS
INSIDE YOU
SASPARILLA
ENLIGHTEN ME
REVERBERATION
PROVE ME WRONG
2,000 LIGHT YEARS
KING OF CASTLE

Dave Morgan "It was awful. I stood outside for most of it."

Mike Moore "I asked Will Sargent for his autograph for my mate who couldn't make the gig. Will refused saying he never did autographs and why hadn't my mate made it. I pointed out my mate was doing 21 months in Dartmoor for armed robbery - 'yeah, sound mate, there you go...' as he signed the ticket"

MARKET TAVERN
COMBERTON PLACE KIDDERMINSTER

HOLOGRAM MUSIC present-
ECHO & THE BUNNYMEN
+ Support
Friday 6th December 1991
Doors Open 7.30pm

UNRESERVED
£4.00 advance

Nº 0100
Retain This Portion   Conditions Overleaf

# Wolfsbane & The Wildhearts

Mark Badgeman "Wolfsbane had been the main support to Iron Maiden on their recent tour. I used to love an angle like that as it generally meant you could guarantee the Shuttle would do a decent piece and people would be talking about it.

Up until this point, every single band had arrived in a van. Not Wolfsbane. They came in a 40ft artic jammed with PA, lights and backline. Their professional road crew thought I was a total idiot. But looking back, so were they because they hadn't told me their gear needed 3 phase power to run. At the Tavern, you plugged into the 13 amp socket on the wall. I didn't even know what 3 phase power was!

I took them into the little brick building outside which housed the electrics for the market. I dread to think what they did but they managed to tail in with some bare ends and proceeded to abstract the electricity required to run their OTT full production. They'd also failed to ask if there was anywhere to hang their myriad lights. The only option I could see was a 'sky hook' so they precariously hung them on a little wooden lip above the bar. Quite how they didn't fall on someone's head, I'll never know.

That gig was also memorable for me because we had a punter in a wheelchair who was being a bit of a nuisance. I wanted to throw him out but wasn't sure if it was discriminatory. I decided all people should be treated the same so I went over and threatened to take his brake off and wheel him out!"

Andrew Wolfman "With Rick Rubin's Def American millions in the bank, Tamworth metal muthas Wolfsbane roared into the Tavern with an articulated lorry full of backline and a double-decker Def Leppard-mobile to transport them down the A453. This was a BIG gig for Kidderminster and Badgeman promised me a tenner and a t-shirt to look after the band for the day. One by one they emerged blinking into the light from their blacked-out battle bus: Jeff Hateley, Steve Danger. I greeted them nervously.

"Hi, I'm Andrew. I'm supposed to be looking after you today. Is there anything I can get you?"
They laughed uproariously, "no mate, but Blaze is in there, and he's in a fooking demanding mood." I was bricking it. This was Blaze Bayley, wild man of rock. What on earth could he want and where could you get it in Kidderminster? A coffin to sleep in? Bats to bite the heads off? Mountains of coke?
Panic was setting in. My mind was running free. Oh God, what if Blaze wants to meet some girls? I am demonstrably not the boy for that job.
I closed my eyes and knocked on the door of the bus. A grizzled face poked out.
"H-h-hi, Mr Blaze... I'm supposed to be looking after y-y-you today..."
"Oh there you are, pal," he smiled hairily, "have you got a plug for me' Game Boy?"

**WOLFSBANE**
## IN ACTION
### THE ALBUM IS
Down Fall The Good Guys

### THE 'SHITHEADS ON SAFARI' TOUR
### GOES DEEPER INTO THE JUNGLE

**DECEMBER**
1 MANCHESTER, International II
2 LEICESTER, Polytechnic
3 CAMBRIDGE, Junction
4 HEREFORD, Park Hall
5 COVENTRY, Polytechnic
7 KIDDERMINSTER, Market Tavern
6 SHEFFIELD, Polytechnic
8 WORKINGTON, Carnegie Theatre
10 LONDON, Astoria
11 FOLKESTONE, Leas Cliff Hall
12 EXETER, University Lemon Grove
13 CARDIFF, Bogey's
14 SUDBURY, Stevenson Centre
15 NORWICH, Waterfront

9

# Show times

**date:** 7/12/91

ON STAGE: **8·15**

WILD HEARTS:

OFF STAGE: **9·00**

# Wolfsbane:

ON STAGE: **9·30**

CURFEW: **11·00**

Andrew Wolfman "Greatest soundcheck I have ever witnessed. Blaze did half an hour of sort-of stand up and set fire to a teddy bear. Well metal!"

James Mitchell (Cake) "Wolfsbane at the Market Tavern was my eighteenth birthday. Instead of Happy Birthday we sang;
We Live our way
Not how you say.
Our blood, our sweat,
We have no regrets.
Tough as steel,
Never show the pain we feel,
Because we were tough as steel."

Neil Archer "Along with Carter USM, Wolfsbane was my favourite gig. I was chatting to drummer Steve Danger at the bar while the support soundchecked. Suddenly a light fitting fell out of the ceiling and dangled between us as we spoke."

Andy Price "I remember Wolfsbane turning up with their 40ft artic and me thinking if they unload that it will fill the room (it didn't)"

Mark Badgeman "Despite the big effort and the massive truck, only 157 people came. The Wildhearts got £50 and I lost £22.50 on the show"

**MARKET TAVERN** COMBERTON PLACE, KIDDERMINSTER.

HOLOGRAM MUSIC present
**WOLFSBANE**
+ WILD HEARTS

**Saturday 7th December 1991**
Doors Open 7.30 p.m.

£5.00 in advance

0112

Dressing Room Copy

# wolfsbane shit heads on safari-tour 2nd leg

## 1st dec~15 dec

| | | | |
|---|---|---|---|
| PROMOTER: | MARK DAWSON | | |
| PHONE: | 0886 5542 | | |
| FAX: | | | |

VENUE DETAILS:

| | | |
|---|---|---|
| GET IN: (TIME) | DOORS: | 7:30pm |
| 12:00 noon | | |
| LOCAL CREW:  2 | SHOW TIME SUPPORT: | 8:15pm off 9:00 |
| SOUND CHECK:  3:30pm | SHOW TIME WOLFSBANE: | 9:30pm |
| | CURFEW: | 11:00pm |
| ACCOMODATION DETAILS:- | NOTES:- THIS IS A SMALL VENU ARE ONLY GOING TO GE | |

THIS PAGE FROM THE ITINERARY REMINDS THEM IT'S A SMALL VENUE!

# SKA AT THE TAVERN

Arguably past their prime, 10 years after their 4 Top 20 hits, and charging at least £900 for a show, The Selecter was a big gamble. But it paid off because it almost sold out twice. Nick Welsh then put Big 5 together which was a Ska supergroup but it didn't do so well with less than 100 through the door. Lessons to learn there!

Mark Venencia "I saw them many times but the first time they played Kiddy was always the best. The whole place was jumping. Top top night. One of my favourite gigs of all time."

Steve Casbierd "I remember pissing Pauline Black off in the bar. I asked her how her job was going at Radio One (she had an evening show) and she stormed off....her bass player then told me she "isn't doing it any more"...oops"

Nick Welsh (The Selecter / Big 5) "Ahh, The Market Tavern! If I drift back in time (as I often do), it's the strangest thing. Although I can't picture it, I can still smell it! Was it next to a farm or something? Maybe I played there a few times with The Selecter? (my recreational pleasure seeking days of the 80's & 90's sometimes has its drawbacks today!) Hold on, maybe they provided us with good food on the 'rider'? That would make sense if it was near a farm, yeah, am I dreaming this or did we have to catch & 'prepare' our own dinner? We must have liked it there because we definitely went back a few times or maybe it was just because we liked Mark? Because of our current plight (virus/lockdown) it seems all so long ago or maybe it just is? I apologise for the many ?'s I have used in my ramblings but it's a very hot Sunday morning & I haven't had my breakfast yet (maybe I should come up & catch myself a nice fresh piggie)"

Matt Davies "One gig had the original guitarist, Neol Davies. I recall Pauline Black commenting "he's not bad is he?.. we picked him up on a YTS scheme!"

Hologram Music..... **present**

2 TONE THE SELECTER

market tavern.

DANCE CRAZE

WED DEC 18

tickets £5.00

A 2 TONE CHRISTMAS SPECIAL

THE SELECTER
EUROPEAN TOUR 1991

**Out on the Streets Again**

Christianne Wakeham "I DJ'ed when the Selecter played. I had never done it before, so I was pretty stressed about screwing everything up. I think it mostly went ok except I got the two decks mixed up for the changeover of one record. Everybody was probably so drunk that they didn't realise anyway - or that's what I tried to tell myself!"

Lou "The Selecter gig was mental! I was helping on the door and trying to keep count of bodies coming in and out was a bit of a nightmare. Everywhere was packed - the gig room, the bar, the stairs, the corridors to the loos, the outside and the car park! We had to turn a lot of people away. They just hung out the other side of the windows where the stage was and danced around in the cold!"

Matt Davies "Big 5 had let it be known that trombonist Rico Rodriguez would be playing with them. Several of us in the audience had turned up hoping to see the great man, including Terry Thomas who ran 'Mr Tee's Rock Shop', a rare records and music memorabilia shop in the town. Mr Tee spoke for many of us when he called out 'Where's Rico?' as the band took the stage. I can't quite remember Jennie Bellestar's response but it left some doubt as to the reason for his absence. To this day I wonder how close we were that night to seeing one of the true legends of Jamaican ska music."

# Big date for the Big 5 . . .

Some of the top names of British ska come to Kidderminster next week with the arrival of the Big 5 at the Market Tavern.
Taking their name from the classic 1972 Prince Buster album, Big 5 is the brainchild of The Selecter's bass player Nick Welsh.
Also a former member of Bad Manners, he has recruited keyboardist Martin Stewart and guitarist Dave Horne from the band, as well as ex-Belle Stars vocalist Jennie B.
Completing the line-up is Perry Melius, former drummer for The On-U-Sound and Eddy Grant, and renowned Jamaican trombonist Rico.
Big 5 play their own brand of dance/ska/ragga and are at the Tavern on January 29, tickets £4.
Support comes from Kidderminster's Stop The World. Doors open 8pm.

# Doctor & The Medics

## Thu 13th Feb 1992
## Thu 18th Jun 1992

SPIRIT · IN · THE · SKY

DOCTOR & THE MEDICS

They had a number one smash with 24 million copies sold yet six years later, they're playing to reduced audiences in a pub. Martin might have booked their return a little too soon but they did Hawkwind covers and you'd have thought that would endear them to the old Omnia Opera crowd.

# BITS AND PIECES

One of the surprise hits of 1986 was the cover of an obscure song from the early 70s by an act who came from nowhere.
The song was Spirit In The Sky, and the act was Dr & The Medics. It zoomed to No 1 for a few weeks, but after that – and without wishing to sound unkind – one-hit-wonderitis set in.
The band's chart career went comatose, but on the live front the diagnosis was somewhat healthier as they're still doing the rounds, of which one is an appearance at the Market Tavern next week.
Spirit In The Sky was a bit of a departure for Dr & The Medics, as their normal sound is more that of Hawkwind, who they have toured with in the past.
It would appear the song has a bit of a hoodoo about it as well. Norman Greenbaum, the guy who scored with it first time round, seemed set for great things but renounced rock'n'roll and retired to a farm in America's Deep South.
Dr & The Medics appear at the Tavern on February 13. Tickets are £4 on the door, which opens at 7.30pm.

Fiona Gordon "Dr & the Medics was a good night. I cooked them veggie lasagne."

Lou "This felt like a real big deal at the time, just because they were a pretty well known name compared to some of the smaller gigs. It was a fun show but I don't remember much because I was pretty drunk!"

By Rich Morley

**Which town were you based in?** Bewdley, Kidderminster

**What years were you active?** 1989-95 and then again 2016-17

**Who was in the band?**
There were a few different members over the Tavern period
1990-92 Rich Morley (Vocals), Garry Todd (Drums), Peter Jones – then Stewart Gordon (Bass), Paul Harvard (Guitar)
92-95 Stewart Gordon (Bass), Paul Harvard (Guitar), Johnny Prince (Vocals), Mick Collett, Sascha Eldridge (Drums)

**What kind of music did you play?**
Haha – this is where and why the split happened in 1992 when original members (Rich and Garry) left – a difference of musical tastes and differences – let's say started off as Goth, indie and then heavier (rock) from 92-95 and then back to their roots 2016/17

**Who were the influences?**
Sisters of Mercy, Fields of the Nephilim, Killing Joke then more Rage Against the Machine, and Motorhead

**What level of success did you achieve?** Flirted with a few promoters and had A&R interest, and were offered a deal to play the UK Uni circuit by one company based in London (after rep saw us at a Tav gig) – destroyed the band as egos and differences came to the fore, so it was turned down. So I (Rich) left.

**What do you remember about playing at the Tavern?** Stan used to love us playing as we 'kept it simple' (his words not mine). I thought I'd played more often than the 5 I did but we were always well supported. One of the gigs I did was packed so I guess we were one of the last local bands to actually do that. We also had lots of smoke and lights so I remember not being able to see much.

**Any memories of the other bands you played with at the Tavern?** Saw loads of bands, Cardiacs and Nik Turner stands out as they were both faves of mine.

**How did the band end?**
The band reformed in 2016 after the death of Paul Harvard. The previous year Paul, Stew and me met up for the first time since the split and kind of agreed to reform. Paul passed away a few months later so we decided we had to do it. Our first gig was promoted as 'Tavern Legends' and we played with The Bullfrogs to a packed Boars Head in the town. I remember Sand Palmer (the owner) rushing up to me panicking as they weren't prepared for such a crowd, at one point they were turning people away. The Pale Kings are still going – it's just the project is on hold at present. Their last gig was in 2017.

**Did anyone go on to further success or have a career in the music industry?**
Stew Gordon went on to join various other bands (he is now based back in Liverpool), he is currently (or was) touring with Famous Monsters (a Misfits tribute band). After 1992 Rich Morley went on to form covers outfit Sister Sandwich (back in the Tav days Sister Savage) and they are still going. Now play with space rock outfit Dr Hasbeen who have included ex Hawkwind members such as Nik Turner and Dave Anderson. Steve Smith before The Pale Kings was with Ambelian and has since joined a reformed Rouen. Marc Temple still plays guitar for Sister Sandwich.

**What else do we need to know about the band?**
The band once headlined a charity concert at Worcester Cathedral and played at major alternative venues such as the local Goth mecca 'The Barrel Organ' and the likes of the 'Hummingbird' in Birmingham. Despite recording various demo's and EP's over the years 'Remembrance', released in 2016, is their first and only album to date.

Richard Hill "I saw these guys a couple of times, loved them. Dark, intense and heavy if I remember rightly. Really cool local band."

Ian Passey "This gig was probably the first time I played at The Tavern, when I was guitarist in Smedley. Rich Morley was always very kind to us, giving us several supports at various venues in the early 90's. Our post C-86 jangle was perhaps not an obvious pairing with their distorted, delay-pedal fuelled goth sound, but I can proudly say we were never bottled off!"

THE PALE KINGS

MARKET TAVERN
KIDDERMINSTER

FRIDAY 31ST JAN
7·30 - 11 p·m
£2·00 / £1·50 TICKETS

THE PALE KINGS

## ATTENTION ALL DAISY CHAINSAW PROMOTERS

I have been informed by DAISY CHAINSAW'S management that they propose to eliminate the usual support act/headline act format for the forthcoming March/April 1992 tour. The following is a direct transcript from a fax sent to me by DAISY CHAINSAW this afternoon (Friday 17 January 1992):

"The show will be an integration of DAISY CHAINSAW and two other acts who will be rehearsing together to create a total coherent form of entertainment.

It is our aim to combine the bands, theatrics, lights and DJ into a whole working unit which negates the requirement of any additional performers/bands etc. Show time is between 2 and 3 hours depending on venue requirements."

### THE VENUE MUST NOT BOOK ANY OTHER BANDS!

Please call me if you need any more information.

Kindest regards

*Robin.*

Robin Catto

Directors: L. PARKER (M.D.)  L. A. PARKER
Licensed by Department of Employment SE 18603 Company Reg. No: 2443774
Registered Office: CONCORDE HOUSE, 1 BARB MEWS, BROOK GREEN, LONDON W6 7PA
Any offer stated in this letter does not constitute a contract

---

Fax to MARK LANGFORD
Fax from MARK BADGEMAN
Date : 21/1/92

Hi Mark

I've actually managed, at long last, to score a Top 40 hit with one of my bands. I've had 'has-beens' like The Primitives and The Bunnymen and obviously Carter and The Senseless Things have gone on to better things but Daisy Chainsaw have charted at 35 this week and I've got them on at the Tavern on Tues 31st March! There's a possibility of a Top of the Pops appearance - I'll know tomorrow about that.

Tickets are £3.50 and will be on sale in two weeks time.

Daisy Chainsaw have come from no-where to be flavour-of-the-month in just 2 months. The single 'Love your Money' was originally released to critical acclaim back in late October. They were the bottom of the bill openers on the recent 'Hole' package tour and began to attract attention. They're now on the Radio One 'A' playlist and the video has been shown on last weeks Chart Show. They played live on last Fridays edition of 'The Word' and MTV love them as well.

The gig is bound to sell-out so can you give it a plug in next weeks paper as they're the most exciting band to play the town since Carter. I've got photos if you want them but give us a ring anyway.

cheers,

Mark

---

Do you remember this band? Of course you don't! One long forgotten single and never heard of again. Why? Because they messed it up. After hitting the giddy heights of number 26 in the charts, they pulled the tour, thinking pub gigs were below them. Instead, they played bigger venues to nobody because they hadn't done the groundwork. You HAVE to play places like the Tavern to build a fanbase. And you can't do it without a local band on the bill. The public aren't stupid. One hyped single won't give you a solid foundation for a lasting career. If they'd played the tour, there was enough interest for them to have sold out every night. From there, the next single might have been a hit (especially if they hadn't refused to sign to Maverick, Madonna's label) and then you can move up to bigger rooms. Total idiots. Shame, because 'Love Your Money' is a filthy-hyped-up-rockabilly-influenced-shredded-speaker classic that's actually worth a listen.

---

ATTN:      MARK DAWSON
FROM:      ROBIN CATTO
DATE:      27.1.92
RE:        DAISY CHAINSAW

Dear Mark,

This is to formally confirm that the Daisy Chainsaw concert scheduled for Tuesday 31st March 1992 has been cancelled and any contract relevant to this date is null and void.

I apologise for the inconvenience this may have caused.

Regards,

*Robin.*

Robin Catto

CONCORDE ARTISTES L
Concorde House, 1 Barb Mews, Brook Green, London W6 7PA   Telephone 071 602 8822   Fax 071 603 235

# Dr. Robert & Indian Summer

Why bother with Daisy Chainsaw when you can replace them with Dr. Robert from the Blow Monkeys?! Now it was my turn to learn a lesson. You can't put a bloke from a shiny pop soul funk band who had massive hits in the 80s on in a dirty rock and roll venue and still expect the audience to come. That sort of act belongs in a nightclub. I don't have any paperwork from the gig but it was poorly attended from memory. But all of that pales into insignificance because of the baked potato...!

James Bainbridge "I recall that the support for Dr Robert was a great pop-funk band called Indian Summer. I know this because I 'played' keyboards at that gig, subbing for the regular player. I say played, but really it was the magic of pre-programming."

David Watkins "Dr Robert threw a baked potato from stage at Stan the PA Man. Who threw it back at him"

Andrew Wolfman "Baked potato-gate Who threw first? Dr Robert or Stan The PA Man?"

Stan The PA Man "The incident with Dr Robert and the potato was one of the weirder things that happened. When he came onstage, he took a baked potato out of his pocket and threw it to or possibly at me while I was mixing. I have no idea if it was to do with the sound, although he didn't say anything about it, or whether it was a comment on the catering or whether he just thought it would be a fun thing to do, but I just caught it and threw it back at him."

1991 / 27737
© EMI RECORDS (UK) – PHOTOGRAPHER: MICHELE SIEDNER
**DR. ROBERT**

## Hologram
### Music Promotions

# PRESS RELEASE

FAX TO:-
FAX FROM:-
REF:-

Dr. Robert is the lead singer with The Blow Monkeys, a band who had a string of top twenty hits in the late eighties with such pop classics as 'Digging Your Scene', 'It Doesn't Have To Be This Way' and 'Celebrate'.

He has now decided to go solo and has signed a new deal with EMI records. They will be releasing a new single around the end of March and Dr Robert has decided to undertake a low-key tour to promote the record.

He will be in Kidderminster on March 31st when the show calls in at the Market Tavern in Comberton Place.

Tickets are a snip at £3.50 and are available from the Market Tavern, Sounds Around, Jukebox, Dead or Alive or Tempest. Support comes from local band, Single Doubt, and the doors open at 7.30pm.

Alice's Cottage, Camp Lane, Shelsley Beauchamp, Worcester, WR6 6RL
Telephone 08865 542

James Kimberley "I got Dr Robert's autograph from the gig at the Market Tavern where he arrived on stage with a potato in his hand..."

79

# THE LAST TEMPTATION OF CAKE

I blame Mark Badgeman. Somehow he and Stan The PA Man had convinced someone from Nation Records, home to the great Fun-da-Mental and Transglobal Underground, to come and run the rule over his teenage sensations Cake (UK). "They're Kidderminster's answer to the Sex Pistols" he would exclaim to anyone that would listen, and then, in a whisper, "and a little bit like EMF."

He had a point. Cake shows were unbelievable. They were snotty and chaotic, music by smart-arse teens for smart-arse teens. The record label guy would surely love it, chart success would be assured, and it would only be a matter of time until we all had Lear jets with our faces painted on the side.

In his svengali-like wisdom, and wanting to make the band look good by putting on a sell-out show, Mark went to the press to fabricate a little filth and fury. "If I told you what Cake were planning to do at The Market Tavern for their Good Friday resurrection, I'd be excommunicated from the Roman Catholic church!!!!!" Screamed the man from the Kidderminster Shuttle.

What had he told them? I mean, sure, the band had plans. New songs had serious bits with mind-melting My Bloody Valentine guitars. Superstar DJ in waiting Ewan Pearson helped us to prepare a nuclear new dance direction. We dropped the dreadful comedy cover of the Sesame Street theme. No more silly bollocks, that was the plan.

While that might be considered sacrilege in certain circles, "Indie band not quite so shit now" is a pretty niche news story, certainly nothing to get too worked up about. A band meeting was convened, probably in the Clock Coffee Shop of The Rowland Hill Centre (don't go looking for it, it's not there any more).

"The paper's expecting something blasphemous to go down on Good Friday, what's going on?"

"Oh don't worry about that. It's just Stan and and Al building a twelve-foot crucifix. They're going to drag it up Comberton Hill and hang Stan off it. Al's going to feed him pints of Mild and throw pickled onions at him when you do the new stuff."

"Oh fine. Wait, what?"

Stan recalls, the construction of the cross, "We built it in Mike the Goth's back garden with his Dad's leftover fence posts. Mr Wakeman provided the tools and a fair bit of advice on how to cut a decent cross lap joint. He wanted a proper job, nothing half-arsed."

The pair set off early on Good Friday hoping to get to the venue in time to make soundcheck, have a production rehearsal and pick up some silverskins. They were met by a picket line of protestors from the local church (including James and Andy from Cake's furious Mum). There were frantically-scribbling hacks from the local press and a very stern-faced Andy Tavern. "Lads, you can't bring that thing in here, we're not that sort of place."

He turned to Al, "and, you can't come in here either. We don't serve sausage rolls."

The local council wanted nothing more than to shut down the Tavern. They were blinded to the cultural capital that it brought to the town, by the fear of chain-fights, widescale juvenile delinquency and (I can only assume) cattle rustling. It certainly had an air of danger

the "cake" indie group

appearing live
friday april 17th 1992
market tavern
kidderminster
two pounds fifty

about it (which gave gigs a frisson of extra excitement) but it was a warm and welcoming place too. If it suspected you of being a weirdo, the Tavern would look out for you.

Andy Tavern always seemed to be being hounded by the council for something. Whether it was monies owed, fights, drugs or toilet-gate. The last thing he needed was the papers and the Pope sniffing around. As Stan puts it, "it was a triple whammy, promoting sacrilege, under-age drinking and novelty indie bands. Stakes just got too high."

Andy finally had to lay down the law.

"Look, you lot. No one gets in tonight without some ID."

No one got in.

Round the back of the venue, the cross was tossed in a bin, while 200 kids had the time of their lives at an impromptu car park rave. Inside, Cake (UK) unveiled their difficult new material to a confused looking A&R man while Stan the PA Man pissed himself laughing.

Shorn of the creative energy of their crowd, Cake tanked hard. It became glaringly obvious that what made this band good in the first place, was the community around it: The joyful, inclusive and downright hilarious scene that dressed up and supported, the talented folk who believed in them and booked their shows, the crazy place that they played. It was barely the band at all (though the singer did have excellent hair).

Forty interminable minutes, two walk-offs and a face-first stage dive on to an empty dance floor later, the band

trudged off apologetically to join their friends. Possibly fearing that his Mum was still outside with an angry placard, James hung back, and went to say, "thanks for coming" to the chap from the record label.

"I don't know what that was all about, but there's something happening here. Maybe we could talk about you doing some demos. It needs a lot of development, but there's a great vibe outside," he allegedly said.

"Thank you, but don't bother," said James. "We just split up."

Aki (Nation Records) "I brought down a A&R man Ian Wilson who used to be a booking agent for Wasted Talent but running a sub label for Atlantic Records. The gig was good but badly attended I recall."

# A big slice of the action with Cake

Local lads Cake and top ska band The Selector renew old friendships when they both return to the Market Tavern.

Cake have reformed again to support Darlington chainsaw outfit Sofahead tomorrow night.

This just so happens to be Good Friday, and I had better not risk telling you about the little stunt Cake were planning to mark the occasion. If I did, I would be risking excommunication from the Roman Catholic Church!

Just to inform you about Sofahead, they were formed from the ashes of the critically acclaimed Dan and are on the road to promte their third album, *Acres Of Geeses*.

Tickets are £2.50 and are available from the Tavern, Sounds Around in Kidderminster and Jukebox Records in Stourport.

Next on the list is Birdland, who play on April 28. From Coventry, they had a Top 30 hit with *Sleep With Me* last year and also have a string of Indie number ones under their belt.

Support comes from Sugarblast, who featured in last week's Spotlight, and Pietra Rosa of Wolverhampton. Tickets are £3.50, available from the above outlets, or £4 on the night.

Finally we come to The Selector, back by popular demand after their hit gig at Christmas.

You can see them on May 1, tickets £5, and I'd advise you to get in fast.

● Birdland, feathering their nest at the Market Tavern later this month.

# Birdland + Sugarblast Pietra Rosa

I'd seen Zodiac Motel in the mid 80s and I had their mini LP and the two 12" singles. I absolutely loved that band. Then they turned up at Nottingham Rock City in 1988 supporting The Damned under the name 'Vicious'. From there, they morphed into Birdland, a fully formed band with bleach blonde moptops and standard indie issue black clothing, signed to Lazy, the home of The Primitives. The first single went to number one in the Indie charts and I presume it was around this time I saw a couple of gigs where the brothers just dived into the audience after two or three songs and started fighting. One was at JBs, but I saw them do it again at the Irish Centre a few days later, which made it feel a bit contrived. They'd get caught out on that these days with the advent of the internet!

I don't remember how I managed to get them on the phone but I asked them about doing a gig and they told me they'd split up. As you may have gathered from the Carter story, I can be a bit persistent so I badgered them and they said if I found them a few more gigs, they'd do it. One was definitely in Rugeley but I'm not sure about the others. So, basically, I got Birdland to reform for these gigs. I was pretty pleased with myself.

Unfortunately, they had a terrible time at the Tavern gig and told me afterwards they'd split up again at the end of the set! I know my memory can be patchy at times, but this is all vivid and locked in. But it doesn't quite make sense when you look at their gigography online because it appears they played a London gig a month later. And then re-emerged the following year with no record deal, a new rhythm section and a lengthy tour that got bad reviews. Did I kill Birdland? Not quite.

BIRDLAND - KIDDERMINSTER MARKET TAVERN - 28.04.92
Birdland were one of those bands that flamed bright and briefly and were all the better for it. They were a foursome from Coventry in skinny black jeans and matching bottle blond haircuts. It was all so perfect, so rock n roll cliche, it was only meant to shine briefly. Live they were a blast to the face. I don't imagine that the set lasted long, which again was spot on. I remember that they used to cover Patti Smith's Rock n Roll ~~Nigger~~, but I imagine they were just trying to be controversial.
We'd had support from Sugarblast and Pietra Rosa, but I have no recollection of either. One of my main memories of this gig was seeing four older people by the bar, with similar haircuts to the band, just greying versions thereof. Given the relative proximity of Kidderminster to Coventry (it was certainly drivable) I always wondered whether they were the band's parents.

*Oops! Not very PC in 2020!*

Kim Thomas "The Birdland gig changed my life, by breaking my nose! I was at the front and somebody jumped off the stage to crowdsurf, as they went over me they kicked me straight on the bridge of my nose. Blood went everywhere and I had to run to the loos. Also a favourite place in the Tavern as there was always such good graffiti to read. Of course when the bleeding stopped we went back out!"

*From Lunchtime For The Wild Youth*

BEN

SNAKE HYDE SALLY

Ben Schrieber "It was the best job in the world. Manning the door at the Market Tavern. Armed only with a clicker, float and repeatedly being told that I was blocking the 'view' of the people crammed in the hallway and on the stairs. Was it the atmosphere, the smell of cow shit or the fact that if the bands went through the wrong double doors they were greeted by a heavy metal jukebox and a swarm of bikers? And I didn't truly appreciate the enormity of the bands themselves from Birdland to the Cardiacs. From Carter USM to The Wedding Present, Chumbawamba to Radiohead. So many bands came, rocked the stage and feasted on Andy's veggie lasagne. A truly magical place where everyone knew everyone and it quickly became the place to be on a Friday or Saturday night in Kidderminster. To go and later play on that legendary stage twice was the perfect ending to an amazing part of my life."

Jon Green (Snake Hyde Sally) "Think we only played at the Tavern a couple of times. We were Kiddy/Stourport based."

Sand Palmer "Think I spent more time there than at home!"

SMEDLEY

Ian Passey (Smedley / Jackpot) "21st Apr 92 - Probably not a gig to go down in Tavern folklore - I seem to recall Smedley being upstaged by the wonderful Teenage Mess! Perhaps more memorable was the soundcheck... After a few minutes of routine monotonous drum thud, the venue doors were flung open and in stormed a bloke from the bar, seething with uncontrollable rage... 'If you hit that fucking snare one more fucking time, I'll shove those fucking sticks right up your fucking arsehole.' He looked like he meant it, too! We very politely apologised, before hiding with the sound engineer behind the mixing desk! Eventually we were informed he'd gone home but still locked all the venue doors before continuing. Our poor, sensitive drummer never really got over it!!"

Baron Webb "I followed Smedley, watching them play with The Pale Kings on a few occasions at the Tavern, 16 years of age and enjoying getting covered in beer..."

Tom Cooke "I loved the Tavern, me and my mate John were underage but with, erm, good 'ID'! We used to go watch loads of bands and have a couple of drinks but never caused any trouble. That was the thing with the Tavern, some people thought it was rough but if you didn't act like a twat it was cool."

Steve Byrne (Bitter Tears) "We supported a terrible metal band called Tantrum. I remember turning up during their soundcheck and they played that 'only the crumbliest, flakiest chocolate' song from the Cadburys Flake advert!! We were in bits!"

# Jon Fat Beast

Andy Barding "Jon Fatbeast and I knew each other as teenagers in Thatcher's Exeter. His fanzine, 'Beast', was a badly-printed, badly-drawn and barely legible organ with violent cartoon strips, local political discourse, tips for squatters and reviews of New Model Army and King Kurt gigs. Essential reading.

Before honing his sticky compere skills with Carter USM, Jon used to present his own live act. It involved a lot of swearing, some rotten poetry and singalongs to ditties about being fat: "I am a flabby bugger/I weigh too bloody much/When I bend over/My feet I cannot touch." Etc etc.

He also used to recite a poem called "Andy Barding, Why Don't You Fuck Off And Die?" which I would smile sportingly through but which was probably, on reflection, only half a joke. I must have been an annoying little bastard back then.

I didn't attend the Kidderminster show - didn't know about it - but I imagine it would have been made up of much the same sweary, messy, half-naked slapstick nonsense as always. Jon would have had a word like 'BUM' scrawled across his belly in marker pen. That was his 'style'.

Way beyond that, though, he was a fantastic, intelligent and sensitive friend, as well as a prolific player on the North London music scene. As Timebox promoter, he brought a torrent of talent to venues like the Bull and Gate throughout the eighties and nineties. He passed away in 2014 aged just 51. I miss him a lot."

Helen Smith "He was an astonishingly creative nutcase."

JON WITH CARTER ON THE INSIDE SLEEVE OF 30 SOMETHING

Without Jon Beast helping me get Carter to play, none of this would have happened. So when he decided he wanted to do a show of his own, I couldn't really turn him down. The problem was, he's not a bonafide act - he was mostly known as an MC who introduced Carter USM in his pants with something stupid written on his chest, normally You Fat Bastard. Nobody could possibly know what to expect. Fruitbat actually told me not to let him do it!

Jon had met Carter when they played Timebox at the Bull & Gate, the club he used to promote. It was an essential place to play in the mid to late 80s. From what I can gather, he did the door, the lights AND introduced the acts. Then he'd keep the mic and heckle the acts. He was genuinely funny and very likeable. At this point, Carter had asked him to stand down as

their career had took off but he was now doing EMF, so he still got to strip down to his pants and do his famous introductions.

When he wasn't working, Jon organised trips to Alton Towers. He loved it there. He'd assemble a little posse and host a really fun day. I was invited to one and went with Mike Parker.

It's testament to the power of the Tavern that anyone came to his show at all. It wasn't busy and I can't remember much of what he did but 'Adult Tiswas' was a good description. I think he spent the entire fee on baked beans which got chucked everywhere! Fortunately(?), there's some recordings from his gigs on Soundcloud so type soundcloud.com/beastofexeterr into your browser if you want to know what you potentially missed.

# SCUMBUG

By Steve Cooper

Which town were you based in? Kidderminster

What years were you active? 1991 - 1992

Who was in the band?
Steve Cooper- Vocals, Brendan Moran- Guitar, Jon Pardoe- Guitar
Dominic James-Moore- Bass, Jonathan King- Drums

What kind of music did you play?
Punk/ metal with a bit of funkiness thrown in now and again

Who were the influences?
We were strongly influenced by numerous bands at the time and the vibe of
the moment (Dance, Madchester, Chili Peppers, Nirvana) but deep down we were
punks/ rockers.

What level of success did you achieve?
Local headline/ support in Kidderminster and the Black Country

What do you remember about playing at the Tavern?
Proper room, proper stage, great vibe, cow piss, the odd nutter

Any memories of the other bands you played with at the Tavern?
Supported Extreme Noise Terror, which was exciting.

How did the band end?
People went to university etc.

Did anyone go on to further success or have a career in the music
industry?
No. Well, not yet!

What else do we need to know about the band?
All of the members have remained musical and are still about. If you fancy an
all- dayer Tavern reunion, give us a shout!

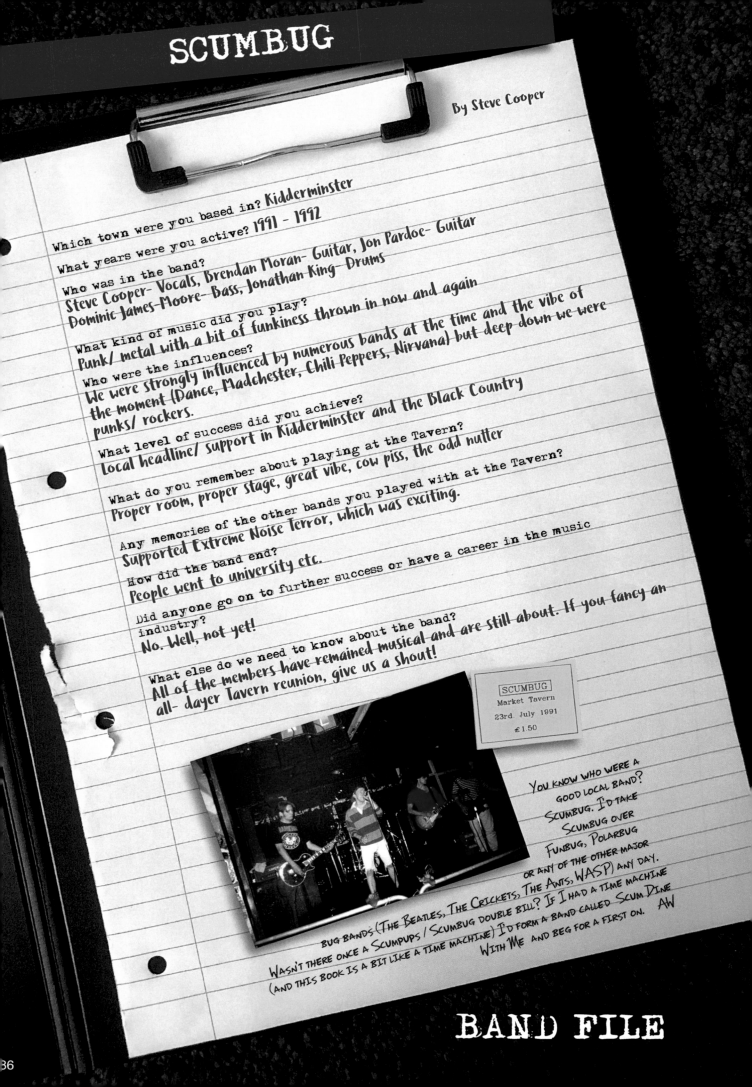

SCUMBUG
Market Tavern
23rd. July 1991
£1.50

YOU KNOW WHO WERE A
GOOD LOCAL BAND?
SCUMBUG. I'D TAKE
SCUMBUG OVER
FUNBUG, POLARBUG
OR ANY OF THE OTHER MAJOR
BUG BANDS (THE BEATLES, THE CRICKETS, THE ANTS, WASP) ANY DAY.
WASN'T THERE ONCE A SCUMPUPS / SCUMBUG DOUBLE BILL? IF I HAD A TIME MACHINE
(AND THIS BOOK IS A BIT LIKE A TIME MACHINE) I'D FORM A BAND CALLED SCUM DINE
WITH ME AND BEG FOR A FIRST ON.   AW

# BAND FILE

36

# Extreme Noise Terror + Headcleaner & Scumbug

## Noise and terror in the extreme at Tavern debut

Two dates coming up at the Market Tavern you might want to keep an eye out for are the debut of Extreme Noise Terror and the return of Midway Still.

Extreme Noise Terror are the first in line, taking the stage next Friday.

Anyone who saw the Brit Awards earlier this year will remember them performing with their great buddies, the KLF, in a decidedly undainty thrash version of 3am Eternal.

Now I'm told ENT might – just might – be joined by some of the KLF at Friday's gig. The only way of finding out is by turning up.

### Expected

Tickets are £3.50 in advance from the Tavern, Sounds Around or The Jukebox in Stourport.

As for Midway Still, they return on June 5 supported by Panic Beach of Stourbridge, of whom great things are apparantly expected.

Admission is £3 on the door, get there for around 8pm.

● Midway Still make a welcome return on June 5, supported by Panic Beach of Stourbridge

I know what it says in that Shuttle article. But I'm sure I didn't say that. I just said there might be some very very special guests that I can't mention and reminded Mark Langford that Extreme Noise Terror had opened the Brits that year with the KLF doing their version of 3AM Eternal. In fact, people were still talking about it - the machine gun, the dead sheep and the abandoned attempt to drown the front row of industry execs in pigs' blood. As someone has suggested on YouTube, this is trolling before it was invented. I may also have written 'All the way from Mu Mu Land' on the flyer too! Anyway, the KLF were never going to come but 164 people did, which is more than would normally have come to see ENT. You always need an angle!!

Lou "Haha OMG I actually did stage security for this gig with another girl called Abi, stood either side of the stage behind the barriers with a HUGE guy between us. I think the idea was that the crowd wouldn't want to cause two chicks any trouble trying to get on the stage. Oh how wrong we were! I got my glasses knocked off within about 4 minutes. The band actually stopped playing, the guitarist grabbed my glasses and put them on the side of the stage saying 'probably safer here luv' and they told the audience to stop giving us shit."

Johnny Vinyl "Extreme Noise Terror were not extreme enough, not noisy enough and certainly not terrorising "

Steve Cooper "As vocalist with Scumbug I was delighted we were supporting a name band. They asked if they could use our bass amp, which was borrowed. With the name they had I was worried that it wouldn't last the night."

Janine Calder "I saw Extreme Noise Terror when I was pregnant and my baby kicked me really hard as I don't think she liked it even in the womb..."

Stan The PA Man "The band had done a track with KLF recently and Mark was a little economical with the truth as to who was playing this gig, telling a number of people the KLF would be at the show, although they never were booked and were less likely to turn up on spec. I have a tape of this show."

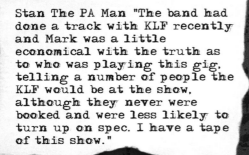

# Get caught in the crossfire!

My Tavern gigs had started at the tail end of 1990 and I spent most of 1991 sussing out what worked and what didn't. Meanwhile, a groundswell of crusty, stripy-legged, big-booted indie kids had made the venue their home and I was trying to make sure each Friday had a suitable act that they'd like. By 1992, there was enough support that you could risk a night with Jon Beast. Or a gig with The Machine Gun Feedback, a little known act I booked solely on the strength of their promo photo as they looked like the sort of band people would like; big boots, Mega City 4 t-shirt, one has dreads, one looks like Miles Hunt. Plus they only wanted £100. Put two great locals on and you've got 75 people through the door on a night where there was no better option available. Ultimately this band did nothing but I expect they now dine out on the story that Oasis supported them at one of their London gigs.

● A burst of musical fire will be let off at the Market Tavern tomorrow night with the arrival of Indie outfit Machine Gun Feedback.
● The band (above) are out on the road to plug their second single, *Hey I'm A Spaceman*.
● It's the follow-up to the debut *Uncle Mikey's Guide To Groovin'*, which made the higher reaches of the Indie charts.
● *Spaceman* is produced by Pat Collier, the knob-twiddler on albums such as The Wonderstuff's *Hup*.
● Support for tomorrow night comes from Stourbridge bands Scrash and Dive.
● Admission is £2.50, and get there for 7.30pm.

# THE 13 WORST BAND NAMES IN THE HISTORY OF THE MARKET TAVERN

They can't all be winners. For every Led Zeppelin there has to be a Limp Bizkit. Here are the thirteen most appallingly named acts to ever grace the Tavern stage:

1    Uncle Ian's Oral Circus
2    Mr Breezy Trousers
3    Psychedelia Smith
4    Emma Gibbs Loves Badges
5    Frank Boff's Big Band
6    Cruella de Villa
7    Sister Savage & The Buggered Nuns
8    Belch Pop Frenzy
9    King Woderick and the Yogots
10   Various Vegetables
11   Ludicrous Lollipops
12   Wench
13   Farter (The Unstoppable Bowel Movement)

# BLOODY FARMERS

The farmers were the common enemy. They really thought they owned the pub. To start with, the back room was just a pub function room but after a few gigs, Andy let us paint it black and put some large band posters on the wall. We eventually got rid of the awful curtains and blacked the windows out behind the stage. I suspect this might be what caused the farmers to up their game and start badgering the council about closing it down.

David Wright "Tuesday daytime at the Tavern was not like any other. I remember my heart sinking as I saw the livestock lorries pulling into the Tavern carpark and realising it was market day.

Market day meant the bar would be full of ruddy faced farmers filling the air with bad smells and bad language. They were gruff and rude. Andy's head barman was banned from the front bar on market day because he would have ended up punching them due to their rudeness.

This meant there had to be three people working the front bar which was generally Andy plus two thick skinned barmaids as the farmers' rudeness was directed at females as well as blokes, in fact if anything in the small-minded world of the farmers, they gave the barmaids the hardest time. They would examine their change and really kick off at the barmaids if they thought they had been short-changed. They would blow a fuse over pennies, or should I say the thought that they had been short-changed by a few pence, as 99% of the time they were in the wrong. So, us regulars soon began to hate the farmers and the chaos of market day.

We did not like the ways the animals were treated either. Entrapped in tiny pens at the back-end of the Tavern where we could hear them baying as we walked towards the toilets on Tuesday-Wednesday nights. As regulars we got used to it but as for the visiting midweek bands, the sounds and smell of the penned in animals were new to them.

Some of the bands verbalised their displeasure and one band that played at the Tavern was called 'Mad Cow Disease' whose poster on the wall in the front bar was noticed by the farmers giving them a good laugh. They weren't laughing a few months later!

One night I was alerted by raised voices coming from the gents' toilet area. The lead singer of a band due to play that particular weekday was being physically restrained from attempting to let the cows out to, in his mind, freedom. It took a few of us a good while to calm him down as he was hysterically crying with anger and sympathy with the cows' plight. We told him we hated it as much as he did, but if the cows were let free, they would panic and just end up being hit by cars on busy Station Hill, which had happened before in the past. He eventually calmed down and I think they did go on."

# REDD KROSS

With
Pop Am Good
+ Identity

Mark Badgeman "I don't recall how I first acquired Third Eye by Redd Kross but I absolutely loved it and I knew I needed to get them to come and play. Problem was, nobody really knew who they were and they weren't getting radio play. In promoter terms, that means nobody is going to buy a ticket. I needed a plan.

By this point, I had a box of demo tapes. Most were on C15 or C30 tapes. The C90 ones were like gold and had normally already been converted to a compilation tape for the camper van. I decided to tape as much of Third Eye as I could onto the remaining C15 and C30 tapes and made a cover that advertised the gig. One or two lucky people were gifted the full album on a C90. Then I just gave them away to the regular punters and told them to give it a listen. Let's be honest, everyone loves a freebie so most people gave it a spin and generally liked what they heard.

When the gig came around, it was busy. But the band couldn't understand why everyone knew the first 3 songs off Third Eye but when they played songs from side two, fewer people seemed familiar with them. I can't remember whether I owned up to what I did. After all, home taping was killing music, right?"

Lou "This was one of my favourite ever gigs at the venue. Mark had introduced me to their music when he booked them and I was singing along like crazy. They had some mad outfits and really brought the Tavern to life that night."

# You'll be Kross if you miss this gig!

## Top US band date a coup for Tavern

The Market Tavern has a nice little exclusive lined up next week with the arrival of American band Redd Kross.

Massive in their homeland but yet to make any commercial headway over here, their gig on June 7 is the only English date outside of London on this tour.

Redd Kross were formed by brothers Jeffrey and Steve McDonald at the height of the American punk era when they were just 14 and 11-years-old respectively.

Just kids playing about? Well, The Osmond brothers of punk cheesed off other older bands by actually being rather good and clinching their first record deal way before their adult counterparts.

As their music progressed from punk to today's Ziggy Stardust-T Rex-Psychedelic Lennon style, they built up a huge following a home.

This included working with Belinda Carlisle, who the brothers first met when she was with Los Angeles all-girl group The Go Go's (There is a very interesting and totally disgusting story about what she once did to Robert Palmer when they toured together, but I'd better not tell it on job-security grounds – let's just say it totally belies her goody two-shoes image of today!)

But here in Blighty their only success has been limited to *Super Sunny Christmas*, which crept into the indie charts on import, although if you saw Teenage Fan Club on tour recently then you will have some idea of what they're like as they were the support band.

Support for the Tavern gig comes from Pop Am Good and Identity. Tickets are available from the Tavern and the usual outlets.

● RIGHT: All the way from the USA, Redd Kross at the Market Tavern next week-end.

Ian Passey (Jackpot) "I've always counted the Redd Kross gig among my all-time favourites at any venue. I don't think I'd heard of them beforehand, but went along as it was obviously a major coup for a band from California to be playing in Kidderminster. They seemed just as delighted to be here as we were to welcome them, which created a fantastic celebratory atmosphere. That, and the fact they were they jaw-droppingly brilliant, of course!"

Andrew Wolfman "Badgeman was pretty evangelical about Cali-punks Redd Kross. They have always been a great band, but were already into their third act by the time they came to Kidderminster. (For anyone taking notes, there was the Black Flag-supporting scrappy-young-kids phase, the garage-y grunge-inventing Neurotica phase, and then the signed-to-a-major-label-but-sent-on-tour-with-much-lesser-bands phase they were in now). Despite being consistently brilliant, nothing the band had done in the last fifteen years seemed to cause more than a yawn in the UK, but thanks to Mark's enthusiasm, Redd Kross were weirdly massive in Kidderminster. Their next record, the hit-stuffed Phaseshifter, was a re-energised return-to-form and, even though The Market Tavern is about as far as you can get from California (physically and philosophically), I consider it a quintessentially Kidderminster album."

Mark Badgeman "I feel like being evangelical about them even now. Go and listen to Third Eye - it's absolutely brilliant! Redd Kross still play gigs and they're making a documentary about themselves, telling the whole story of how they started when Steve was just 11 years old, playing with Black Flag and antagonising the underground scene until they found their feet and were able to write proper songs. If the Tavern was still there today, I'd be trying to book them for their next tour and banging on your door until you agreed to buy a ticket to come and see them!"

REDD KROSS 👁 THIRD EYE

That's Sofia Coppola naked on the cover!

REDD KROSS - KIDDERMINSTER MARKET TAVERN - 06.92
One that appeared lateron in the gig book, out of sequence. I evidently suddenly remembered that I'd seen Redd Kross in June, but with no ticket stub or internet, the actual date is lost in the mists of time.
I have such a love of bandslike Redd Kross, who play sometimes slightly glam, no nonsense power pop. Its basically no frills fun, with wonderful melodies and a joyous outlook.
What the Californians made of the Market Tavern and Kidderminster is anyone's guess, but if they had a problem visiting the arse end of nowhere they certainly didn't show it. I suppose that's the thing with power pop, it can work in any venue, big or small.

LTFTWY

BY JASON

**Which town were you based in?** REDDITCH WHERE KEVIN TURVEY COMES FROM!!

**What years were you active?** IDENTITY STARTED IN 1987 BUT CHANGED OUR NAME TO FUNBUG BECAUSE LOOKOUT RECORDS SAID THERE ARE TOO MANY BANDS WITH THE NAME IDENTITY. WE FINALLY SPLIT IN 2011 BUT I'D REFORMED IDENTITY IN 2007 FOR OUR JAPAN TOUR AND RECORD DEAL. IT WENT ON / OFF FOR YEARS.

**Who was in the band?** ALWAYS STEVE REES ON BASS / BACKING VOX AND TALKING A LOT, ORIGINALLY MALC REES ON DRUMS / BACKING VOX / CHATTERBOX... THE CLASSIC MARKY MARK ON DRUMS AND SINGING / HI ENERGY PERSONALITY, AND ADUM SHIT ON DRUMS, AND ME JASON GUITAR GYMNAST AND CRAP SINGER!!

**What kind of music did you play?** SKATE PUNK WITH A COUNTRY TWANG

**Who were the influences?** ELVIS PRESLEY, DESCENDENTS, GREEN DAY, MEGA CITY FOUR, THE HARD ONS, THE STUPIDS, HUSKER DU

**What level of success did you achieve?** WELL I GUESS THE BIG ONE IS SUPPORTING GREEN DAY IN THE EARLY DAYS, TOURED WITH THE DICKIES, PLAYED WITH EVERYONE FROM NOFX, MISFITS, ALL, HARD ONS, GBH, GRANT HART, BAD BRAINS, BUZZCOCKS, 88 FINGERS LOUIE, DID 2 EUROPEAN TOURS, TOURED JAPAN, GOT A FEW RECORDS OUT WE DIDNT REALLY CARE ABOUT RECORDS AND BEING POPULAR WE HAD LOTS OF INTEREST BUT WE COULDN'T GIVE A SHIT, MY ONLY AMBITION WAS TO GET ON LOOKOUT RECORDS AND FUCKEN DID IT.

WE GOT A RECORD DEAL WITH GOLF RECORDS, IT WAS SHIT, NEVER HAD A PENNY OFF THEM!? BUT FIXING A HOLE RECORDS IN JAPAN SIGNED US AND PUT OUT OUR BACK CATALOGUE, AND NEW STUFF WHO WE LOVE!!!! ALSO SPEED-O-WAX

**What do you remember about playing at the Tavern?** I LOVED PLAYING THE TAVERN CUZ ITS A NICE PLACE TO DRIVE TO. AND AS A HARD CORE VEGAN ANIMAL RIGHTS ACTIVIST I FELT PRETTY BAD PLAYING THERE HA HA. BUT I GREW UP IN THE COUNTRY AND WORKED ON FARMS ALL MY LIFE. I REMEMBER BEING ON LSD AT A GIG AND WE GOT INTO THE AUCTION AREA SOMEHOW AND I WAS CONVINCED THERE WERE COWS THERE??, I THINK I CAME UP WITH THE SONG SUNSHINE (ATE MY BRAINS) AT THE MARKET TAVERN WHEN WE WAS OUTSIDE FUCKING ABOUT DRUNK WITH PSEUDO HIPPIES. THE 1st TIME I SAW JOHN OTWAY WAS THERE, WAS BRILLIANT! JIM McDONALD FROM REDD KROSS BOUGHT THE 'BROWN' FUNBUG T-SHIRT THAT WE COULDN'T SELL!! WE SOLD MORE T-SHIRTS THAN THE BUZZCOCKS ACCORDING TO MARKY MARK OUR DRUMMER. THE BEST WE PLAYED APART FROM THE BUZZCOCKS GIG WAS AN ALLDAYER AND WE PLAYED OUTSIDE AND THAT WAS THE DAY I MET ADAM VEEVERS FROM SKIMMER!! WHO'D BECOME MY BEST FRIEND AND BROTHER IN LAW.

**Any memories of the other bands you played with at the Tavern?** LOADS... BEING BACKSTAGE WITH THE BUZZCOCKS AND PETE SHELLEY REALLY LIKED ME AND KEPT GIVING ME CHAMPAGNE AND WAS REALLY FRIENDLY I THINK HE WANTED TO BUZZ MY COCK!! STEVE DIGGLE IS A GOD, BLYTH POWER WERE A REALLY GOOD LAUGH TO PLAY WITH, OF COURSE ANOTHER FINE MESS!! I'VE GOT A BAD MEMORY AND WAS PRETTY MUCH PISSED UP ALL THE TIME AND HAVING GREAT FUN WITH DRUGS...HA HA!!

**How did the band end?** FUNBUG LAST PLAYED IN REDDITCH SUPPORTING THE CRACKED ACTORS AT THE QUEENS HEAD SAT 10TH MARCH 2010? I JUST HAD ENOUGH AND QUIT AT THE LAST SONG. WE'RE STILL MATES AND HAVE THE ODD KNOCKABOUT NOW AND THEN.

**Did anyone go on to further success or have a career in the music industry?** MALC PLAYED BASS FOR THE JOYCE MCKINNEY EXP, THEN BECAME THE SENSELESS THINGS MERCHANDISER WHEN THEY GOT BIG. AND NOW HE'S BEEN "THE CRAVATS" DRUMMER. STEVE RUNS TOP BANANA REHEARSAL STUDIOS IN REDDITCH WHICH IS A MASSIVE HELP FOR ALL LOCAL BANDS!! BUT NO WE WASN'T INTERESTED IN THE MUSIC INDUSTRY WE WANTED TO "KEEP LIVE MUSIC SHIT!!" WHICH WE'VE CONTINUED TO DO WITH "THE VEEVERS" AND "THE FUR CUPS....FROM REDDITCH!!"

**What else do we need to know about the band?** THE ONLY REASON I WANTED TO BE IN A BAND WAS TO GET INTO AND PLAY GIGS FOR FREE!!! xXx

**FUNBUG**
KEEPING LIVE MUSIC SHIT.

**FunBug**

LTD. EDT.

TEZBINETOP ep

Mark Badgeman "Green Day's favourite UK band - as I never tired of telling people!!"

FUNBUG

STEVE

Oh Shit It's **FUNBUG**

**FUNBUG**
KEEPING LIVE MUSIC SHIT

"LOOK MOM! NO BRAINS!!!"
**FUNBUG**
"STUPIDER THAN THOU"

Oh Shit It's **FUNBUG** AGAIN!!

**FUNBUG**
KEEPING LIVE MUSIC SHIT

Live at the Market Tavern video on YouTube

**FUNBUG**
KEEPING LIVE MUSIC SHIT.

**FUNBUG**
FUCK OFF AND SMILE

Andy Price "I was looking for a pub to run and saw the Market Tavern was being advertised. Previously I'd been running a nice restaurant in Bath and there was a venue nearby that was always busy, so I was looking for somewhere that bands could play. When I came to see the Tavern, I saw the back room and that was the only reason I wanted it. I thought if I couldn't fill that three or four nights a week, I might as well give up, although I didn't really know how to go about getting the bands.

The previous owners had been making their money from the old licensing laws when market pubs were allowed to open all day. The Tavern was busy on market days because all the other pubs had to call last orders in the afternoon. That all changed in 1988 when all day drinking came in, so they were looking to get rid of it.

Martin had come up from Bath to visit me and decided to have a go at booking some bands, then Mark walked in not long after and he seemed pretty serious about it too. Unfortunately, the council had got it into their heads that I was going to turn it into a fine dining restaurant. I mean, seriously, would you take your wife to a restaurant that had toilets like that? Plus it stank. I was gobsmacked. There was no way you could open a restaurant there. I didn't con them over it, they'd just asked what my background was and I told them. I never said I was going to run a restaurant.

When we started putting the bands on, the market supervisor, who had an office upstairs, absolutely hated it. He could hear them soundchecking and then there'd be the remnants from people enjoying themselves the previous night when he came in the next morning. He definitely started the complaints to the council. The farmers thought they owned the place because it was the market licence that had made it a busy pub in the 80s. But now that trade had gone, and there was no way you could run a pub that just catered for a handful of farmers twice a week.

Their tactic was to try and get me out over the state of the toilets. The lease said they were responsible for the upkeep, but they were only expecting to do it after market days and not after busy gigs on a regular basis. So they tried to get me to do it. They sent solicitor's letters and it was costing a fortune trying to deal with it. That's why Mark did the benefit gig. What they should have done was send the fire brigade down on a busy gig because we were always over the official capacity. They never thought of that!

The farmers hated the jukebox in the front bar as well. Originally, it just had normal pop music on, but I asked one of the regulars to do a list and we got things on it like The Jam, which weren't on other pub jukeboxes at the time. And it was loud! It attracted people the farmers didn't like. And the council didn't like them either. They wanted it to be a middle class place for the auctioneers and somewhere the farmers could be comfortable because they lived in the middle of nowhere and only saw other people once or twice a week.

Eventually, it cost so much money that I went bankrupt and sold the pub to David Cox who was the only person willing to take it on. Some guys from Worcester were interested, probably the Jolly Roger ones, but they were concerned about the way the council were behaving. The markets were getting less and less busy so there was no trade there. In hindsight, I wonder if their endgame was to shut the pub down so they could build the flats."

# The Kidderminsters are united

**KIDDERMINSTER MARKET TAVERN** could close as a live venue, following an eviction order served on landlord Andrew Price by the local council, who own the building.

The Market Tavern, formerly a pub, was converted into a 300 capacity live music venue some two years ago, and has subsequently become a crucial part of the UK club circuit. Price told NME this week that although a high court appeal will prove costly, he plans to "fight the eviction order every inch of the way".

Promoter Mark Badgeman is currently organising a petition with the help of local music fans desperate to keep the Market Tavern, the only live music facility serving the Kidderminster area, fully operational. Badgeman has already received pledges of support from Pop Will Eat Itself and Ned's Atomic Dustbin, who played their first ever gig as the current line-up at the Market Tavern. Carter USM and Senseless Things manager Adrian Boss also voiced concern at the continuing erosion of the live music circuit in the UK.

● Meanwhile, Pop Will Eat Itself issue their first new 45 in 12 months through RCA this week. The double A-sided single 'Karmadrome'/'Eat Me, Drink Me, Love Me, Kill Me' serves as the first taster from the Poppies' upcoming 'The Looks Of The Lifestyle' LP, which is scheduled for release in September. Twelve-inch and CD formats also carry 'Pweization' originally featured on their '89 'Very Metal Noise Pollution' EP. As previously announced the band also warm-up for their appearance at the New York New Music Seminar next month with five consecutive shows at London's Marquee (June 2, 3, 4, 5 and 6).

DJs POP WILL EAT ITSELF

# SCORPIO RISING
Panic Beach (playing live)
Wednesday 10th June £3.50Adv

# DUB MERGE
+ The NOT FOR BABIES
Sound System
Saturday 20th June £2.50

The Market Tavern is currently under the threat of closure from Wyre Forest District Council. We intend to fight this every inch of the way but legal battles are costly. These benefit gigs are to help raise enough money to beat the council and keep the Tavern open as a fully operational live music venue. The bands have given their time for free so please support us in our hour of need - Kidderminster needs live music!

# The MARKET TAVERN Benefit gig will take place on June 10th
## Featuring
# DJs PWEI
## POP WILL EAT ITSELF
and at least two top Indie bands playing live and possibly more celebrity DJs

The future of the Market Tavern is in doubt as the local council are trying to evict us. Please support this benefit gig to help us raise our legal costs.

£3.50

## Keep live music urges top agent

**By MARK LANGFORD**

A talent scout for a leading record company has joined the fight to keep live music at a Kidderminster pub whose landlord is threatened with eviction.

Charlie Pinder, an artist and repertoire agent for London-based East West Records, urged Wyre Forest District Council to consider the implications if the Market Tavern ceased to be a venue for live bands.

Landlord Andrew Price and partner Gail Russell have been told by the council, who

### RECORD CHIEF BACKS TAVERN

own the lease to the Comberton Place pub, they could have to quit after a row over rent arrears and the state of the toilets.

But the couple claim the real reason is the council does not like them hosting live music because of the crowds it attracts.

Mr Pinder, whose label records artists such as Simply Red and Tori Amos, said he had been to the Tavern several times, and if this was the case the council would be making a mistake.

He said: "The Market Tavern is

a very good little venue. Kidderminster is not a big place, yet it attracts a calibre of bands it should be proud of.

"Obviously the council has to consider any possible nuisance it could cause to the people who don't use it, but you generally find the people using places like this go to see the bands and not to cause trouble.

"I think very often people just don't realise the importance of places like this."

Council estates officer David Coleman was unavailable for comment but a spokesman for the Market Tavern said the matter was still being dealt with by their solicitors.

It's ironic that when the Tavern reached the peak of its popularity, we were having to do a benefit gig to raise money for Andy's legal costs to stop it being shut down. I don't remember how we used to get Pop Will Eat Itself to come and DJ but that was a massive draw as they were a major Top 40 act. Scorpio Rising had done some great gigs, Scrash and Panic Beach were local but Stranglmartin were American and had never played before. At 286 tickets, it was another 'almost sold out' show.

Mickey Banks (Scorpio Rising) "I think we drove from another gig in London. Brought watermelons."

## Flash in the pan as landlord and council clash

# PUB MUSIC FACING ITS WATER-LOO

● Gail Russell and Andrew Price outside the Market Tavern.

Lou "This was such an awesome event, Scorpio Rising were brilliant and really getting some attention on the scene at the time - all the girls were in love with Mickey the singer."

Live music at a Kidderminster pub could be flushed down the pan because the licensee faces eviction by Wyre Forest District Council in a row over the state of the toilets.

Andrew Price and partner Gail Russell agree the toilets at the Market Tavern are unhygienic, but accused the council of not doing its agreed share of the cleaning duties properly.

Mr Price said they cleaned the toilets three days a week and the council the other four.

He said: "In the lease they are responsible for supplying toilet paper, soap and roller towels but they very often don't do it."

Eviction proceedings were started by the council because of this and the couple, who took over the pub two years ago, falling behind with the rent on their ten-year lease.

Mr Price admitted the arrears but said they would be able to pay them off in the next three weeks.

### By MARK LANGFORD

He said they felt a major reason the council wanted them out was it did not like them staging live bands for youngsters in the area

"Eighteen months ago an enforcement officer came down and said he did not like what we had done with the pub or the kind of people we were attracting. It was meant to be a pub for farmers.

"But we've spent a lot of money doing this place up. When we took over no-one had spent a penny on the place in 20 years, glass in the frontage that had been

kicked in 15 months previously had not even been replaced," said Mr Price.

Talks between the council and the couple's solicitors in the hope of reaching a solution are now under way.

Top names who have played at the Market Tavern include Robert Plant, Carter – The Unstoppable Sex Machine and The Selecter.

Regulars have now organised a concert on June 10 featuring members of Top 20 Dudley band Pop Will Eat Itself to raise money for the couple's legal costs.

District estates officer David Coleman disagreed the state of the toilets was the fault of the council, adding they had nothing against live bands playing at the pub.

He said: "Tenants have their problems from time to time and we appreciate that.

"But we are talking about community charge payers' money and if we've got a tenant who doesn't meet his covenants, then we'd rather get rid of them and get in someone who does."

Mark Badgeman "I used to turn up around 2pm to get ready for a gig because the farmers would be drinking in the venue at lunchtime and they'd leave straw all over the place. I had to sweep it up and take the tables and chairs out. Sometimes, the farmers were still there around 3pm when bands were trying to load in, absolutely slaughtered but about to drive their cattle lorries back to their farms. I remember one of them moaning about being caught drink driving. 'I don't understand why the copper stopped me - he could see I was a farmer'! I hated them, they were rude, ignorant, arrogant and a total pain. They were instrumental in getting the council to boot Andy Price out. I still have an irrational hatred of farmers to this day!"

Andy Barding "Stranglmartin were one of those bands that, once seen, begged to be seen again. Not that, on paper, they were particularly original - this was a trio of vaguely punky/indie rockers from Lexington KY with a handful of good songs. Fair enough. But in practice... WOW.

A lot of the charm fell to David Butler, the band's affable and compelling frontman and left-handed guitarist. He could get sounds out of his instrument that I simply hadn't heard before. Cartoon sound effects, explosive twangs and the like. All of which lent songs like 'Crabs', 'Stop Interrupting Me' and 'I Hate Your Guts' a quite unique appeal.

The night they played Kidderminster I hopped in my work pool Fiesta and drove up from Wales for the pleasure of a repeat of the Newport TJs experience, which had gone down so well a night or two beforehand. I slept in that Fiesta, too. There was an impressive bar tab for the taking at the Market Tavern, as I recall. And David bought me a Chinese takeaway. Good band, good man, good times."

Mark Badgeman "It would have been my idea to do the benefit gig and it was definitely a forerunner of the all-dayers, which didn't start until 1993. I needed the bands to play for free but I needed a name. Scorpio Rising had played with Fretblanket and that was a pivotal gig for them as we got 200 in. They had another gig in London on the same day, but it was either a support or an early finish so they jumped straight in the van and drove to Kiddy, which was on their way home anyway. Along with the Poppies on the decks, that was enough to ensure we'd get a good crowd. Adding two popular local bands, Panic Beach and Scrash, would have boosted the appeal, which meant there was room for Stranglmartin who were from Kentucky and had no connection whatsoever to Kidderminster, but were looking for a gig after supporting Redd Kross in Newport the night before.

Looking back over my notes, it appears everyone did it for free, including Stan the PA Man. We raised £1180 for Andy's legal costs and that helped us stay open a bit longer. I think the threat of closure must have died down a bit following the gig, especially after the Shuttle ran it on the front page, as we eventually made it to the start of 1994. But Wyre Forest District Council should forever hold their heads in shame at what they did to the Tavern. It was mean and petty and deprived the town of a brilliant venue."

Andrew Wolfman, Tim from Freek Downward Thing & friends

# DUBMERGE

By Marcus

**Which town were you based in?** Kiddy / Hereford / Ludlow / Worcester / Bromyard / Leominster

**What years were you active?**
1991-20?? Around ten years, but I managed about 7 years and they continued for a bit after I left

**Who was in the band?**
Version 1 : Lofty, Steve, Jon, Trevor, Dom, Marcus
Version 1: Lofty, Nigel, Lou, Jon, Trevor, Dom, Marcus
V2: Lofty, Paul, Jon, Trevor, Dom, Marcus, Kenny, Matt on sound
V2.5: Lofty, Paul, Jon, Trevor, Dom, Marcus, Kenny, Ben Matt on sound
V3: Lofty, Paul, Steve, Barney, Marcus, Kenny Matt left and was replaced by a Welsh rasta bloke called Shaun
who always wore a red gold and green string vest and insisted he always ate chicken on the rider. We missed a
ferry once because he demanded a chicken take away.
Then I left and there were other versions of the band.

**What kind of music did you play?**
Crusty Dub Rap Dance Hiphop Dub-hop, Dancehall, Shouty dub

**Who were the influences?**
Dub syndicate, On-U sound, RDF, RATM, Beastie Boys, Citizen Fish, Culture shock, a lot of Roots Reggae,
a lot of leftfield Rap and Hiphop, Disposable Heroes of Hiphoprasy, Ragga Twins, we went a bit jungle a few
times.

**What level of success did you achieve?**
We played a lot out of the Uk in Europe on tours that were a mix of squats, venues and festivals, we did
one or two support tours, we had a good Uk festival following because we had a current sound at the time
and did something interesting with it..

**What do you remember about playing at the Tavern?**
Andy who ran the place, always seemed reasonable and decent, but the venue never paid that much.
Beamish on draught was a winner.
'Epic' the album by Faith No More was a massive favourite on the juke box in 1990 and seemed to be on repeat.
The sound was always pretty good, if we were lucky we would have our own sound man or sometimes Stan the
Man who was brilliant.
I don't remember a dressing room…was there one?
Not sure if we were ever asked for a rider or if we got one? It probably didn't matter tho as we much
preferred playing really high rather than drunk.
If you were in the venue mid-week and went for a piss, it would be really unusual if you didn't hear a cow
mooing from inside the market building which connected through a corridor where the toilets were. Probably
an animal that didn't get sold because nobody wanted it.
If you were hungry / desperate there was always chips after the show from Captain Cods opposite but the
food there was disgusting before quite a few pints.
It had a special smell.
Badgeman owes us £40 for the last gig we did in 1995

**Any memories of the other bands you played with at the Tavern?**
Citizen Fish- excellent of course
RDF- Classic dub-crust-dub
The Selector regulars at the pub and always brilliant

# BAND FILE

**How did the band end?**
I left, they carried on....not sure what happened after me.

**Did anyone go on to further success or have a career in the music industry?**
Kind of yes for a while.

**What else do we need to know about the band?**
I joined the band shortly after their inception , at the time they were called 'Tribe' and I had a live tape recording of a very early gig which was my introduction to the whole thing. The singer's van got broken into before the gig and on the tape you can hear him shout angrily into the mic : "My white escort van just got broken into. Thank you very much" or something like that.
We weren't signed or managed, we had had a few booking agents on and off, we recorded and distributed all of our own music which came out on quite a few self released tapes and CDs. We were very much a DIY band. Studio time and manufacturing of tapes and CDs paid by shows. We had no interest in the trappings of a record deal .
Looking back now I think we did really well without the benefits that came along with a record deal in the 1990's.
All we really wanted to do was play gigs around the UK and abroad and get stoned. We succeeded brilliantly at that.

DUBMERGE

+ Friendly Fire Sound System

Friday 20th August

MARKET TAVERN
KIDDERMINSTER

# Adorable + The Wishplants & Pietra Rosa

Adorable should have been a legendary Market Tavern gig. Lots of interest, a great debut single that hit number one in the Indies, but then the music press turned on them and their tour to promote the second single was a struggle. We only got 60 in despite two good supports.
Adam Hammond from Isolation Records explains what happened...

Theirs is a fascinating story. Adorable wrote some great songs, played some electrifying gigs and at one time appeared to have the world at their feet, but their star was short-lived. Falling foul of the all-powerful British music media, they were shunned, ridiculed and ignored. Theirs is a tale of how not to promote a band. How not to do an interview and how to pick your timing extremely badly.

Inspired by artists such as Echo & The Bunnymen, The Jesus & Mary Chain and The Psychedelic Furs, Adorable arrived on the scene just as Shoegaze was waning and just before Britpop really took off. It was easy for lazy journalists in the media to label them as just another band hanging on to the coattails of a fading genre, yet it would have taken only one gig for them to realise that Adorable were as far removed from Shoegaze as the Ramones were from Prog. This was not a band creating soundscapes whilst staring at their feet introvertedly. Adorable weren't a band shrouded in doubt and uncertainty. Adorable were bursting with confidence, self-assurance and totally in your face. They exuded belief, and backed it up with aggressive live performances. They had the tunes, the look, the attitude and the talent to make it all the way to the top. And they so nearly did.

'Sunshine Smile' was the band's first single, released in April 1992 on Creation Records after Adorable had toured supporting the hugely popular Curve. The single made Record Of The Week in the NME and topped the independent singles chart, yet little did the band know this would represent the high watermark of their musical career. It was all downhill from here.

The problems really began in the band's first series of interviews with the music press. Many groups at the time would go into print slagging off the music of the day and emerge as admirable anti-heroes. Adorable came over as arseholes, posh kids talking about French cinema and the writings of Proust while dismissing their peers, branded in their first NME interview as "the cockiest new band in pop" and "cocksure, throat-grabbing, individualist, sun-shines-out-of-my-ass limelight muggers". The first quote from them came from Wil and little did he know at the time that he was hammering nails into his own coffin. "I'd not only encourage people to stop buying records, but I'd encourage them to go en masse back to the record shop with their record collections and return them. Even if they won't give you a refund. No-one's doing anything that's worthwhile. They shouldn't be taking up space in your rooms."

If the press hated their attitude, Creation's Alan McGee loved it and would work to promote the band in that light, producing promo pictures of the band overlaid with a sign that said 'Arrogant'. A Creation press release declared, "Adorable have established a dangerous reputation as the cockiest band in pop music. Their self-confidence transcends mere enthusiasm, rivalling the insolence of bands like The Sex Pistols." It was a tactic that would backfire massively, and the negatives began almost immediately with a live review by Paul Lester in Melody Maker (18th April 1992) declaring, "Schoolkids in a scout hut playing Echo tracks with feedback is not what I dashed across London for, believe me. Adorable aren't sassy, they're not sexy, they're not sharp, they don't even slouch with style. And they career through every title in their set at the same breakneck speed, at the same deafening volume, all of which, not surprisingly, makes all the songs sound the same."

It got worse. Creation chose to release 'I'll Be Your Saint' as the band's second single containing the legendary lyrics, "I'll be love, I'll be your god." Oops. It was the ultimate bad luck that the review copy fell into the hands of Melody Maker journalists The Stud Brothers, ludicrously intelligent and thoughtful writers who had a fascination for innovation and style, and ones who couldn't see anything new in Adorable, certainly not enough to justify the rhetoric.

For the full interview, go to www.isolationrecords.co.uk/adorableinterview.html. Many thanks to Adam for allowing me to use this abridged version of his article.

adorable
Glorious
Cut #2

crash sight
saint
sunshine smile
fallen idol
homeboy
sistine

i'll be your sa
available on 7" + 12

101

# adorable

At soundcheck

# adorable

## i'll be your saint
available on 7" · 12" · cd;   out 13th july

live dates: july 8 · aberdeen pelican  9 · gourock bay hotel  10 · carlisle pagoda
11 · hull adelphi  13 · nottingham imperial hotel  14 · reading 21 south street
15 · newport t.j.'s  17 · exeter cavern  18 · aldershot buzz club  21 · trowbridge psychic pig
22 · tamworth arts centre  23 · windsor old trout  24 · kidderminster market tavern
25 · bedford esquires  27 · stoke wheatsheaf  28 · leicester princess charlotte
29 · southampton joiners  30 · chelmsford y club  august 1 · london underworld
a creation records product.

# FRI 24th JULY
# MARKET TAVERN
# KIDDERMINSTER

Huge thanks to Nicola Smith for the Adorable photos!

## market tavern kidderminster
### tel: 0562 752590

| | | |
|---|---|---|
| FRIDAY 22nd May | All the way from Mu Mu Land — EXTREME NOISE TERROR + HEADCLEANER + Scumbug | £3.50 Adv |
| FRIDAY 29th May | DF 118 — Ex Radical Dance Faction + The Stratosphere rave and sound system | £2.50 |
| FRIDAY 5th June | MIDWAY STILL + PANIC BEACH | £3.00 |
| SATURDAY 6th June | RYTHM-ITES | £3.50 |
| SUNDAY 7th June | FROM LOS ANGELES — ReDD KRoSS + POP AM + GOOD + IDENTITY + Stroke Bagpuss | £3.00 Adv |
| FRIDAY 19th June | sensitize / Sugarblast + MINT 400 (Ex Spiny Dogfish) | £3.00 |
| FRIDAY 3rd July | Special double heading — FRETBLANKET / PANIC BEACH + Monsterland (From America) | £2.50 |

Look out for Adorable, Scorpio Rising, Th' Faith Healers

tickets from: market tavern, sounds around, jukebox (stourport) dead or alive (worcs) or tempest (b'ham)
1 min from the station. Last trains: B'ham 23.02  Worcs 00.01

---

## market tavern kidderminster
### tel: 0562 752590

| | | |
|---|---|---|
| FRIDAY 19th June | sensitize / Sugarblast + support | £3.00 |
| SATURDAY 20th June | Benefit gig (Save the Tavern) — DUB MERGE + the NOT FOR BABIES Sound System | £2.50 |
| WEDNESDAY 1st July | Whiskey Priests | £3.00 |
| FRIDAY 3rd July | FRETBLANKET + LUDICROUS LOLLIPOPS + IDENTITY | £2.50 |
| FRIDAY 10th July | SCORPIO RISING + CURVEBALL + MANIC THING | £3.00 Adv |
| FRIDAY 24th July | adorable + Pietra Rosa + Bathchair Suicide | £3.00 |
| FRIDAY 21st August | BACK TO THE PLANET | £3.00 |

support the Tavern — don't let the council close us down

tickets from: market tavern, sounds around, dead or alive (worcs) or tempest (b'ham)
1 min from the station. Last trains: B'ham 23.02  Worcs 00.01

---

## market tavern kidderminster
### tel: 056. 752590

| | | |
|---|---|---|
| FRIDAY 17th April | SOFAHEAD + CAKE + reverse | £3.50 Adv |
| TUESDAY 28th April | BIRDLAND + + Sugarblast | |
| FRIDAY 1st | the return of... STOP THE WORLD — BANK HOLIDAY SPECIAL | |
| FRIDAY 15th May | MACHINE GUN FEEDBACK Scrash + dive | £2.50 |
| FRIDAY 22nd May | All the way from Mu Mu Land — EXTREME NOISE TERROR + HEADCLEANER | £3.50 |
| TUESDAY 2nd June | FROM LOS ANGELES — ReDD KRoSS + POP AM + GOOD | |
| FRIDAY 5th June | MIDWAY STILL + PANIC BEACH | |

Look out for Sensitize, Rythm-ites, Th' Faith Healers

tickets from: market tavern, sounds around, jukebox (stourport) dead or alive (worcs) or tempest (b'ham)
min from the station. Last trains: B'ham 23.07  Worcs 23.49

---

## market tavern kidderminster
### tel: 0562 752590

| | | |
|---|---|---|
| FRIDAY 8th May | Ex Carter — Jon 'FAT' Beast a night of sex, madness, magic and fun | £2.50 |
| FRIDAY 15th May | MACHINE GUN FEEDBACK Scrash + dive | £2.50 |
| FRIDAY 22nd May | All the way from Mu Mu Land — EXTREME NOISE TERROR + HEADCLEANER + Scumbug | £3.50 |
| FRIDAY 29th May | DF 118 — Ex Radical Dance Faction | £2.50 |
| FRIDAY 5th June | MIDWAY STILL + PANIC BEACH | £3.00 |
| SATURDAY 6th April | RYTHM-ITES | £3.50 |
| SUNDAY 7th June | FROM LOS ANGELES — ReDD KRoSS + POP AM + GOOD + IDENTITY | £3.00 Adv |

Look out for Sensitize, Scorpio Rising, Th' Faith Healers

tickets from: market tavern, sounds around, dead or alive (worcs) or tempest (b'ham)
1 min from the station. Last trains: B'ham 23.07  Worcs 23.49

---

## market tavern kidderminster
### tel: 0562 752590

| | | |
|---|---|---|
| SUNDAY 7th June | FROM LOS ANGELES — ReDD KRoSS + POP AM + GOOD + IDENTITY + Stroke Bagpuss | £3.00 Adv |
| WEDNESDAY 10th June | Benefit gig — DJs POP WILL EAT ITSELF / PANIC BEACH playing live (plus another band to be confirmed) | £3.50 Adv |
| FRIDAY 12th June | Stratosphere | £2.00 |
| THURSDAY 18th June | Dr and the Medics | £4.00 |
| FRIDAY 19th June | sensitize / Sugarblast + support | £3.00 |
| SATURDAY 20th June | Benefit gig (Save the Tavern) — DUB MERGE + the NOT FOR BABIES Sound System | £2.50 |
| FRIDAY 3rd July | Special double — FRETBLANKET + LUDICROUS LOLLIPOPS | £2.50 |

Look out for adorable, Back to the Planet, Scorpio Rising

tickets from: market tavern, sounds around, jukebox dead or alive (worcs) or tempest (b'ham)
1 min from the station. Last trains: B'ham 23.07  Worcs 23.49

---

## market tavern
### comberton place, kidderminster  tel. 0562 752590

| | |
|---|---|
| Fri 31 Jan | PALE KINGS/SMEDLEY |
| Sat 1st Feb | U.X.B./RANSOM |
| Fri 7 Feb | SCORPIO RISING |
| Sat 8 Feb | POINTED STICKS |
| Tues 11 Feb | UNCLE IANS ORAL CIRCUS |
| Thurs 13 Feb | DR + THE MEDICS |
| Sat 15 Feb | CRAZY LITTLE SISTER |

Coming soon: Crazyhead, Ruthless Blue Band and Cardiacs

---

## market tavern
### comberton place kidderminster  tel: 0562 752590

| | |
|---|---|
| FRIDAY 24th July | adorable |
| SATURDAY 25th July | STRATOSPHERE RAVE |
| FRIDAY 31st July | ILLUSTRIOUS |
| SATURDAY 1st August | AMBUSH |
| FRIDAY 7th August | PALE KINGS |
| SATURDAY 8th August | NEW CRANES |
| FRIDAY 14th August | SCUMBUG |

---

## market tavern

| | APRIL | | MAY |
|---|---|---|---|
| 3 | Destination POP disco featuring CARTER THE UNSTOPPABLE SEX MACHINE — hear the new single, 'The only living boy in New Cross' | 1 | May Bank Holiday special THE SELECTER 2 TONE |
| 10 | STOMP Disco | 8 | to be confirmed |
| 17 | Sofahead | 15 | to be confirmed |
| 28 | BIRDLAND + Sugarblast | 22 | Extreme Noise Terror! |
| | | 29 | MIDWAY STILL / PANIC BEACH |

---

## market tavern
### comberton place, kidderminster  tel. 0562 752590

| | |
|---|---|
| Sat 18 Jan | EGYPT |
| Sat 25 Jan | ERIC BELL |
| Fri 31 Jan | PALE KINGS |
| Sat 1 Feb | U.X.B. |
| Fri 7th Feb | SCORPIO RISING |
| Sat 15 Feb | DANGEROUS |
| Fri 21 Feb | PANIC BEACH |

---

1992 FLYERS & ADS

# BOFF

Johnny Vinyl "Frank Boff's Big Band, if my memory serves me well, a large American/Japanese frontman (probably from Cheltenham) backed with nasty, funky beats and with saxophone. Was the saxophonist dressed as a nun? Maybe she was a nun. Or maybe that was another band entirely? Either way... I bought the 12" 'Xcite The Girl'... (Ah the merch table),. they were actually far better live than their recorded material. Though 'Broola' (on the b-side) was captured well and at the Tavern we went ballistic when they played it and carried on singing the chorus line into the next track. Or maybe they had finished and we carried on. Not unusual. Top tune...Top band!"

John Peutherer (Stop The World) "Musically the band I always thought were a mix of Bad Manners with The B52's. They were an absolutely terrific act. Catchy tunes, great playing, humour... really superb. They played quite big gigs at the Bulldog Bash. I know they released a 12" ep because I still own it!!"

Stan The PA Man "One of my very favourite gigs was the Frank Boff Big Band on Christmas day in 1992. What else would you do on Christmas night? Nothing funny happened and there were no problems I just remember it being a proper good night with a great vibe and everybody having a good time. We should have done it more often."

Stig "It's my birthday and I'm friends with the Stop The World chaps. Dave Cooper STW singer asked FBBB if I could announce the bands onto the stage as a birthday treat. I did so nearly stripping my throat and damaging the mic. But great gig, drank a shed load of Yorkshire Bitter and FBBB gave me signed copies of their EP. A much missed venue."

## The Frank Boff Big Band

XCITE THE GIRL
JAMES ?
c/w
BROOLA
XCITE THE GIRL
RIBBED & READY MIX

BOFF :-
TRUMPET GEOFF
TROMBONE BONES
KRANOV SAX/VOCAL
ROB BASS
GRUNKEE DRUMS
KAFAI VOCAL
FORDY GUITAR

INFO/CONTACT :
CLEGG BADLANDS RECORDS, 11 ST GEORGES PLACE, CHELTENHAM, GLOS. GL50 3LA. Tel 0242 227725

THANKS :-
JOYCE, EAGOR &
BADLANDS

---

The one thing that let the Tavern down in the early days was the lights. I used to rent them in to start with but it was expensive. I knew Bryan Leach, later to become Coldplay's lighting designer, who told me he had some parcans and an old Strand dimmer for sale. They seemed pretty cheap. A parcan is the old fashioned single colour light that you'd see millions of at any 80's rock show. I drove to London to pick them up. Turns out he was selling me the actual housing (which is technically the parcan) and not the lamps that actually produce the light.

So we had 8 empty parcans and no light coming out of them! We couldn't afford to get the Par lamps at first so I got a piece of ply and screwed a household light fitting to it and we lit the bands with 100w bulbs. It just doesn't work! Especially if you put a coloured gel over it. The name Par actually stands for 'parabolic aluminium reflector' which is essentially what a torch is. Our household bulbs had nothing to reflect the light so I put some kitchen foil at the back. I remember Redd Kross's singer commenting 'these hi-tech lights are killing me'

Eventually we got the real thing, which meant someone could have a go at operating them. If the gig wasn't so popular, they'd just get left on. If it was a bigger show, someone would have a go at flashing the buttons or pulling the faders. Occasionally, a band brought their own lighting designer with them and you'd see the difference it makes having a professional do it, even with just eight lamps wired in pairs.

lists of my Friday nights... in retrospect it didn't actually matter who was on as I always seemed to end up there anyway (or on the roof)"

Sue Gardner "The Tav was a place I loved and went to regularly. It was a working man's social club style place built onto a cattle market, so the farmers would be in there for a drink during the day. It could be rather fragrant at times too. It was frequented by bikers and basically anybody that was in the least bit alternative for any reason. There was a regular alternative night called, The Ectoplasmic Sonic Stomp, which I think gives you a good insight into what kind of a night it was. Loved it!"

Steve Cooper "The best place to assess the cultural weather in those days was to check flyposters in the subways at the bottom of Comberton Hill. Kidderminster's own NME!"

Julie Marshall "Sensitize played to three of us stuck to the bar at the back (the youngest of us being chased around the Tavern by the landlord for being 17) and one hammered middle-aged man playing air guitar in the middle of the room. I think he may have had a stetson."

Sally Lacy Kerr "I said 'Ooo stop the world - I wanna get off'. Wasn't it the dogs bollocks of a place - smelt a bit like them too!"

Ray "I remember drinking Special Brew and scrumpy snakebites for two or three hours before the Rhythm-ites came on and two minutes into their set, collapsing, head down onto a table. Birdie and Tracie very kindly led me to their wagon outside and I drifted into a booze coma for the rest of the night. Missed it all."

Chris Perks (Dive) "It was an absolute institution and completely unique, and as 17-year olds (COUGH), sorry, 18-year olds who loved music, beer, and fun, there wasn't anywhere you'd rather be. I don't think there was another venue that could attract big names and still give young local bands the chance to play on a Friday and Saturday night."

Daz Rogers "It was great seeing all these cool bands without having to worry about the last train home."

Dom Dunlea "Very few lucid memories, apart from the sobering smack of 'eau de cowshit' enhancing the toileting experience. Definitely remember seeing Carter twice."

Fiona Gordon "I worked in the cafe for a while & I remember a lady called Jean who was there for years. I was a barmaid for a few years too."

Kev Wheeler "I was pretty much a permanent fixture there so saw most of the bands, but tight fisted enough to stand in the stairwell for some of them."

David McCaskill Elliott (Spike) "Who was the guy who wore the black leather jacket with band names written on it? It had Gaye Bikers On Acid and Lesbian Dope Heads On Mopeds. That always used to make me laugh."

Matt Taylor "I described it to someone a while back as like an indoor festival complete with cowshit, straw and crap cider in plastic glasses. Headlined by Midway Still and The Family Cat."

Johnny Vinyl "The band I always wanted to see at the time, I don't think ever played The Tavern... AK 47's. Their album 'Don't Call Me Vanilla' was up there with RDF and others. I might have even bought the LP at the Tavern (at some anarchic gig)"

Jon Herbert (about the flyers) "Brilliant. You forget how many good bands played the Tavern back in the day. Great to see!"

Simon Glenister (Paintbox / Tunng) "Played many times in Paintbox, got banned once - it was a big block of cheese, I'm saying no more."

# Back To The Planet

Mark Badgeman "If I wasn't fact-checking this, I'd tell you Back To The Planet played loads of times and that the Poppies loved them so much when they DJ'ed for them, they took them out on tour. Turns out I might have made this up. I wondered why the band had no recollection of playing Kiddy. It was just one of hundreds of venues they played, even though they were great gigs for us.

Both Tavern gigs sold out, which puts them in a very select group of acts who actually shifted all 300 tickets (Carter, Chumbawamba, Buzzcocks, The Wedding Present and Robert Plant). We had other busy gigs, but often we were a handful short of selling out. BTTP were the perfect Tavern band though. They had proper crusty credentials (formed in a squat, played Castlemorton Free Festival and the Deptford Urban Free Festival as well as countless Glastonbury appearances on the tiny stages) melding punk, ska, techno and pop perfectly. It would appear I described them to the Shuttle as a cross between EMF and the Selecter. Not unreasonably so. At this point, their only recorded output was one 12" and a couple of cassettes sold at gigs, so it was remarkable how they'd become so popular.

The Christmas gig on the poster was cancelled at the last minute, leaving Madhalibut with a very busy headline show. They were also a perfect fit for the Tavern and supported on several occasions, including the return of BTTP."

Lou "This gig was RAMMED! Back To The Planet were doing loads of gigs and festivals at the time and I think they'd just had a pretty successful single release, so it was packed full of fans and people singing along. Loads of 'new age travellers' turned up, so the car park was full of vans and trucks."

Johnny Vinyl "I remember Madhalibut supporting Back To The Planet and they were crustie progsters. Not everyone's cuppa but I liked them enough to buy the cassette! BTTP were always good and a crowd pleaser... and made it into the RECORD MIRROR... booo!! Next time I saw Madhalibut, it was supporting The Sea... who I actually didn't see as I'd staggered off outside for a joint... and returned in time for last orders!! Often, we missed the support and sometimes the main event! That'll be the drugs."

## BACK TO THE PLANET
(Levellers support band)

## +SCRASH + STATE OF GROOVE

## +guest DJ's from P.W.E.I.

FRI 21st AUGUST 1992
Market Tavern
Kidderminster £3

Special Christmas gig with...

BACK to THE PLANET

MadHalibut
Wednesday 16th December
MARKET TAVERN
KIDDERMINSTER
£3.50                    7.30-11.00
Only 1 minute from the station. Last trains: B'ham 23.02  Worcs 00.01

# Chumbawamba

Fri 11th Sep 1992
w/Credit To The Nation

Fri 19th Feb 1993
w / Papa Brittle

Tue 14th Sep 1993
w/Credit To The Nation

Tracey Brookes "Best place ever to see Chumba. Crawl out a sweaty, jibbering, very very drunk mess."

Mark Badgeman "Here we go again! If you'd asked me before I bothered to check, I'd have told you that the Tavern had become a crusty hotspot with sellout gigs from the likes of Back To The Planet well before Chumbawamba called me. But once again, it turns out it's not true. We'd done RDF, but the first BTTP gig was only a month before Chumbas first played. I remember the phone call though. Dunstan wanted to know why I never booked them. I absolutely loved the band, I'd been to their gigs and I knew they were worth tickets. So much so, I assumed I couldn't afford to get them to come to Kiddy. 'How do you know you can't afford us?' asks Dunstan who then suggests they'll play for a door split to take the pressure off. Unbelievable! That never happens.

I remember being a little bit wary of them at the first gig. I thought they'd all be militant vegans and would pull me up on having leather shoes or something. But the opposite is true and from memory, they weren't even all veggie. It was no surprise that they were totally professional and put on a storming show. This was classic Chumbas too with the costumes and what I consider to be the best line-up.

They'd insisted on having a young rapper called MC Fusion from Walsall on the bill with his band Credit To The Nation. He was managed by former Chumbawamba associate, Simon Commonknowledge, and they did a song together in the set. Enough Is Enough later became a big smash on the alternative scene, even reaching number 56 on the real charts.

When Chumbawamba were massive, they came back and did a huge sellout show at the Tavern, with Credit To The Nation again. We sold out really fast. I was used to people turning up early to get the last few tickets, but this one was weird because there were hardly any ticket holders at the venue when we opened. I started to panic, thinking I'd miscalculated the sales. Hundreds of ticketless fans were hanging around on the stairs and outside so I let a few of them in. Whoops. When all the ticket holders turned up fashionably late, it was a bit of a squeeze to get everybody in!"

Lou "Bloody awesome night! Chumbawamba were MASSIVE so it was a really packed gig with loads of atmosphere, a proper sweaty, bouncy night of madness. Credit to the Nation were fab too - a great support act and a friendly bunch of guys. I went to see them at the Hummingbird in Birmingham with Mark soon after this as they put us on the guest list."

Woz "Saw Credit To The Nation in Kiddy McDonalds before the gig"

Julie Marshall "I BLOODY LOVED CHUMBAWAMBA AT THE MARKET TAVERN. They got shit much later than that. When their anti-gay-bashing song became a drinking song."

The Head Barman "I remember being on stage with a few others doing security and the crowd bumrushed the band."

David Wright "I remember one part of the gig when I thought they were doing the Hari Krishna chant, which briefly caught my attention. I later found out, after they had really made the 'big time' and I had some of their albums, that they were singing 'Harry Roberts' (not Hari Krishna), the guy who killed 2 coppers while on his way to do a bank job."

Dunstan (Chumbawamba) "In the early 90s Chumbawamba were the most unfashionable of bands who always tried to play in the most unfashionable of places. The majority of us were from towns like Burnley, Barnsley and Billingham (it's near Middlesbrough) so we totally understood and appreciated the importance of bands coming to play in places like these and the huge impression it can leave on anyone who went to a gig there.

In fact Harry and Mave had never stopped talking about UK Subs playing at Barnsley Civic in the very early 80s and how it had impacted on them so much. Even now the Subs still seem to have that same punk philosophy which rightly raises Charlie Harper into some sort of revered Punk God-like status.

So playing in Kidderminster was as important to us as playing in London where weirdly we were never cool enough for the music press. To be honest I think we always felt more at home in those forgotten towns as they reminded us all of growing up in some similar cultural backwater (no offence Kidderminster).

Driving into the town and seeing all the carpet shops and warehouses we were taken aback to realise that Kidderminster was the hub of the Carpet World. An industry town; we felt at home immediately. And then to see this brutal concrete building parked awkwardly next to the local cattle market was the sort of weird and wonderful venue we thrived in.

We played at the Market Tavern at a time when it seemed like there was an appetite in the country for politics, after a long spell of it being ignored. NME and Sounds and that lot were putting Credit To The Nation on their front cover and there was a resurgence of people in music talking about the BNP and opposing them. Bands like the Manics, Back To The Planet, Pop Will Eat Itself, Blaggers ITA to name but a few. It was around the time of us doing Enough Is Enough; our anti-fascist 'anthem' if I may be so bold to call it such. We were riding on a mini-wave it would seem.

But either way we were writing and singing stuff like Homophobia and gigs like the Market Tavern sort of shocked us a bit that we were being picked up on by this newly-political student and non-student audience of kids, lots and lots of them.

We would have been doing the Shhh and Slap stuff too; a time when we were properly having fun with the songs and the stage show, all that Mrs Meta Battle stuff, aeroplanes on heads, Danbert shuffling on stage as Jesus, Alice blaspheming as a whisky-swigging, chain smoking nun and Elvis appearing for the encore to perform an awful rendition of 'Can't Help Falling In Love' then coaxing a member of the audience on stage to do their own Elvis cover.

The Market Tavern really felt like one of those places where you were playing at a party, to your friends. I think we might've even had the cheek and temerity to play there twice in one year; we loved it so much. In this day and age it's easy to be all dewy-eyed nostalgic about gigs like those but I am completely unashamed to be so. In the words of the legendary Nigel Tufnell and David St Hubbins of Spinal Tap 'Great days! Great days!'"

(written with much needed help from memory-man Boff)

PHOTOGRAPHER : CASEY ORR

chumbawamba

One Little Indian Records

**\*\*\*\*P R E S S   R E L E A S E\*\*\*\***

CHUMBAWAMBA 1993... time to open the lid on the band that still thinks it's an underground terrorist organisation.

1993... CHUMBAWAMBA unashamed bandwagon jumpers somehow accomplished the incredibly difficult feat of getting dropped from a record label which they themselves own. Lou Watts, AGIT-PROP partner, CHUMBAWAMBA keyboard player, vocalist and dab hand with a spanner explained the decision to dump the band: "Basically, they - or should I say we - are awkward and bloody-minded. We found that we just couldn't work with ourselves anymore."

1993... CHUMBAWAMBA are on the verge of signing with another independent label. Lou Watts speaking on behalf of AGIT-PROP said of the move: "Good riddance to bad rubbish... the label will find they've signed a bunch of petulant demanding troublemakers." Danbert Nobacon of CHUMBAWAMBA added: "We're coming out of the closet. We're in the market place now. We've got the politics of popular culture in one hand and a copy of KLF's "How to Make a Hit Record" in the other. We've put an advert in Exchange & Mart: Reliable runner. One previous owner."

1993... CHUMBAWAMBA are now working with Concorde Booking Agency and claiming that the crate of Jack Daniels they've added to their rider is: "neccessary if we want to look like we're living out the rock 'n' roll lifestyle - that there's no tomorrow and hardly anything left of today... "

1993... CHUMBAWAMBA are trying to get on the Scottish leg of the Guns n Roses world tour. "Axl needs us. We could help him get over his homophobia with a spot of aversion therapy... " said Danbert.

1993... CHUMBAWAMBA are working on a new album 'ANARCHY' as a follow-up to 1992's 'SHHH'.

CHUMBAWAMBA are available for comment at the following gigs:

Friday 5 February - CARDIFF Treforest   University of Wales
Saturday 6 February - SHEFFIELD   Leadmill
Friday 12 February - LANCASTER University   Sugar House
Friday 19 February - KIDDERMINSTER   Market Tavern
Saturday 20 February - HARLOW The Square
Saturday 27 February - HEBDEN BRIDGE   Trades Club
Wednesday 3 March - BARNSTAPLE   Club Chaos
Thursday 4 March - EXETER   Cavern Club
Friday 5 March - EXETER   Cavern Club
Thursday 11 March - BRIGHTON   Pavilion
Friday 12 March - BRENTWOOD   Anglia University
Saturday 13 March - TRURO
Sunday 14 March - DERBY   Wherehouse
Wednesday 17 March - WARWICK   University
Saturday 20 March - WOLVERHAMPTON   University
Friday 26 March - DUDLEY   JB's

For interview, information or a good time contact CHUMBAWAMBA on the following hot lines: tel: 0532 790739 or fax: 0532 781993

109

# Credit To The Nation

Fri 11th Sep 1992
w/ Chumbawamba

Fri 23rd Oct 1995
w/ Rhythm-ites

Sat 1st May 1993
w/ Fun-da-mental

Tue 14th Sep 1993
w/ Chumbawamba

Andrew Wolfman "Credit to the Nation deserve credit (sorry) for more than just confusing the nation's indie discos with their is-it? isn't-it? Teen Spirit-sampling hit 'Call it What You Want'. Kidderminster didn't have much of a history of hosting fiercely anti-fascist Walsall-based rap trios before Credit To The Nation came to the Tavern (and not much of one afterwards tbf).

I would love to be corrected on this, but I can't see that many (any) significant black artists had played in town since Farley 'Jackmaster' Funk at the end of the eighties, and before that, Jimmy Cliff at the Town Hall in 1967(!) In many ways Matty Hanson was a pioneer, breaking down barriers in traditionally indie territories. The Market Tavern adored him and treated the band like the big stars they never quite became."

"call it what you want"

Mark Badgeman "We never did a Credit To The Nation headline? What was I thinking? I'm still not sure where I was going with the Rhythm-ites support. That was a brave attempt at mix 'n' match that probably didn't work. One thing I remember is Simon Commonknowledge, their manager, offering to 'test' Ben's weed then smoking it all!"

# SINGLE OF THE WEEK

**CREDIT TO THE NATION: Call It What You Want**
*(Rugger Bugger)*

You can't keep a great riff down! When fresh-faced *NME* cove and erstwhile DJ John Harris was recently accosted behind his wheels of titanium alloy and entreated to "play some f—ing dance music", our man gallantly responded by slapping 'Smells Like Teen Spirit' onto the deck – whereupon The Kids, uh, danced. It's that simple, sometimes. And if they aren't already doing so, right-minded jocks the country over will soon be wearing out this positively *'whaaat?'*-tastic slice of vinyl.

For 'Call It What You Want' is based around a direct sample of the riff that started a cultural revolution, that catapulted Nirvana into ionospheric realms of megadom and heralded the dawn of that recently deceased marketing phenomenon some chose to call grunge.

Hell, it's not just lurking subliminally round the back of this West Bromwich rap crew's second 45 – it's there at the beginning, swiped directly and unapologetically, as fresh as the fateful day when Kurt Cobain laid down the chords a million other bands had tried and rejected for being much too cheesy. Law suits? Just try it, sez Credit's manager: "Nirvana are welcome anyday to pop round my house in Gipsy Hill to sort it out."

Frankly, they ought to be flattered, for this is perhaps the most urgent freaked-out pop blast of the year so far, a classic single in the truest spirit of the genre where for the duration of the needle's journey across the seven-inch vinyl (you remember them?) sheer raw adrenalin is the sole item on the agenda. And what happens once the needle's stuck in that run-out groove after three or so minutes? Yep, you put the thang back to the start, again and again and again.

The looped *"da-nana/da-nanana/da-nana/da-nanana"* of air guitar heaven soon gives way to a righteous hardcore bustle that sounds a ringer for PE's 'Welcome To The Terrordome', and MC Fusion's zealous jive-talk. This boy may have stolen the guts from the proto-slacker anthem of the decade but slack he most certainly ain't. The flip 'The Lady Needs Respect' is almost inevitably less compelling than the main track, but then we are talking about a musical theme originally swiped from Boston's 'More Than A Feeling', so whaddya expect?!

And we can call it what we want. How about Single Of The Bloomin' Week for starters...

Ben Schrieber "Credit to the Nation were supporting Chumbawama for the second time. Rapper Matty Hanson (AKA MC Fusion) appeared dressed in a black tee and red dungarees (with the now essential one strap hanging down). Flanked on each side by his identically dressed friends/dancers and occasional backing singers Tyrone (T-Swing) and Kelvin (Mista-G) they proceeded to whip the Tavern crowd up into a jumping fist-pumping frenzy.

The synchronised dancing is impressive but it's MC Fusion who steals the show, dropping between conscious lyrics then left wing political viewpoints. Highlights include the Nirvana/Public Enemy sampling 'Call It What You Want', 'The Lady Needs Respect' and their own mini anthem 'Teenage Sensation' with its catchy whistling hook.

MC Fusion makes a re-appearance during Chumbawumba's set for their anti-fascist collaboration 'Enough is Enough'. Everyone in the Tavern felt like they'd witnessed something special that night but back then for Matty, Tyrone & Kelvin it was Straight Outta Kidderminster and Straight Back to Walsall."

THE SCOTTISH Sex PiSTOLS

ANOTHER FINE MESS

CRYSTAL INJECTION

SAT 31ST OCT

MARKET TAVERN KIDDERMINSTER

Mark Power "Started going there late 80's early 90's, that long ago time deceives me.....
Saw loads of punk bands there, UK Subs, GBH, Vibrators, Lurkers etc etc...but probably the funniest band I saw was The Scottish Sex Pistols! Fucking funny...Ah well time to be nostalgic..
The walk to the toilets through the lakes of piss was always fun!!"

Mark Badgeman "I thought this would do better than 153 people. Tribute bands were all the rage but generally I steered clear of them. At the time, the Pistols hadn't reformed so this was the only way you were going to exclusively hear their songs played live and the band were all dressed up, so it looked like a good laugh.
I may have this wrong as I can't find reference to it now, but I think they were managed by Tam Paton, the 'Scottish Jimmy Saville', who'd famously managed the Bay City Rollers. I can't say more as the courts found him not guilty."

John Combe has passed away now but he wrote two great books about the Kidderminster music scene. He was also the promoter in town when I was young. We all went to see his gig by The Alarm at the Town Hall in 1983 and they were fantastic. But John was losing money and eventually stopped promoting. I don't know why, but for some reason it really bothered me. I didn't know him, and I never met him, but I always had this ludicrous idea that it should be me doing it, not him! That way Kiddy would still have decent gigs and we wouldn't have to keep getting the train to Brum to see bands. I think it was a bit of teenage punk rock attitude still railing against the dinosaurs, but John graciously admitted in his book that he wasn't keeping up to date with the latest trends and was getting a bit too old for the cutting edge acts. When we spoke for his piece on me in his book, he was surprised at what had happened at the Tavern and the level of bands who'd played. But looking back, it took an astonishing amount of effort to make sure the word was out about each gig. If only someone had thought to invent the internet!

Vol 2 GET YOUR KICKS ON THE A456

Written by John Combe

Illustrated by Charlotte Combe

The books seem to be sold out at the moment, but keep your eyes open for secondhand ones if you don't already own them as they are the definitive text on the local music scene. John details the great bands that played Kiddy in the 60s and the 70s as well as the local acts. The Tavern provides but a footnote to the great rock n' roll history of this town that has previously hosted gigs by Gene Vincent, the Rolling Stones, The Who, Yes, The Kinks, Tyrannosaurus Rex, Squeeze, Dexy's Midnight Runners and U2.

# mike peters

*from the ALARM*

I'm NOT ENTIRELY SURE I KNEW WHO THE ALARM WERE BEFORE WE ALL WENT TO SEE THEM AT KIDDY TOWN HALL IN 1983. I REMEMBER THE EXCITEMENT THOUGH. WE KNEW THEY WERE A BIT PUNKY AND THAT, FOR KIDS MY AGE, IT WAS THE FIRST TIME A 'PROPER' BAND THAT WE ACTUALLY MIGHT LIKE HAD COME TO PLAY IN THE TOWN.

THE ROCKETS SUPPORTED, NOT SURE IF I'D ALREADY SEEN THEM AT THE MARKET TAVERN AT THAT POINT, BUT I LOVED THAT BAND. MIKE SANCHEZ WENT ON TO FRONT THE BIG TOWN PLAYBOYS WHO WE USED TO GO AND SEE ON WEDNESDAYS AT THE THURSTON IN BEWDLEY BEFORE THEY WENT ON TO BIGGER AND BETTER THINGS.

THE ALARM WERE INCENDIARY THAT NIGHT AT THE TOWN HALL. AN ABSOLUTELY BRILLIANT BAND BURSTING WITH PUNKY ENERGY, RABBLE ROUSING SONGS BUT WITH A SOLID SUBSTANCE BEHIND THEM. I WANTED TO BUY THEIR 7"s FROM THE MERCH STALL BUT BY THE TIME I'D WANDERED OVER AFTER THE GIG, THEY'D PACKED UP. I'VE LONG SINCE REGRETTED NOT OWNING THE ORIGINAL 'UNSAFE BUILDING', BUT THEY BECAME ONE OF MY FAVOURITE BANDS AND I BOUGHT PRETTY MUCH EVERYTHING ELSE THEY DID UP TO THE SECOND ALBUM.

WHEN MIKE PETERS SPLIT THE ALARM UP ON STAGE AT BRIXTON ACADEMY IN 1991, I'D LONG SINCE LOST INTEREST, BUT WHEN I GOT THE CHANCE TO BOOK HIM A YEAR LATER, I WAS ABSOLUTELY DELIGHTED. IT FELT RIGHT THAT HE SHOULD COME AND PLAY KIDDY AGAIN.

FOR ME, HE WAS THE BIGGEST STAR TO HAVE PLAYED AT THAT POINT. HE'S A VERY HUMBLE MAN BUT AT THE TIME, I COULDN'T BELIEVE HE FELT IT NECESSARY TO INTRODUCE HIMSELF TO ME. HERE'S A GUY I'VE SEEN ON STAGE AT THE TOWN HALL, B'HAM UNI, THE ODEON ETC — I KNOW WHO YOU ARE!! THEN HE ASKED ME IF I KNEW WHERE THERE WAS A 5-A-SIDE FOOTBALL PITCH THEY COULD USE, WHICH THREW ME SOMEWHAT. I WASN'T EXPECTING THAT!

THE GIG WASN'T AS BUSY AS IT SHOULD HAVE BEEN. AS FAR AS I WAS CONCERNED, IT SHOULD HAVE SOLD OUT. INSTEAD, WE DID 204 BUT I PAID HIM THE RIGHT FEE SO I MADE SOME MONEY OUT OF IT. I'VE WORKED WITH MIKE A COUPLE OF TIMES SINCE AND HE'S A LOVELY MAN. — MARK BADGEMAN

## and the poets of justice

# MARKET TAVERN KIDDERMINSTER
# FRIDAY 6TH NOVEMBER

Information and Free Fan Club Contact: (M.P.O.) P.O. Box 709 Prestatyn Clwyd LL19 9YR Wales U.K. Tel (0745) 888911

# Cardiacs

Tue 3rd Mar 1992
w/Pietra Rosa & Conch

Wed 25th Nov 1992
w/Honeyblades

Tue 7th Dec 1993
w/Ship Of Fools

BARNEY MARSH: "IT WAS A RATHER A LONG TIME AGO, SO MEMORY IS SKEWED BY RECOLLECTION AND TIME. IT WAS THE ONLY TIME I WENT TO THE MARKET TAVERN: MY GIRLFRIEND, A GROUP OF MATES AND I HAD DRIVEN FROM BIRMINGHAM IN MY CLAPPED OUT BEETLE. I ONLY HAVE MEMORY SNAPSHOTS: I WAS A RECENT (BUT COLOSSALLY FERVID) CARDIACS FAN.

MY FIRST IMPRESSION WAS OF THE EXTRAORDINARY ATTIRE THAT PEOPLE WORE. CONCERTS AT THIS POINT FOR ME WERE USUALLY MARKED BY THEIR COMMONALITIES – EVERYONE WEARING A VARIATION ON A THEME. BUT HERE THERE WERE STUDENTS LIKE US, METALLERS, INDIE KIDS, PUNKS – I EVEN SAW A COUPLE OF PEOPLE IN SUITS. IT JUST FELT A LOT MORE ALL-ENCOMPASSING THAN MOST CONCERTS I'D BEEN TO. SIMULTANEOUSLY LESS INSULAR BUT EVEN MORE CLIQUEY – WE WERE ABOUT TO EXPERIENCE SOMETHING THAT MOST PEOPLE WOULDN'T UNDERSTAND.

ANOTHER SNAPSHOT – THE BAND. ON STAGE. NO CONFETTI – APPARENTLY BANNED BY THE MANAGEMENT – BUT ENORMOUS COOLING FANS. TIM. SHOULDER LENGTH HAIR. SOME SORT OF COAT. SINGING AND PLAYING AS IF HE WAS STANDING IN A GALE. MUCH MORE GUITAR THAN I HEARD ON THE EARLIER RECORDS, WHICH APPEALED TO MY ROCK SENSIBILITIES. COLOSSAL PASSION. A STRANGE, QUASI-AUTHORITARIAN VIBE. ALL THOSE PEOPLE WRITHING AND MOSHING TOGETHER (A PREVIOUSLY STAID LOOKING SUIT-TYPE HAD REMOVED HIS TIE, AND WAS FLAILING ABOUT IN THE MIDDLE WITH THE REST OF US).

IT WAS THE FIRST TIME I'D REALISED IT WAS POSSIBLE TO POGO TO RIDICULOUS TIME SIGNATURES, IF EVERYONE KNOWS THE TUNES. AND, OF COURSE, WE ALL DID."

## "IT WAS UTTERLY, UTTERLY GLORIOUS."

John Daniel (Cardiacs TM) "We always enjoyed coming to the venue. Nothing was too much trouble."

Andrew Wolfman "The Cardiacs always strike me as a very Tavern band. Venomously derided in the music press, routinely ignored by the world at large, their helium-voiced high-art punk/prog skronking seemed to make perfect sense here."

Barney Marsh "My first Cardiacs gig. Tiny mind blown."

Mark Badgeman "I first saw Cardiacs at Junction 10, the satellite JBs venue in a desolate car park near, you guessed it, junction 10 of the motorway. What a band! Totally insane. Live, as the full six piece, they were like a grotesque carnival. Musically, they had basically invented their own genre - prog punk!

When Derek Kemp from The Agency called me about booking them, I was absolutely delighted. He had a funny and slightly annoying way of selling you a show whereby he'd give you a slow and methodical rundown of why you should book the band without ever saying who they were. Then he'd tell you once you'd given him a clue that you were interested, at which point it was hard to say you wanted to pass. It was like a game of poker! I'd probably pestered him about Cardiacs but I'd have known straight away from his patter who he was talking about this time.

By the early 90s, Cardiacs had slimmed down in number and used tapes in place of the missing musicians. Proper tapes. Reel to reel ones that sat behind the drummer. The band were so tight musically. They also ran a tight ship financially. I'd have to sit down at the end of the night and go through the figures with a fine-tooth comb. Big bands get a guaranteed fee plus a percentage of the profit. To calculate the profit, you need to prove your costs incurred in staging the gig. Mine were a bit slack because how do you calculate an actual cost on six trips to Brum to put up posters and distribute flyers for a variety of gigs, a couple of trips to Worcester, the time spent plaguing the Shuttle to do a bigger feature and all the paper and toner that went through my photocopier? But John, their tour manager, wanted actual receipts. You can't really knock it because it's the correct way to do it, but I wasn't used to it as no other band had anywhere near that level of professionalism.

It was really sad that lead singer Tim Smith died as I was putting this book together. He'd been ill after a heart attack and wasn't able to move or communicate very easily, despite being fully coherent. I'm sure he'd have been astounded to see his death covered in all the national newspapers."

Jim Smith (Cardiacs) "I remember the walk up to the venue from the car park, a very strong odour of cows and their issue. There were a lot of cattle pens set up and I distinctly remember Tim, during a soundcheck, once commenting that he could hear cows mooing in his monitor. We had a good laugh at him telling him that it was probably the tormented souls of cows long passed, but it turned out to actually be cows outside! Would you Adam n Eve it! Always a good place to play though."

Sandra Gardner "I remember Tim Smith saying that he could hear mooing during their soundcheck... I doubt that was a regular occurrence at other venues they played at!"

Stan The PA Man "My very favourite band to play the Tavern were the Cardiacs. I was a fan in the first place and I was a little surprised when Mark asked us to do it but we got in a better desk and we got away with it. The band would turn up with a reel to reel tape machine with backing tracks on it which weren't very keen on being damp, which when the venue got full of sweaty punters was exactly what happened as the venue was prone to condensation, which was the same issue Carter had with their DAT machines. I still have tapes of the Cardiacs shows and still listen to them to this day. I recorded several of their shows and are without doubt the tapes I listened to more than any other. While I have been writing these bits down Tim Smith has passed away and it makes this particularly sad to write."

Peter Moltesen "I remember seeing Cardiacs supported by Ship of Fools at the Market Tavern. It was just after Zappa passed away as Timmy dedicated a song to 'Uncle Frank'."

David Watkins "The Cardiacs were really, really great"

By Damon

**Which town were you based in?** Wolverhampton

**What years were you active?** 1990 til 1993

**Who was in the band?**
Stuart Robertson, Damon McNally, Steve McCalmont, Jon Cockburn

**What kind of music did you play?**
Indie Rock / Punk

**Who were the influences?**
The Clash, The Damned, Bauhaus, The Fuzztones, Iggy and the Stooges, Killing Joke, Roxy Music, Pixies

**What level of success did you achieve?**
Many great support slots - many at the Tavern: Cardiacs, Dodgy. Also: Ned's Atomic Dustbin, Long Pigs. The Sandkings, Kingmaker, PWEI, The Cygnet Ring, Sultans of Ping FC.
Our song 'Round & Round' was included on the compilation album "Demise Of The Executive Perambulator" in association with Brum Beat

**What do you remember about playing at the Tavern?**
It smelled of cow shit! Great vibe, all bands helped each other out, very friendly atmosphere, exciting venue to catch a new band.

**Any memories of the other bands you played with at the Tavern?**
Cardiacs were awesome. Big fan then, big fan now. Was great to have met and discussed musical influences with Tim Smith. Lifelong inspiration.

**How did the band end?**
Fizzled out, lost traction.

**Did anyone go on to further success or have a career in the music industry?**
Damon and Stuart briefly set up "Freebass" (before Peter Hook and Mani took the same name) with Glen Dodd (Sandkings) and Daz Groucutt (Sing Sing)
Stuart and Steve went on to record/ gig with Gravity Wheel including Glen Dodd and Dave Brown (Sandkings) and DJ Peza.
Damon is currently in The Sensation Seekers who have released the album 'Jerk Beat' and a single and have had airplay on 6Music and other stations around the globe.
Stuart is now Technical Director of the Young Vic Theatre in London. Jon plays in a cover band called The Chapel Ash Clash based in Wolverhampton. Steve does production work on events such as Lovebox.

**What else do we need to know about the band?**
First spotted and managed by Kevin Moberley (Stage Audio Sound). Then Managed by Nick Moore. Nick was cutting his teeth in the music industry at the time and getting the band fantastic support slots/ exposure. A legend/ the 5th member.
Tom Carson (Mad Carson now MC16) often guitar teched and helped out.
Stew Talbot Guitar tech/ drum tech/ van driver/ calmer of all disputes.
Rehearsed and tattooed at The Attic Studios Wolverhampton.
We had a large following of hunt saboteurs (crusties). They drank bottles of Thunderbird before our gigs then danced it off! We penned the tag S.O.S Shitfaced On Sherry just for them.

Mark Badgeman "You can't see it very well but here's me in my prized Pietra Rosa long sleeved t-shirt. Great band!"

# Terrorvision + Shutdown & Teenage Mess

## Fri 13th Nov 1992

**TERRORVISION**

## ON TOUR IN NOVEMBER

9 LEICESTER, Princess Charlotte
10 BRIGHTON, Concorde
12 LONDON, Islington Powerhaus
13 KIDDERMINSTER, Market Tavern

For further information please write to:
Total Vegas Recordings, P.O. Box 30,
Batley, West Yorkshire WF17 6XA

Sometimes you need to do a favour for a booking agent. Derek Kemp booked the Cardiacs and was looking for a show for his new rock act. Yep, go on, I'll give Terrorvision £50 - they sound quite good to me. They could go places! We might have only done 56 through the door but I still managed to make £11 profit for a bag of chips on the way home. Terrorvision did slightly better, scoring three Top 10 hits including 'Tequila' that got to No 2 in 1999.

Neil Cox (Shutdown) "They had plenty of coke as I recall!"

### Friday 13th: Tavern hosts Terror night

Friday the 13th this month sees the Market Tavern play host to an outfit called Terrorvision, but don't be deterred by the date.

Their track record so far shows them to have supported Zodiac Mindwarp, L7, a slot at the recent In The City music festival in Manchester and a booking to back The Ramones next month.

Consisting of vocalist Tony Wright, bassist Leigh Marklew, guitarist Mark Yates and drummer Shutty, the band (above) have received various pats on the back from the music papers for their current single My House which is taken from the forthcoming album Formalde-hyde.

Tickets are available from the Tavern on Kidderminster 752590.

Jamie Nicklin "I remember watching Terrorvision play and it was obvious that the lead singer was really pissed 'this song rhymes with basin, it's called Jason'. As the gig came to a close, the singer took a run and jump off the stage, landing on the empty dance floor on to his bum. Oooooooo.... me and my mates grimaced as he landed, he just sat there laughing and gurning through his long sweaty hair."

On Sat 7th December we had biker faves Dumpy's Rusty Nuts and then Genital Deformities on the following Wednesday. I'm surprised the Shuttle didn't go into meltdown over band names that week!

Andrew Wolfman "Genital Deformities were proper fit-inducing crust-punk / grindcore players from Kingswinford. A band who, in their day, could give Napalm Death a run for their money. They sounded a bit like Celtic Frost and a bit like someone chewing glass and trying to kick you in the throat. I once caught the train from Kiddy to Stourbridge with them, and found them pleasantly un-stabby."

# Sebadoh + Cooler Than Jesus

## Sat 14th Nov 1992

## US guitar crew gig a big coup!

This weekend sees the Market Tavern clinch a little exclusive and wave two fingers at the bigger musical venues of the Midlands.

Kidderminster's answer to the Hollywood Bowl will be the ONLY venue between London and Yorkshire where you can catch American guitar outfit Shebadoh, who are in Britain on a mini-tour to plug their new album *Sebadoh vs Helmet*.

Formed by ex-Dinosaur Jr bassist Lou Barlow five years ago, Sebadoh have in that time recorded a pretty respectable tally of material – 100 tracks divided between three albums, a tape and a few singles, and even the seven inch releases have eight or nine tracks on them.

The sound of Sebadoh has been compared to that of *Double Nickels on the Dime* by The MinuteMen, a band Sebadoh regard highly.

They play the Tavern on November 14. Tickets are £3.50, available from the Tavern, Sounds Around or Tempest in Birmingham.

Andrew Wolfman "Convincing seminal US indie-rockers Sebadoh to play at The Tavern remains the greatest feat of local venue booking I have ever seen.

Still seething from being unceremoniously dumped out of Dinosaur Jr just as the grunge-icons blew up globally, Lou Barlow rallied his influential but reclusive sideband Sebadoh, signed to Sub Pop and decided to... play in Kidderminster.

This, in turn, caused the Kidderminster Shuttle to print the words 'Minutemen,' 'Double Nickels on the Dime' and 'lo-fi' for, one assumes, the first and only time in its history. Until now, I have never known how Badgeman managed to make this minor miracle happen.

Lou Barlow explains: "I thought Lemmy was from Kidderminster." (He's not, he's from Stoke, though his surname was Kilmister, which does sounds a bit like it.) "Kidderminster, near Birmingham. I thought I read that he was from there. Never mind." Never mind, indeed. Thanks for coming Lou!"

If I could second guess what the audience were thinking, I'd be a millionaire promoter. 'Freak Scene' by Dinosaur Jr was a massive hit whenever it was played at the Stomp. So surely everyone will want to come and see Lou Barlow's new band? I mean, for £3.50, you can be in the same room as the guy who played bass on that monumental track. Nope, Kiddy scores one of its biggest coups and only 132 turn up. I still don't understand that.

Support came from Birmingham's Cooler Than Jesus who put out a single on Radioactive and featured Simon White who later went on to play with Brit-poppers Menswear.

Dinosaur Jr

# Sebadoh
(U.S.A)
+ cooler than jesus

## ★ Sat 14th Nov 1992 ★ £3.50

# MARKET TAVERN
# Kidderminster

# SISTER SAVAGE & THE BUGGERED NUNS

By Rich Morley

**Which town were you based in?**
Bewdley, Cleobury, Highley

**What years were you active?**
1992 – present day

**Who was in the band?**
When we played at the Tavern: The Sister (Rich Morley), Dan Tarbotton, Toby Hardwick, Simon Wild – also Speed
Harris (Dean Morality), Sister Gonzo

**What kind of music did you play?**
Comedy Covers – at the time we just took the piss out of everybody – hang on we still do!

**What level of success did you achieve?**
4 albums, 1 compilation album, several EP's, 150 or so gigs later the band are still serving up their unique
blend of food-based parodies, the odd straight cover or reworked pop hit.
Over the years we have gone on to support some big names – The Beat, Dreadzone, Senser, Inner City Unit
(Nik Turner), Eat Static, Spunge, Bentley Rhythm Ace – played all over the place, anywhere and
everywhere; base of Snowdon, in barns, big tops, biodomes – mainly parties and DIY festies.

**What do you remember about playing at the Tavern?**
We played a couple of gigs supporting Pop Am Good and also did some all dayers, the last one sticks out in the
memory bank. The stand-in bass player went totally AWOL at the end of the gig and beat his girlfriend up, by the
time we got to her he had run away. A few hours in A&E sobered us up and needless to say that was the last we
saw of that bass player – we thought it would also be a good time to change the name of the band (to Sister
Sandwich & the Buttered Buns) – mainly for that incident plus we had the 'Christian Mafia' on our backs and
had threats of legal action because of the band name.

**Any memories of the other bands you played with at the Tavern?**
We played with local bands mainly but did one gig with Pop Am Good and Funbug – Quite liked Funbug.

**How did the band end?**
It didn't – obviously there has been a few changes over the 28 years but we refuse to go away!!!

**Did anyone go on to further success or have a career in the music
industry?**
Speed Harris (Dean Morality – younger brother of one of the girl singers in Omnia Opera) went on to play
with a renowned Iron Maiden tribute band (Hi-on Maiden)

**What else do we need to know about the band?**
Unsurprisingly, as the band enter their 28th year, they have undergone many a line-up change, but since
2013, with original singer 'The Sister' still at the helm, the boys have had a settled line up and have
continued to dazzle, amaze and bewilder many a crowd on the live music scene.
Originally set up as a non-serious joke band, ripping into well known jukebox faves and adding their
unique punky flavour to the likes of the teen pop of East 17 and Gina G, they mixed this up with their
own blend of favourite rock and punk covers. As 2020 arrives the band has continued the original
ethos and flavour. Yes, the food and kitchen related parodies are more prevalent than ever, with the
likes of ZZ Top's 'Fresh Baked Flan', the Eurhythmics 'Cheese Dreams' and some 4 years prior
to LadBaby's 'I love Sausage Rolls' was being chanted out at many an over enthusiastic
sandwich fan based audience. The energy is still evident as the band's live shows no sign of
slowing down, unabated fast paced drums, driving, rolling bass, and the coruscating guitar of
'Marcoroni cheese' added to the animated, nervous energy of their leader, dressed in a foam
sandwich suit, their raucousness at live shows, are widely renowned.

## EAT
### + Pietra Rosa + Various Vegetables
### Friday 27th November
## Market Tavern
### KIDDERMINSTER
7.30 - 11.00 £3.50

Mark Badgeman "I had the offer of two different headliners for this date and, as far as I could see, there was nothing much to choose between them. Sarah Blackband hated Pulp at the time so she convinced me to book Eat. Whoops! Wrong decision. They might have been a year away from breaking the Top 75 but that's my biggest regret as a promoter."

Mark Badgeman "I'd seen Brum punk rockers GBH at Digbeth Civic in 1985 with Peter & The Test Tube Babies and had played my 'Catch 23' single to death, so when they asked if they could play, I was open to the idea but wary because the old punk bands weren't pulling enough punters to make their fees viable. I agreed a door split with Jock, but he wasn't happy when only 80 turned up as their share was less than he was hoping. I didn't think it was particularly punk rock when he started complaining about paying his mortgage but I might be a bit more sympathetic to his plight these days!"

CATCH 23/HELLHOLE

# market tavern
# kidderminster
## tel: 0562 752590

| FRIDAY 11th Dec | Punk special with **G.B.H.** + Genital Deformities | £3.50 |
| SATURDAY 12th Dec | **FREE DISCO** playing Levellers, Ozrics, Orb, Moonflowers, Back to the Planet, Senser, RDF, Chumbawamba, Dub Merge!, Rhythm-ites, Spiral Tribe, etc......... | free!! |
| WEDNESDAY 16th Dec | Christmas special with... **BACK TO THE PLANET** Also playing at Birmingham Edwards on Dec 3rd | £3.50 |
| FRIDAY 29th Jan | **BIG 5** Featuring Jenny Belle Star, ex-Selecter members and ex-Bad Manners playing original ska based stuff! Single out in January | £4.00 |
| FRIDAY 12th Feb | **RADIOHEAD & FRETBLANKET** | £2.50 |
| FRIDAY 19th Feb | **CHUMBAWAMBA** + Papa Brittle | £4.00 |

last trains: B'ham 23.02 Worcs 00.01
one minute from the station

*The prices listed are advance prices. It may be more expensive on the night.*
**advance tickets from :**
**Market Tavern, Sounds Around, Tempest (Bham)**

## GBH of the ears!

GBH of the eardrums is on its way to the Market Tavern as one of Birmingham's finest gets into action next weekend.

The band is G.B.H., at the forefront of the 'second wave' of punk rock so to speak, circa 1980.

As one who was developing his musical tastes in that fair city at the time G.B.H. hit the scene (i.e. I was at school), I remember well how it became de rigeur to have their name scrawled all over your rucksack.

Only problem was this was about the same time the Mods and Rockers were re-emerging, and they usually took 'G.B.H.' as an invitation to indulge in it with you - nostalgia, eh?

Anyway, I digress. G.B.H. (above) are vocalist Colin Abrahall, Jock Blyth on guitar,

Ross Lomas on bass and drummer Joe Montanaro.

Inspired by the initial wave of punk on both sides of the Atlantic, their first release in 1981 – the 12 inch *Leather, Bristles, Studs & Acne*, was well received by the critics.

The following year saw international success in America, Canada and most of Western Europe, as well as their debut LP *City Babies Attacked By Rats*.

They have kept a pretty solid soundbase over the years, but this has been bolstered by their discovery by fans of the new metal, thrash, hardcore and grunge bands who have cited G.B.H. as an influence.

They play the Market Tavern on December 11. Admission is £3.50 on the door.

By Roland

**Which town were you based in?** Worcester

**What years were you active?** Oct 1990 - Nov 1995

**Who was in the band?**
Simon Pitt - Vocals, Steve Badsey - Rhythm Guitar / B Vox, Roland Link - Bass / B Vox, Stuart Jones - Lead Guitar / B Vox, Steve Makepeace - Drums / B Vox

**What kind of music did you play?** Melodic Punk / Pop Punk (although I hate the expression)

**Who were the influences?** Buzzcocks, Ramones

**What level of success did you achieve?**
We toured Germany four times and got to play shows in Holland and Poland.
We featured on lots of compilation cassettes (you remember those) and CDs in the UK, France, Germany and Japan. A German label also released a split single along with Liverpool's Mere Dead Men.
We released one album, A Million Smiles, in 1992. It was re-released by Japan's Fixing A Hole Records in 2019 as the double CD A Million Smiles ... And A Few Smiles More. Along with the original album, all the band's demos and tracks which were included on compilations were also gathered together and featured on the second disc..

**What do you remember about playing at the Tavern?**
I have many great memories of playing the Tavern. Supporting The Vibrators and being told by Knox that we sounded like the Buzzcocks in '78, only better. Steve Badsey was walking round with a very pleased look on his face for the next few days.
I recall a gig with Stop The World at which I felt we'd held our own. That was until the curtains behind the stage were pulled back as they were playing and they'd got a fire eater outside performing during their set. Fantastic!
Performing in the back / gig room as a fight broke out in the front bar between the bikers that used to frequent it. Tables, chairs and fists were flying. We carried on, as did everybody else.
I'll always cherish the memory of supporting Dr Bison. I loved that band. I was sat chatting with Chepstow Reg their bass player in the backstage area and he picked up his ukulele and played me a little tune. Whenever I listen to their track Fractured Jaw (which has him playing the ukulele on it) it takes me right back to that moment.

**Any memories of the other bands you played with at the Tavern?**
Pop Am Good were a great band, great guys and always stayed with us. Funbug and Stop The World were our buddies and we gigged many times together at The Tavern and elsewhere. Scottish Sex Pistols were a good laugh. Again, they partied with us in Worcester afterwards and stayed with us. I had to send the one guy one of his boots bach! Dr Bison loved 'em. Dickie Hammond what a guitar player and gentleman.

**How did the band end?**
Fell apart at the end of a Polish / German tour at the end of '95.
Too much booze and other substances. Sick of each other.
Although we did reform for a sold-out show at Worcester's Marrs Bar in November 2005 and have played together sporadically since.

**Did anyone go on to further success or have a career in the music industry?**
Roland Link became an author, writing several books including:
Kicking Up A Racket - The Story Of Stiff Little Fingers 1997 - 1983 (Appletree Press)
What You See Is What You Get - Stiff Little Fingers 1977 - 1983 (Colourpoint)
Love In Vain - The Story Of The Ruts & Ruts DC (Cadiz Music)
Children Of The Boneyard Stones - The Story Of The Screaming Dead (Kicking Up A Racket)

Since 2017 Roland Link has toured and recorded as the bass player for the internationally known Inkubus Sukkubus. Simon Pitt, Steve Badsey and Steve Makepeace play together in Trevino Slaxx. Steve Badsey and Steve Makepeace were in the Worcester band The Miffs. Stuart Jones is now a lecturer at Cardiff University teaching recording and production.

ANOTHER FINE MESS
+
FUNBUG
(FORMERLY IDENTITY)
VE: + SUPPORT
ARKET TAVERN
KIDDERMINSTER
AT 3RD OCT

POP AM GOOD
+
STOP THE WORLD
+
ANOTHER FINE MESS
PLAY THE
MARKET TAVERN
KIDDERMINSTER
Friday 20th September
£2    8.00 PM

THE MINGERS
ANOTHER FINE MESS
LOST SOUL
THE MARKET TAVERN
KIDDERMINSTER
THURSDAY 23RD JAN
8.00 PM    £2 DOOR

STOP THE WORLD
AND
ANOTHER FINE MESS
PLAY AT
THE MARKET TAVERN
KIDDERMINSTER
FRIDAY 21st JUNE
.00 PM    £1 on door

LONDON'S POPCORE KIDS PRESENT...
PSEUDO HIPPIES
PLUS
ANOTHER FINE MESS
+ FUNBUG
Sat 23rd Jan
IF U DIG the RAMONES...GREEN DAY...BUZZCOCKS...the ONLY ONES...
PRIMITIVES...MC4 and other BOUNCY fuzz POPCORE then hear US!!
MARKET TAVERN
KIDDERMINSTER

ANOTHER FINE MESS
+
FUNBUG
+ the ADVOCACY
SAT 17TH APRIL
MARKET TAVERN
KIDDERMINSTER

POP AM GOOD
+
STOP THE WORLD
ANOTHER + FINE MESS
PLAY THE
MARKET TAVERN
KIDDERMINSTER
Friday 20th September
£2    8.00 PM

AT THE TAVERN

123

# Radiohead + Fretblanket Melon

**Fri 12 Feb 1993**

## Tavern double delight

Tomorrow night sees two bands at the Market Tavern that really seem to be going places at the moment.

They are Radiohead and Fretblanket, of Oxford and Stourbridge respectively and of whom great things are expected.

Radiohead are signed to EMI and are veterans of tours supporting the likes of The Frank and Walters, Sultans of Ping PC, and Kingmaker.

They earned much praise with their second single *Creep*, which the NME hailed as one of the Top 10 of 1992, and a third entitled *Anyone Can Play Guitar* is due for release shortly if it isn't already out now.

As for Fretblanket, they have the admiration of fellow Stourbridge denizens Miles Hunt of the Wonderstuff and and John from Ned's Atomic Dustbin.

Many of you will no doubt recall they were the stars of a centre page spread in the NME and having earned rave live reviews are tipped as a band to watch.

And that is just what you can do by trundling along to the Tavern for 7.30pm, admission £2.50. Kidderminster's Melon start things off.

Mark Badgeman "Radiohead were just an up n' coming Indie band when I booked them - they cost me £100. I didn't fancy their chances at pulling a decent crowd so I did a double header with Fretblanket, who were the hottest local band at the time, and added Melon as the opener. They were touring in support of the 'Anyone Can Play Guitar' single and when they got their midweek chart position, it was clear it was heading for the Top 40. The Tavern gig was just before the charts were announced but even so, there was a bit of a buzz.

Then, on the morning of the show, I get a phone call from Radiohead's agent to say they were cancelling because Thom had a sore throat. I couldn't believe it. I was convinced they were trying to 'do a Daisy Chainsaw' on me and I recall making enough fuss to ensure they rescheduled for a couple of weeks later.

It was too late to cancel the gig as, pre-internet, it was impossible to get the word out at short notice. So I ran it with Fretblanket and Melon, dropped the price and it was brilliant, 225 through the door and hardly any disappointed punters.

When the rescheduled date came around, 'Anyone Can Play Guitar' had already reached 32 in the charts and 'Pablo Honey', their first album, was about to chart that week (ending up at 25). Surely it was going to sell out? No - we inexplicably had a quiet one with 123 through the door. Well done Kidderminster! Those kind of things make you want to give up. For years I've been telling people I lost a fiver on that gig but I've just checked the accounts and we actually made £34."

Lee J Biggs "Good night. Melon were great."

# •Radiohead• FRETBLANKET & melon Friday 12th February MARKET TAVERN KIDDERMINSTER

**£2.50**

**7.30-11.00**

Last trains: B'ham 23.02   Worcs 00.01   Only one minute from the station

# Radiohead make it up to fans

I HAVE good news if you were one of the many left distinctly preeved by the last-minute cancellation by Radiohead of their recent Market Tavern gig.

Fret not, because it has now been rescheduled for March 2, with humblest apologies sent from the band.

A sore throat caused lead singer Thom to strain his voice at a gig the previous night, so to avoid total loss altogether, the plug had to be pulled at the Tavern.

Still, at least you still get the chance to see a band for whom life is looking pretty good at the moment.

With the Top 40 success of *Anyone Can Play Guitar* and the expected release of the debut album *Pablo Honey* this week, most of the dates on this tour have sold out.

They are also due to appear on France's prestigious Black Session, a 40-minute live gig from Paris aired on the country's national France-Inter radio station whose recent guests have included Suede and Paul Weller.

Back to March 2 at the Tavern, and support comes from Tansads. This is a urban-folk type band, late of Glastonbury, who have just released its second LP.

Called *Up The Shirkers*, it's produced by Philip Tennant of Levellers and Waterboys fame, and is a taste of what attracts 1,000 plus people to their gigs in the North West.

Tickets for Radiohead and Tansads are £2.50 IN ADVANCE, and are available from the venue.

■ Take Two – Radiohead at the Market Tavern on March 2.

Andrew Wolfman "Main support was a band called The Tansads. They were supposed to be one of the two big bands from the new scene in Wigan, and we excitedly assumed they'd be widdly, wide-eyed space-rock, like The Verve. Turned out that they were a crap crustie cross between The Beautiful South and an episode of Last of the Summer Wine, with a song that went 'Chips and egg would make us high / But God has poked us in the eye'. Truly the bitterest of symphonies."

Nick Broome "I love them now but at the time watched them for 20 mins & went into the other room to play pool. Ha!"

Jo Deakin "I remember Thom Yorke hanging off the ceiling and being completely OTT and me thinking they were shit! I was a bit wrong there!"

Lou "I think this was one of my top three favourite Tavern gigs ever. I was 17 and helping out. I ended up being put in charge of cooking the freshly prepared lasagne and some baked potatoes for Radiohead, and then joined Helen for the interview after too. It's one of my favourite 'claims to fame' haha. The Tansads were ace, and I think I actually enjoyed their set more than Radiohead's in a way as they were more bouncy and energetic. Radiohead had not long released 'Anyone Can Play Guitar' I think, so it was a big deal for us to have them."

"RADIOHEAD, THE BAND WHO FIT NONE OF THE CURRENT INDIE-ROCK TRENDS, STILL SEEM SET TO RULE IN 1993" (EXPOSED)

"SO F***ING SPECIAL" (ALBUM NETWORK, USA)

"HIGHLY POSSIBLE THAT RADIOHEAD COULD BE HUGE" (DEADLINE)

"UTTERLY MEMORABLE SONGS" (SHEFFIELD TELEGRAPH)

"NOT FAR BEHIND SUEDE IN THE BEST-NEW-BAND-IN-BRITAIN STAKES" (TODAY)

"RADIOHEAD, IN A PERFECT WORLD, WOULD BE THE PERFECT POP BAND TO BE HEARING ON THE RADIO ANY TIME, ALL THE TIME" (THE LIST)

"RADIOHEAD MAKE MY BALLS ACHE AND LEAVE MY SPINE IN BITS. LIKE ALL THE BEST SHAGS" (INDIECATOR)

"PRIMED TO BLAST ON TO THE AMERICAN SCENE" (BILLBOARD)

Paul Evans "Not the best claim to fame - having a piss standing next to Thom Yorke from Radiohead in the cow dung smelling bogs."

Mike Moore "Radiohead being surprisingly quiet despite having 4(?) guitarists."

"THE YEAR'S MOST PROMISING NEW BAND..." (WHATS ON)

"ONE DAY RADIOHEAD WILL RULE THE WORLD..."

"SOMEBODY HAD TO COME ALONG AND REMIND US WHAT GREATNESS LOOKS LIKE. SO THANK GOD IT'S RADIOHEAD" (NME)

"ONE OF BRITAIN'S BEST KEPT SECRETS..." "A GROUP SET TO BE ONE OF THE MOST SUCCESSFUL ROCK BANDS IN BRITAIN..." "THERE'S A TOUCH OF GENIUS ABOUT THEM" (HIT CD)

"ALL HAIL THE NEW KINGS OF GLUM" (HITS, USA)

"A CREDIBLE, COOL, UK GUITAR BAND YOU CAN GENUINELY BELIEVE IN, WHO ALSO HAPPEN TO BE DISTURBINGLY FUCKIN' GOOD" (M8)

"IF SUEDE ARE THE 90s SMITHS THEN RADIOHEAD ARE THE CLASH AND REM ROLLED INTO ONE" (N. LONDON INDEPENDENT)

"YORKE IS AN ARTICULATE, FRIGHTENINGLY TALENTED SONGWRITER AND THE UNCANNILY POLITE RINGMASTER OF 93'S MOST DEVASTATING BAND" (SHEFFIELD STAR)

"THE IMPRESSION CREATED WITH COMPLETE INGENUOUSNESS IS OF A COMPLETE AND MATURING BAND WITH SOME GREAT SONGS BESIDE 'CREEP' AND ON THEIR WAY TO BECOMING HUGE"

"THE BUZZ ON THIS BAND IS SO LOUD THAT WE STARTED TO THINK KILLER BEES HAD REACHED L.A."

"THE FIRST TRUE STAR IN AGES TO EMERGE FROM THAT GLAMOUR-DESERT INDIE-ROCK. STEP FORWARD THOM YORKE OF RADIOHEAD. ONE DAY THE WHOLE WORLD SHALL FEAR YOUR NAME" (SELECT)

Kim "Fretblanket were going to support Radiohead, still not big but had heard of them and then they pulled out. So when they rescheduled, Tom and I sat at the side determined to hate them, sitting down (unheard of in the gig room) arms crossed, I remember saying to Tom 'they're quite good aren't they?'"

David Wright "Eric Bell played there on a Wednesday night to about 40 people, and after the gig he was in the kitchen having a smoke with Andy plus the rest of his band. I was still hurting from my relationship break up and was on my own in the back (music room) stood at the bar having a drink, when Eric Bell came out to me with a spliff (Andy must've told him about my situation) and gently spoke to me in his soft Irish accent about women, how he could relate to my pain, how I was still a young man and would fall in love again. Out of all the musicians who I had crossed paths with whilst working at the Tavern he was the most egoless, sincere one I had the pleasure to meet and he must have spent around 45 minutes taking time away from the party in the kitchen to listen and generally give his wisdom he had picked up about relationships over the decades, telling me about his own experiences from his 30/40 yrs on the road after turning his back on Thin Lizzy in their prime. Eric Bell is the most thoughtful/kind musician I ever met at the Tavern."

David Watkins "Eric Bell ignored the nice vegetable lasagne on the rider and sent me off to score some squidgy black, as it was then. We spent the entire gig waving at him to turn down his huge Marshall amp. He grinned and ignored us, lost in himself, throughout."

# The God Machine + Bathchair Suicide Appleberry Crescent

## Fri 12 Feb 1993

Andrew Wolfman "The God Machine might have been the best show I saw at the Tavern, one of the best I've seen anywhere. They are criminally under-rated now, their tragic demise obscuring the memory of just how good they were.

That said, the number of people I've spoken to from local bands who claim to have supported them in 1993 (you didn't, it was Bathchair Suicide, of course it was Bathchair Suicide) is proof of how highly they were regarded by 'the heads' back then. Cranked through Stan the PA Man's mighty rig, the 'hit' single 'Home' had a riff that other riffs would call 'Sir'. You could be forgiven for thinking you were watching the best band on the planet, in the back room of a pub on a cold night in Kiddy."

THE GOD MACHINE

Friday 12th March + Bathchair Suicide + Appleberry Crescent

MARKET TAVERN KIDDERMINSTER
£3.00 Adv
7.30-11pm

THE GOD MACHINE

1. OUT
2. I'VE SEEN THE MAN    5:08
3. THE DESERT SONG    2:39
4. IT'S ALL OVER    5:12
5. HOME    5:55
6. THE PIANO SONG    5:20
     4:57

Fiction

Polydor
POLYDOR LIMITED

James Cole "The God Machine. Amazing gig. Way better than Radiohead."

## Converts bring back blend

Camden converts The God Machine will be appearing at Kidderminster's Market Tavern this weekend.

The band, who formed in San Diego two years ago but then moved to the trendy London suburb of Camden, will be bringing their blend of spacious psychedelic grooves, heavy metal riffs and bleak vocals to the Tavern tonight (March 12).

Support comes from the new-look Bathchair Suicide, who are currently going through an experimental phase, while London-based Appleberry Crescent complete the line-up. Doors open at 7.30pm and admission is £3.

# Dodgy + Pietra Rosa Emission

## Fri 5th Mar 1993

Late 80s Redditch band Purple pre-date my tenure at the Tavern but had they been around in the 90s, I'd have expected to have received a demo tape looking for a support. Nigel and Matthew from that band moved to outer London and I found myself with a copy of their demo by their new band, Dodgy. It was good! We reviewed it in Straight Elephant.

By 1993 and their 4th single, 'Water Under The Bridge', interest was picking up. Emma Banks was their agent so I happily gave them £100 (plus VAT - bloody record deals caused some bands to be VAT registered!) and hoped they still had some mates left in Redditch. We only did 82 people but I made £8.50 profit for a bag of crisps on the way home. Three years later with several Top 40s under their belt, they scored the hit of the summer with 'Good Enough' which peaked at No 4, making them one of the most successful bands to have played the Tavern.

*From Straight Elephant in 1991*

### DODGY DEMO

One of the few sixties revivalist groups that I've heard recently that actually sound that they have a feel for the genre. These boys are groovy!

All those great psychedelic records made by people who had served their apprenticeships in beat groups, learning to sing three part harmonies and play R & B riffs. Then when they got loose and discovered all kinds of studio trickery the records had a quality that its hard for someone coming from another era to recreate.

Somehow these boys manage it... the harmonies on 'Lovebirds' are Beatlesque and Matthew on drums sounds like Mitch Mitchell. Andy's guitar work, too, occasionally doffs a hat to Hendrix, but it's to his more melodic, song based material rather than the solo work-outs beloved of 'Metal-heads'.

Of course the lyrics are nonsense, as one would expect, but so are most of the original lyrics in songs of the genre. Being in possession of some killer songs is probably the one thing they lack, but at least they all sound right.

'Searching for lost souls' is a mini-epic with what could be tablas, simulated backwards oriental-sounding guitar and studio effects that would have sounded state-of-the-art in 1968.

Only question is...when are they going to go to India, discover that all this Eastern Mysticism lark's a big con, and start wearing suits?

James Attlee

THE CORRACH

# 'Dodgy' homecoming

WATCH out for some 'Dodgy' boys hitting Kidderminster tomorrow – they are bound to take the town by storm.

Math, Nigel and Andy, better known to the pop world as Dodgy, are appearing at the Market Tavern.

They had an unusual 1992, which included getting arrested trying to stage a gig at Speakers Corner in Hyde Park, supporting Ozric Tentacles on tour and appearing at Glastonbury Festival.

To welcome in 1993 they have brought out their first release, which can be described as Sixties influenced, Byrds-style, jingly pop music.

To promote *Water Under The Bridge*, the Redditch lads are returning home as part of their tour – well almost.

A lack of suitable venues in Redditch means they are counting Kidderminster as their homecoming.

Tickets are £3 and support is supplied by Emmission, a new up-and-coming Stourbridge band, and Pietra Rosa, who also have a session being broadcast on Radio WM in the near future.

Tickets are £3. Call the Market Tavern for more details.

● Math, Nigel and Andy, appearing at the Market Tavern.

Andrew Wolfman "One of the least essential jobs I've ever had was as a security guard for Dodgy. Whenever a band member tried to get backstage, I'd block their way and say, "sorry, Sir you can't come in."
"Why not?"
"You're dodgy."
The hours just flew by."

Woz "I remember sitting down as there weren't many there to be fair and they were great. Saw them many times after that. Water Under The Bridge had just come out. Was only 16 so had a few cheeky cider cans before getting in and caught the bus back to Stourport after the gig."

THE 'DODGY' DEMOS ‹1›
1. Love Birds
2. Summer Fayre  3. Searching
Contact Win Management 071-241 1893
Dolby B   RMS Copying
BASF Chrome   ©1990
Win Management   071 241 1893

*water under the bridge*

**dodgy**

the d-tour the dodgy way!

**NEW SINGLE**
from **dodgy**
water under the bridge
22·2·93

the d-tour
dodgy play their instruments
and sing LIVE! @:KIDDERMINSTER

MARKET TAVERN, 5th MARCH

**China Drum
Guns n' Wankers
The Pale Kings**

**Fri 23rd Apr 1993**

Leatherface should have played the Tavern in 1991 but the gig never happened. If it had, they'd have been touring 'Mush', an album The Guardian described as 'that rarest of musical gifts, the truly perfect album'. Allmusic called it 'one of the best albums of the decade'. By 1993, they were on the verge of splitting up. The gig did just shy of 200 tickets which I was happy with. China Drum were produced by Frankie Stubbs, the singer of Leatherface and were a great addition. Guns n Wankers was Duncan from Snuff's new band. This was a punk rock super-bill!

**LEATHERFACE**

Sarah Sutherland "Saw Leatherface there with Guns n' Wankers supporting - it was a lively night!"

# Leatherface bring Geordie grunge!

A GEORDIE outfit described as the Motorhead of the Grunge scene descends on the Market Tavern next weekend.

The outfit is Leatherface, currently out on the road and arriving in Kidderminster next Friday, having supported Senseless Things and appearing at last year's Reading Festival.

Descriptions vary for this lot — hard nuts and headbangers are but two.

Perhaps *Melody Maker* put it the best: "We have rainforest problems because

Leatherface have eaten all the trees." Quite.

Off stage though Leatherface lead singer Frankie Stubbs proved he was no Leatherhead by making a name for himself as a producer.

So far he has produced Midway Still's new album and has been working on demos with several new northern bands.

If you fancy seeing these hardy ambassadors of the North, it will cost you £3.50 in advance from the Tavern.

▶ **Leatherface: The Motorhead of Grunge.**

Kev Wheeler "I think the best thing about the Tavern was the fact that it was a bit like Cheers. Although a biker pub by association, no matter who you were, you were always welcome! You were always greeted at the bar by a regular who would attempt to spark up a conversation. I remember there was no discrimination there. However, if you stepped out of line, it would kick off in an instant, get dealt with and generally those involved would shake hands and have a pint afterwards.

The one place in Kiddy I miss the most, even after 23 years since it closed, even after enjoying other places since, there will only ever be one "Market Tavern" (home) and nothing will ever replicate it.

It was my life for a good 7 or so years. 7 nights a weeks when I was legally old enough to attend with the best down to earth people you could ever wish to meet... The music brought me in at the beginning but the pub family kept me going back until the doors finally shut. I can't imagine there will ever be a place like it again, which is such a sad thing for the younger generations in Kiddy."

# Stourbridge Big Night Out

*Fretblanket, Scrash, Babylon Zoo & Indigo Jane*

**Fri 16th Apr 1993**

The 'Stourbridge Big Night Out' was just my marketing trick to attract a bit more attention for what was essentially an all-star local band night. The Wonder Stuff, Ned's and the Poppies had created an expectation that Stourbridge could produce one more big band and everyone was looking to see who it might be. You always need an angle, right?

Fretblanket were the biggest draw, especially after standing in for Radiohead two months earlier and playing to a packed room. I think it was my way of easing them into becoming fully-fledged headliners. Plus they were the most likely of the Stourbridge bands to break through.

But hold on, who's that third on the bill? Babylon Zoo? The band who had the biggest selling debut single of all time with Spaceman in 1996? That song off the Levi's ad? They played third on the bill on the local band night?

Never one to miss an opportunity, when the single was number one, I got Peter from the Express & Star to run a story about how they'd played their first ever gig at the Tavern, albeit without Jaz, as Kerry, formerly of Yeah God (the band who'd stood in for Pop Will Eat Itself when they cancelled on me at Murdochs), was singing that night.

A quick factcheck to get the full story for this book reveals the story I told the Express & Star had some flaws. It's taken 25 years for the truth to surface on this one. Kerry explains what actually happened...

Kerry 'The Buzzard' Hammond "That was a Culo Avalanche gig. I'd left Babylon Zoo by then with one of the other members and we were carrying on with the original BZ blueprint, which I felt had become compromised. The only Babylon Zoo gig I played was at The Princess Charlotte and was a bit of a mess. I never played Spaceman but I do remember Jaz playing me the demo he had recorded in the studio / shed we built in his garden.

The Market Tavern gig was not our best. We had all sorts of freakish tech issues and had to pull the show after 3 songs as I recall. We didn't play any BZ songs, writing with BZ was a bit of a nightmare. With the talent onboard, it should've been a doddle but it never really worked. Within two weeks of forming Culo Avalanche we had ten songs, pretty much an album and a 70 minute live set. We did some dates supporting Pop Will Eat Itself, seem to remember Manchester Uni, we played a good set but the locals were largely unimpressed.

I'm pretty sure that gig was when Clint first asked if I was up for joining PWEI. Previously Graham had always been the one to push for me to join.

However, Culo Avalanche ranks among the best bands I've been involved in. We absolutely fired up live and when we got it right, it was awesome. All the songs were heavily improvised, often we just took a ton of speed & weed and let rip, but because we had done exactly this for months in rehearsal, we had a brilliant understanding of what we could and couldn't get away with.

Unfortunately, with bands so heavily fuelled by drugs, it started falling apart but we did have major label interest at one point. Around that time I got asked to audition for the Nine Inch Nails guitar job and also for The Wildhearts, pretty much the same week. I ended up eventually joining PWEI, which was a bit of a disaster, as I basically left one mad druggie band that was imploding for an even druggier more imploding band. Ho hum.

My abiding memory from the Babylon Zoo project was that it never had an identity beyond the 'local supergroup' bollocks. For sure there was some talent, I loved working with Mark the drummer (from Drop) & H the bass player, but it never ever felt like a band to me and though Jaz & I did work quite well together and he was, at that time, potentially a great frontman and singer, it never quite worked."

**MARKET TAVERN**
**KIDDERMINSTER**
tel: 0562 752590

| | | |
|---|---|---|
| Saturday 3rd April | 'Putting the House in Order' Charity show PANIC BEACH & melon & emission | £2.50 |
| Friday 9th April | Back to the Planet + Madhalibut | £3.50 |
| Friday 16th April | STOURBRIDGE - 'The Big Night Out' featuring Fretblanket + SCRASH + Babylon Zoo + Indigo Jane | £2.50 |
| Friday 23rd April | LEATHERFACE + Guns 'n' Wankers + Pale Kings | £3.50 |
| Saturday 24th April | Bathchair Suicide & Madhalibut | £2.50 |
| Saturday 1st May | Fun-da-mental + Credit to the Nation | £3.00 |
| Saturday 8th May | DUB MERGE | £2.00 |
| Friday 14th May | MIDWAY STILL & PANIC BEACH | £3.00 |
| Friday 4th June | U.S. Hardcore ALLOY. Funbug Ex members of Cro-Mags, Articles of Faith, Uniform Choice, Dag Nasty | £3.00 |
| Saturday 12th June | CHUMBAWAMBA Tickets only! On sale now | £4.00 |

To be confirmed: Warm up date for THE BUZZCOCKS - Tuesday May 11th

last trains: B'ham 23.02 Worcs 00.01
one minute from the station

The prices listed are advance prices. It may be more expensive on the night.
advance tickets from:
Market Tavern, Sounds Around, Tempest (B'ham), Magpie (Worcs)

# Fun-Da-Mental + Credit To The Nation

Aki Nawaz - AKA Propa-Ghandi (Fun-da-mental) "Life in Fun-Da-Mental is not normal. Political thoughts are stretched to the limit and sometimes very uncomfortable for society's indoctrination, not just for the host nation, which is drunk on its own consumption of ideology and worth, but also from our own romantic notions of culture and faith from which we emerged.

Our history in this land does not start with just our realities but with that of our parents' and ancestors' who were also subjugated and imprisoned by the 'Great British Colon-(y)' from which we emerged disadvantaged and burdened by its simple outlook that we were somewhat inferior, a classic psyche of Empires throughout history, I assume.

All this anger and confusion was brought to the forefront and displayed in all its nakedness on stage for Fun-Da-Mental. Uncomfortable for some, outrageous to others, however liberating for us and some of the natives.

Fun-Da-Mental also carried its internal fault lines. The music industry created a false projection as the wheels began to capitalise on a new 'politic of dance and sounds'. We had created something different, a landscape of sounds

clashing and lyrics which were telling stories of the past but also attempting to warn of the future, much of which I can gloat about and say came true. We were changing the conversation but not many were listening.

We had just gone through a 'silly' break up with the original line-up after a fantastic life challenging trip to Pakistan, all expressed in a write up in Melody Maker by David Simpson. The video for 'Countryman' had been a success, clouded only by false accusations, which, if the story could be told in all its truth, would be comical in its conclusion, but that's for another day.

The Kidderminster Market Tavern concert was on the radar and frontmen had been auditioned desperately, from memory (do not trust it), we took on Imran, a rapper and toaster from Kilburn in London to front the band and Dave Watts and I worked out our manic / militant Bucks Fizz dance routines.

Imran possessed great skill (i.e. he remembered his lyrics, came in and out at the correct point and had a better conscience of the FDM concept than the previous 'donkey' fronting the band.)

As we left London towards Kidderminster it became apparent that this was a 'global' gig for

PHOTO: STEPHEN SWEET 071-265 9842

Imran. He had never left his postcode since his birth and a motorway was like the path to the afterlife for him. Many rappers, although I respect their artform, are usually not as 'seasoned' as they appear. They have the gift of memory and lyrical genius, but life is a literally a postcode.

The Tavern gig was an important date for alternative culture, it was on the circuit of 'good gigs' to play, I had been there previously with the band Giant International, who I managed, and it was a fab place.

Our Bucks Fizz dance routine was energetic, but, in all honesty, bloody knackering. It possibly looked very frightening too for peaceniks, and, to be honest, I would have frightened myself watching me, but the Tavern hosted concepts which were offkey, so we felt empowered to just destroy any 'Ghandite' notions of our community. We were gonna act like 'savage beasts,' but not the ones that lose like in the Disney films.

As the concert went into overdrive with slides from history projected behind us, it was time to introduce Imran onto the stage for his track. We had not really done any full-on concerts with him previously and I do not think he had even seen us as a live band, but he saw me and Dave Watts showing some headbanging skills during the set. When he came on stage, what he did, we did not expect, or even in our wildest unconventional creative minds, imagine. Even Motörhead fans would have been shocked!

On the way home it was quiet in the van. If it were not for the engine I am sure the noise from the air going to our 'back passages' would be loud. We dropped off Imran from his global tour of Kidderminster and thanked him. "What do you think Ak?" Dave asks, "I never imagined that we would have 'Skippy the Kangaroo' fronting Fun-Da-Mental!" The van stopped and we rolled out onto the pavement in tears of laughter.

Imran was unique and remains so!"

**PEACE LOVE OR WAR**

**FUN'DA'MENTAL**

Tarina Steward "I was there. It was brilliant xxx"

# NATION RECORDS
## & Q.F.M. PUBLISHING

Tel : 071 229 4604
071-792 6167
071 221 7931
Fax : 071 792 2654

### FUN-DA-MENTAL

FUN-DA-MENTAL formed in August 1991, specifically to perform at London's Notting Hill Carnival. The response of their live performance, and the style of music they created, meant that the band continued into their philosophy of sound - creating music with a message.

Made up, originally, of four Asian men, the band has recently changed personnel and include a West Indian DJ; frontman with a ragga attitude BAD-SHA LALLAMAN, who raps and toasts in Punjabi and English; Indian percussion, tabla player and co-vocalist GOLDFINGER MAN-THAROO; DAT operator and political orator PROPA-GANDHI; and turntable wizardry courtesy of DJ BLACKA-DEE.

The line-up is now featuring three members, raised and educated in the North of England, namely Bradford and Leeds, though born in Pakistan and India and a West Indian raised and educated in London.

The philosophy, which forms the foundation of the band - the Fundamentals - is to highlight the various forms of traditional classical Asian sounds and rhythms to incorporate them into hardcore rap and ragga music, whilst also promoting the beauty of Islam, Seikhism and Hinduism, as well as anti-west political oration, which forms an integral part of the band's make-up.

Using sampled speeches of such world leaders as MALCOLM X, Nation of Islam leader MINISTER LOUIS FARRKHAN, leader of the African National Congress, NELSON MANDELA and 'man of cloth' MAHATMA GANDHI. The band also use controversial speeches such as Enoch Powell's infamous 'rivers of blood' speech of the seventies and Le Pen's right wing politics which are so apparent and prominent within Europe.

FUN-DA-MENTAL have been open to criticism regarding the contents of their lyrics. The band express their views through this musical vehicle tending to be quite frank, honest, in their opinions, often alienating some and outraging others. However, it is fair to say the the band face each criticism head-on giving reason for such strong opinions.

Their belief that there should be no boundaries in music is quite apparent in their sound. Classical Asian music absorbs the dub of the Carribean and the dance vibe of the West.

Since formation the band have released two single, "JANAAM - THE MESSAGE/RIGHTEOUS PREACHER" and "GANDHI'S REVENGE/AZAAN - THE CALLING". Both singles have enabled the band to carve a very solid niche within the current music scene within UK and have been opened many doors for the band within Europe and beyond.

Directors : K.Canoville & A.Nawaz.
Nation Records Ltd / Q.F.M. PUBLISHING. 19 All Saints Road. London W11 1HE. ENGLAND.
Registered Office  19 All Saints Road. London W11 1HE. Vat No : 539 1350 47. Co, Registration Number: 2452382.

# Buzzcocks + Funbug

This was a vindication. They could have played anywhere. This wasn't GBH or The Lurkers, this was a first division punk band with seven Top 40 hits. We sold all 300 tickets!

## Buzzing back in

The Buzzcocks, one of the most famous bands of the punk era, will be continuing their much vaunted revival with a warm-up appearance at Kidderminster's Market Tavern on May 11.

The group, who reformed in 1990, are shortly embarking on a 35 tour date of Britain and Ireland to coincide with the release of their 'Innocent' single and the 'Trade Test Transmission' album which is out on May 17.

A limited number of tickets priced at £5 are available from the Tavern, Sounds Around, Magpie and Tempest but the show looks set to sell-out. Doors open at 7.30pm.

## Punk not dead

Music
The Buzzcocks
Kidderminster Market Tavern

While the heady days of punk may never be revived to their former glories, the return of one of the scene's most influential architects gave a welcome reminder that the music which launched a thousand anarchists will never roll over and die.

The Buzzcocks' visit to Kidderminster was dubbed a warm-up gig for their forthcoming national tour, but while the band took to the stage amid a host of smiles, one look at the audience showed it was to be a far from light hearted affair.

The fans were not disappointed as the band launched aggressively into both old and new material dispelling any fears that they may have passed their sell-by date.

Despite its classic 'Buzzcocks' sound many of the 'original' fans in the crowd seemed reluctant to embrace the new material and for a while proceedings dulled.

While Pete Shelley and co no longer have age on their side, they still retain a talent and enthusiasm which will continue to ensure that punk is not dead.

Julian Safe

Steve Cooper "It was electric and I was 16 again down the front! Afterwards I had the pleasure of meeting them. I shook Mr Shelley's hand and heard some ace stories from Steve Diggle"

Darren Poole "Was great! Remember being backstage with them, eating stuffed peppers and drinking champagne... Rock n Roll!"

The Head Barman "Lots of tv screens."

Simon Holder "That was a great night!"

Roland Link "Had a broken leg and got Pete and Steve to sign me cast. We (Another Fine Mess) supported them the month after in Worcester. Great guys."

Kate Holden "Only one I remember is the Buzzcocks because I met them and personally my impression was they were a bunch of old twats. I felt a bit sorry for them stood in the back room pretending to be big rock stars, thinking mate, you are at a cattle market in Kidderminster...!"

Special Warm-up show...

# BUZZCOCKS
(Featuring Pete Shelley)
## TUESDAY 11th MAY
## Market Tavern
### Kidderminster

A limited number of advance tickets on sale now (£5.00) from Market Tavern, Sounds Around, Magpie, Tempest, Way Ahead, H.Q. and Plastic Factory

# Bang Bang Machine

Sat 4th May 1991 (support unknown)
Sat 14th Aug 1993 (festival)
Fri 5th Nov 1993
w/ Tribute To Nothing & The Berts
Fri 26th Jan 1996
w/ Frisbee & Iris

Mark Badgeman "Bang Bang Machine's history may or may not offer any clues to their wonderful jumble of ambient-dub-goth-pop-rock.

Steve Eagles was previously in 1976 Evesham punk band Satan's Rats who released 3 singles, played the famous punk rock festival in Birmingham and supported the Sex Pistols in Wolves. That band morphed into The Photos, a new wave act fronted by Wendy Wu, who had a Top 10 album in 1980 but ultimately never achieved their full potential.

Steve Lee was previously known as Marc Angel and played bass in Wrathchild. I loved that band, the UK version of Kiss with cheap pyro and outrageous costumes! Stakk Attakk is an essential album.

For Bang Bang Machine, they were joined by drummer Lamp and vocalist Elizabeth Freeth and released the self financed 'Geek Love', a beautiful ten minute sensual pop song that John Peel loved so much he said 'Even if they never made another record, they'll have achieved more than most of us do in our entire lives'. Listeners agreed and it topped the Festive Fifty in 1992.

The subsequent album had big choruses and giant riffs but was unafraid to slip into blissed-out dream pop that brought comparisons to the Cocteau Twins. Elizabeth was endlessly compared to Siouxsie Sioux which was inevitable but did her a disservice. Comparisons to shoegazing bands were way off the mark in my opinion. Live, they were powerful. As such, they always went down well at the Tavern. Their appearance at the Free Festival was a highlight."

Lamp (Bang Bang Machine) "We always enjoyed playing the Market Tavern. It was just down the road and we were always treated well."

# Moonflowers

Sat 13th Jul 1991

Wed 2nd Jun 1993

Mark Badgeman "I can't do the Moonflowers justice here but I fear they might get forgotten altogether if I don't at least try. They were a Bristol based psychedelic, hippy, jazzy, funky, fiddly, slightly baggy outfit who had no problem stripping off or covering themselves in dayglo paint to decorate the records that they put out on their own PopGod label. Guy Garvey from Elbow cites them as a major influence. Don't let that put you off though and check out their joyous Damned mash-up 'Disco-Man' which you'll find on Spotify. We did over a hundred tickets for the 1993 date as this was an excellent gig for the free-festy crusty crowd, especially with Madhalibut on the bill."

133

# THE TIME I SWINDLED A SEX PISTOL

BY DEAN MORAITY

## Glen Matlock & The Mavericks
### + The Advocacy

### Sat 3rd Jul 1993

I was a massive Sex Pistols fan as a teenager (still am!). In 1993 I was 17 and extremely excited when I learnt that Glen Matlock was touring with his new band, The Mavericks, they may not play punk, but it was a chance to see a real live Pistol play in the flesh (remember, this was before the reunion shows that started in 1996). I had somehow managed to get in contact with the band's manager, Guy Ford, (god knows how, this was pre internet...) and after telling him what a massive Pistols fan I was, I managed to blag free tickets to their show at JB's in Dudley.

I kept in touch with Guy in the run up to the show and I jokingly said that it would be awesome if Glen came and played at my local, The Tavern. Guy said "I'll speak to Glen and see what he says, I'll tell him you're a massive fan - it doesn't harm to ask". A few days later I get a call from Guy telling me Glen said he'll do it! The only problem was the band were charging £1000 per show. However, as I was such a fan, Glen said they'd do it for £200 and treat it as a warm up for the bigger shows they had coming up. SHIT! Things just got real.

I had no experience putting on or promoting shows, sure, I played in my own punk band but promotion for that just involved pasting up a few posters in the subway tunnels around Kiddy. So I turned to Mark Badgeman, first to get the ok to put the show on at The Tavern and secondly to ask how the fuck I go about making this happen, promotion-wise. Mark was ace, sorting out poster and flyer printing and steering me in the right direction with everything else.

The day of the gig came and I was nervous as hell. Glen and his band arrived later than scheduled due to traffic and rushed to soundcheck. All went smoothly and the band sounded ace. My band were supporting (obviously) so we quickly soundchecked then went to hang with Glen. He was a really nice bloke and chatted to us for ages about his time in the Pistols and posed for photos.

I couldn't hang around with him for too long though as I had to help man the door (one of the conditions of putting the gig on and to keep personnel costs down...). We opened the doors and there were about 5 people queuing up to get in. Good sign I thought... However, as time ticked on, only a few more punters arrived... We held off going on stage as long as possible to allow it to fill up a bit, but it never did; I think we played to about 16 people. We finished our set and went back to the dressing room. Glen came over to me with a concerned look on his face: "not many in is there?" I optimistically said I was sure more people will come in as they were probably waiting in the bar until his band went on.

Alas, this wasn't really the case. A few more did roll in, but not many. The Mavericks took the stage and tried to make the most of it. There's a video of the gig knocking around and you can hear the singer taking the piss about the turnout. They cut the set short and trudged off stage back to the dressing room.

I was back at the door with Mark Badgeman counting up the takings; it wasn't good. Mark reminded me that we had to take out the printing/promotion costs. Oh, and pay the soundman... I took what was left and went to the dressing room. Glen came out to see me. I apologised for the poor turnout but he took it really well, saying these things happen and it wasn't my fault etc. However, his demeanor changed when I handed him the envelope with the money in explaining that all that was left after costs was £22.50... The rest of the band were similarly displeased, with the singer moaning that it didn't even cover the fuel up from London. They wanted the full £200 but I had no means of getting it for them so I told them to take it or leave it. They took it. Packed their gear up rather sharpish, jumped in the van and drove off. Needless to say, I didn't promote any more gigs at The Tavern.

In 2016 I went down to London to see the Professionals (Paul Cook from the Pistols band) with Glen Matlock's The Rich Kids supporting. As I walk towards the entrance of the venue I see Glen sat outside having a fag. I walked straight up to him and shook his hand saying "you don't remember me do ya?" He looked at me puzzled and I said "I put you on at The Market Tavern, Kidderminster..." You could see the cogs turning then he said "It's you, you fucker! You owe me money!"

Jim Henderson "Back in 1992, I'd started (at the age of 16) a Sex Pistols fanzine called "Never Trust A Hippy"! I found out via NME that Glen Matlock's then band The Mavericks were playing at the Market Tavern on Saturday 3rd July 1993.

I was in contact with Glen so arranged to meet and interview him prior to the gig. As well as Glen on bass, the band consisted of vocalist Gerry Foster, guitarist Paul O'Brien, and drummer Paul Simon (ex-Neo / Radio Stars).

The crowd was pretty sparse that night, but the band put on a great performance - 11 songs in total, including the track 'Burning Sounds' which was originally recorded by Glen's post-Pistols band Rich Kids. The band later renamed themselves The Philistines and released a CD called 'Hard Work', which featured studio versions of most of the tracks that they played at this gig."

NEVER TRUST A HIPPIE

Jim & Glen

Jim & Glen

Dean on the door

Dean & Glen

Jim & Glen

135

## market tavern kidderminster
### tel: 0562 752590

|  |  |  |
|---|---|---|
| Tuesday 2nd March | RADIOHEAD + The Tansads | £2.50 |
| Friday 5th March | DODGY + Pietra Rosa + Emission | £3.00 |
| Friday 12th March | THE GOD MACHINE + Bathchair Suicide + Appleberry Crescent | £3.00 |
| Friday 19th March | R.D.F. & The Ancient Ones (ex Hippy Slags/Hawkwind) + Jerk Frenzy | £3.50 |
| Friday 26th March | POP AM GOOD + Funbug + Sister Savage and the Buggered Nuns | £2.50 |
| Friday 2nd April | CITIZEN FISH & SPITBOY (U.S.A.) | £3.50 |
| Friday 9th April | Rescheduled Date... BACK TO THE PLANET +Mad Halibut | £3.50 |

last trains: B'ham 23.02 Worcs 00.01
one minute from the station

The prices listed are advance prices. It may be more expensive on the night.
advance tickets from:
Market Tavern, Sounds Around, Tempest (Bham)

## MARKET TAVERN
### KIDDERMINSTER
### tel:0562 752590

|  |  |  |
|---|---|---|
| Saturday 3rd April | 'Putting the House in Order' Charity show PANIC BEACH & melon & emission | £2.50 |
| Friday 9th April | Back to the Planet + Madhalibut | £3.50 |
| Friday 16th April | STOURBRIDGE 'The Big Night Out' featuring Fretblanket + SCRASH + Babylon Zoo + Indigo Jane | £2.50 |
| Friday 23rd April | LEATHERFACE + Guns 'n' Wankers + Pale Kings | £3.50 |
| Saturday 24th April | Bathchair Suicide & Madhalibut | £2.50 |
| Saturday 1st May | Fun-da-mental + Credit to the Nation | £3.00 |
| Saturday 8th May | DUB MERGE | £2.00 |
| Friday 14th May | MIDWAY STILL & PANIC BEACH | £3.00 |
| Friday 4th June | ALLOY + Funbug Ex members of Cro-Mags, Uniform Choice, Dag Nasty | £3.00 |
| Saturday 12th June | CHUMBAWAMBA Tickets only! On sale now | £4.00 |

last trains: B'ham 23.02 Worcs 00.01
one minute from the station

The prices listed are advance prices. It may be more expensive on the night.
advance tickets from:
Market Tavern, Sounds Around, Tempest (B'ham), Magpie (Worcs)

## MARKET TAVERN
### KIDDERMINSTER
### tel:0562 752590

|  |  |  |
|---|---|---|
| Friday 23rd April | LEATHERFACE + Guns 'n' Wankers + Pale Kings | £3.50 |
| Saturday 24th April | Bathchair Suicide & Madhalibut | £2.50 |
| Saturday 1st May | Fun-da-mental + Credit to the Nation | £3.00 |
| Saturday 8th May | DUB MERGE | £2.00 |
| Tuesday 11th May | Special warm-up show... THE BUZZCOCKS | £5.00 |
| Friday 14th May | MIDWAY STILL & PANIC BEACH + Elizabeth Jane | £3.00 |
| Friday 28th May | THE LURKERS | £3.00 |
| Friday 4th June | U.S. Hardcore ALLOY + Funbug Ex members of Cro-Mags, Articles of Faith, Uniform Choice, Dag Nasty | £3.00 |
| Friday 11th June | The Selecter (featuring Pauline Black) | £5.00 |
| Friday 18th June | LEVITATION | £3.50 |

last trains: B'ham 23.02 Worcs 00.01
one minute from the station

The prices listed are advance prices. It may be more expensive on the night.
advance tickets from: Market Tavern, Sounds Around, Magpie (Worcs)
Birmingham outlets: Tempest, Swordfish, Way Ahead, Plastic Factory, H.Q.

## MARKET TAVERN
### KIDDERMINSTER
### tel:0562 752590

|  |  |  |
|---|---|---|
| Friday 2nd April | Citizen Fish + Spitboy (USA) + Preacher | £3.50 |
| Saturday 3rd April | 'Putting the House in Order' Charity show PANIC BEACH & melon & emission | £2.50 |
| Friday 9th April | Back to the Planet + Madhalibut | £3.50 |
| Friday 16th April | STOURBRIDGE 'The Big Night Out' featuring Fretblanket + SCRASH + Babylon Zoo + Indigo Jane | £2.50 |
| Friday 23rd April | LEATHERFACE + Guns 'n' Wankers + Pale Kings | £3.50 |
| Saturday 24th April | Bathchair Suicide & Madhalibut | £2.50 |
| Saturday 1st May | Fun-da-mental + Credit to the Nation | £3.00 |
| Saturday 8th May | DUB MERGE | £2.00 |
| Friday 14th May | MIDWAY STILL & PANIC BEACH | £3.00 |
| Friday 4th June | U.S. Hardcore ALLOY + Funbug Ex members of Cro-Mags, Articles of Faith, Uniform Choice, Dag Nasty | £3.00 |

last trains: B'ham 23.02 Worcs 00.01
one minute from the station

The prices listed are advance prices. It may be more expensive on the night.
advance tickets from:
Market Tavern, Sounds Around, Tempest (B'ham), Magpie (Worcs)

## MARKET TAVERN
### KIDDERMINSTER
### tel:0562 752590

|  |  |  |
|---|---|---|
| Friday 19th March | R.D.F. + The Ancient Ones + Jerk Frenzy | £3.50 |
| Friday 26th March | POP AM GOOD + Funbug + Sister Savage and the Buggered Nuns | £2.50 |
| Friday 2nd April | Citizen Fish + Spitboy (USA) + Preacher | £3.50 |
| Friday 9th April | Back to the Planet + Madhalibut | £3.50 |
| Friday 16th April | STOURBRIDGE 'The Big Night Out' featuring Fretblanket + SCRASH + Babylon Zoo + Indigo Jane | £2.50 |
| Friday 23rd April | LEATHERFACE + Guns 'n' Wankers + Pale Kings | £3.50 |
| Saturday 24th April | Bathchair Suicide & Madhalibut | £2.50 |
| Saturday 1st May | Fun-da-mental + Credit to the Nation | £3.00 |
| Friday 7th May | DUB MERGE | £2.00 |
| Friday 14th May | MIDWAY STILL & PANIC BEACH | £3.00 |

last trains: B'ham 23.02 Worcs 00.01
one minute from the station

The prices listed are advance prices. It may be more expensive on the night.
advance tickets from:
Market Tavern, Sounds Around, Tempest (B'ham), Magpie (Worcs)

## market tavern kidderminster
### tel: 0562 752590

|  |  |  |
|---|---|---|
| Friday 29th Jan | BIG 5 Featuring Jimmy Belle Star Rico - the legendary trombonist, ex-Selecter members and ex Bad Manners playing original ska based stuff Single out in January | £4.00 |
| Friday 12th Feb | RADIOHEAD & FRETBLANKET + melon | £2.50 |
| Friday 19th Feb | CHUMBAWAMBA + Papa Brittle | £4.00 |
| Friday 5th March | DODGY + support | £3.00 |
| Friday 12th March | THE GOD MACHINE + Bathchair Suicide + Appleberry Crescent | £3.00 |
| Friday 2nd April | CITIZEN FISH & SPITBOY (U.S.A.) | £3.50 |
| Friday 9th April | Rescheduled Date... BACK TO THE PLANET +Mad Halibut | £3.50 |

last trains: B'ham 23.02 Worcs 00.01
one minute from the station

The prices listed are advance prices. It may be more expensive on the night.
advance tickets from :
Market Tavern, Sounds Around, Tempest (Bham)

## market tavern
### comberton place kidderminster
### tel: 0562 752590

|  |  |  |
|---|---|---|
| Friday 12th March | Indie | GOD MACHINE |
| Saturday 13th March | Biker Rock | CUM TO BEDLAM |
| Thursday 18th March | Irish Folk | TIN DRUM |
| Friday 19th March | Reggae | RADICAL DANCE FACTION |
| Saturday 20th March | Disco | INDUSTRIAL NIGHT |
| Friday 26th March | Indie | POP AM GOOD |
| Thursday 1st April | Indie | BLAB HAPPY |

1993 FLYERS & ADS

BATHCHAIR Suicide

ANOTHER FINE MESS

ANOTHER FINE MESS

ANOTHER FINE Mess

Dec 29th '93

# TAVERN MEMORIES

Keri-Jane Herman "I remember people on the roof and falling off."

Mervyn Weaver "I remember an interesting night when halfway through the show the drummer came flying off the stage & started getting stuck into someone in the crowd. Real scene from a western movie... and the band played on!"

The Head Barman "I think we had the loudest pub jukebox in the UK!"

Kim "One night I'm sure Andy Tavern wouldn't let us in as we were underage and the band, possibly Cake, turned and played facing out the window."

Sand Palmer "Remember working the last night that Andy had it... Arrived... Only cans behind the bar. Nought else which was a bit strange..... There was quite a big band playing .. (memory shit - can't remember who), so filled up quite quick... Then a LOAD of police arrived... asking what was going on and looking for Andy... We hadn't seen him... Police told us he had sold the Tavern 2 weeks before so we were all trespassing... But when they realised how many people were there, they turned round and said... We'll come back at 2am when you're all done and take the keys off you.. haha.. T'was a wicked night at the end."

Baron Webb "Playing there was very special and exciting, especially as it was the place that we'd heard about throughout our young lives as being the local music Mecca. I went on to be lead singer/guitar in a few local bands with John Peutherer (Stop The World/Dr Bullfrog) Neil Archer and Steve Bray (trombone player in Frank Boff Big Band). We were called Johnny 5 & also The Supertonics."

Matthew Edwards "This place was responsible for me dropping out of college three years running. I only wish I were there in the days of Radiohead getting heckled. Best band I saw there would have to be Downward Thing, they played on my 17th birthday and they were fucking awesome. Catatonia were shit. Can't remember any of the other bands I saw there, but there were many. This place was mental, I wish it were still there."

Lou "I helped Mark out at gigs for a couple of years, working on the door, heating and serving food for the bands, sweeping floors, acting as roadie and occasionally interviewing bands - they were some of the best years of my life!"

Andrew Wolfman "On my (let's say) eighteenth birthday, Andy Tavern bought us all a round of 'Satan Spunk' whiskies. This is the only time I have ever tried to steal a tractor."

Paul Chance "The first time I went I was 14 so 1987. I had a bottle of Newcastle Brown and smoked furiously. I was with a guy who wanted to hold a 60s disco in the back room."

Steve Cooper "I went in for a pint in the afternoon on a Good Friday. The pub was supposed to be closed by law. I said 'So you're open then, yeah?' Andy replied from behind the bar 'I'm not closing my pub just because some cunt got nailed to a piece of wood two thousand years ago!'."

Lou "Mark basically WAS the Tavern - along with Andy and Gail the landlords. I think he had more groupies than most of the bands haha!"

Katherine Alker "I loved the Market Tavern: Fretblanket, Chumbawamba, Back To The Planet, Pietra Rosa, Ned's. Chatted to Clint Poppie one night in the bar too!"

Lee Biggs (Dive / Love Buzz) "I remember Radiohead, Fretblanket, God Machine. I think we played with Back To The Planet, Korova Milk Bar. I played with Love Buzz. It was our second and final gig."

Stuart Crompton "There was a nipple sucking contest on one memorable occasion with one lucky female punter and a few friends, probably not printable."

Dr Marc Price "I have fond memories of milling around after a gig at the Tavern and finding myself in an impromptu breast kissing competition. I didn't win, but who cares!"

137

*By Luke*

**Which town were you based in?**

Stourbridge

**What years were you active?**

Approx '91 - '95

**Who was in the band?**

Mike Fox, Darren Pataki & Luke Sweeney

**What kind of music did you play?**

Industrial Indie Techno Dance

**Who were the influences?**

PWEI of course & the Wonder Stuff & Plenty of Nine Inch Nails with a dash of KLF & Apollo 440 to name a few..

**What level of success did you achieve?**

Not as much as we fantasised about as we were scuppered by Musicians Union Lawyers trying to be too helpful... Our crowning glories (apart from Tavern Gigs...) were supporting PWEI at Aston Villa Leisure Centre & The Town & Country Club on 3 consecutive nights & then an amazing support slot at the Marquee for them on The Looks or the Lifestyle tour.

**What do you remember about playing at the Tavern?**

Being very nervous then very drunk to cope but absolutely loving the hostile crowds, one gig – an all dayer I think – with Rich March & Adam Mole DJing (poss others too) we really gave it everything & virtually destroyed the main band's drum kit (well we only had about 6 feet square to use) and the Poppies threw a load of clothes they were selling at the gig at me saying I effin well deserved them! You can imagine how chuffed I was. Possibly at the same gig one of our managers – Bones – wandered into the Farmers Boy after & got the crap beat out of him – served him right probably, was being extremely drunk & obnoxious!

**How did the band end?**

Mental Illness of the bass player – I was gutted but you cannot argue with a sick mind :(

**Did anyone go on to further success or have a career in the music industry?**

No! I think we all tried different bands & me and Mike wrote a few songs but it was never the same.

**What else do we need to know about the band?**

We got a real drummer half way through our career – Tim – he was ace & made us sound great – I had roadied for his band in the past.

Andrew Wolfman "I live by a hospital in the middle of a global pandemic and still, whenever I hear a siren, I think oh shit, Scrash are coming on."

# TIMES

| Stage one | | Stage two | |
|---|---|---|---|
| 10.30 | Hair & Skin Trading Co | 8.00 | Pink Dandelions |
| 9.30 | Bang Bang Machine | 7.00 | Funbug |
| 8.30 | Joyce McKinney | 6.10 | Melon |
| 7.30 | Family Go Town | 5.25 | Magic |
| 6.30 | Midway Still | 4.40 | Tribute To Nothing |
| 5.45 | Panic Beach | 3.55 | Tanglefoot |
| 5.00 | Emission | 3.05 | Another Fine Mess |
| 4.15 | Scrash | 2.20 | Weird's War |
| 3.25 | F.M.B. | | |

## Coming soon at the Tavern...

**Tue 14th Sept** - CHUMBAWAMBA & CREDIT TO THE NATION (Tickets on sale now)
**Fri 1st Oct** - SENSER (tbc)
**Fri 8th Oct** - CROPDUSTERS (Crusty folky band) + Madhalibut + Chuck (ex-Resque)
**Thu 14th Oct** - F.M.B. (Yes - they're coming back!! Tickets on sale 23 Aug)
**To be confirmed** - Citizen Fish, The Tansads, The Sea, Psychastorm, Mega City Four

# MARKET TAVERN
## KIDDERMINSTER
### tel: 0562 752590

# FREE FESTIVAL

Hello, and thanks for coming to our first festival. Or should I just be honest and call it an all-dayer?

When we first dreamt the idea up about four months ago, we wanted to have a nice outdoor stage, lots of stalls and all the usual festival stuff. However, as we got nearer to the day, things started to go wrong. First bands started pulling out, then we couldn't transport the stage blocks from Wordsley without hiring a removal van, then we were forced to move the outdoor stage to it's current position which is by no means an ideal spot. It's probably raining now. Still, what did you expect for nothing?

Maximum respect to all the artists and crew who are doing this for absolutely nothing, they're not even getting expenses. In fact, everyone involved with this project has given their time for free, so be patient if things aren't going to plan.

We lost a lot of bands on the way so in case you're wondering ... The Jacobites are in Lithuania, Madhalibut and Bitter Tears have members away on holiday and Credit to the Nation and The Wishplants are down in London supporting Hawkwind!

We apologise for the lack of facilities but the cafe is on stand-by should the weather take a turn for the worse (or the if neighbours take offence!) and for one reason and another we couldn't invite any stall holders.

If this all goes well, maybe next year we can really go for it with a big event but in the meantime enjoy yourselves because we've still got some great bands playing throughout the day.

Special Note

This is an ego-free event which doesn't have a headline act to ensure that you've got quality entertainment on hand all throughout the day.

# Saturday 14th August 1993

**The Pink Dandelions**
Folky rockers from Birmingham in the same vein as The Levellers, who should have you all dancing in the car-park!

**The Hair & Skin Trading Co**
Avant Garde rock from ex-Loop members Neil Mackay and John Willis sounding closer to Curve and The Jesus and Mary Chain according to the NME! Currently on tour to promote their new single, 'Go Round'

**Another Fine Mess**
Poppy punk 4 piece from Worcester who have been name-dropped by Clint Poppie in Select, mentioned in the Phoenix programme as one of the best support bands on this year's Buzzcocks tour and gigged their arses off in every Worcestershire pub that'll have 'em

**Magic**
A 3 piece London indie guitar outfit who had the sleeve of their single recently reviewed in the NME but not the music. The sleeve got a right slagging!

**FMB**
Stars of Channel 4's 'The Next Big Thing', FMB had the nations pop kids glued to their sets on Sundays throughout the summer as Rags and the boys struggled in the face of adversity for that elusive big break. They've been packing venues around the country and there should be a single out fairly soon.

**Funbug**
In their former incarnation as Identity, this Redditch power pop trio could have been huge if they'd caught the same train to fame as their contempories, MC4 and the Senseless Things. Instead they toured Germany and farted around before signing to the Lookout label in the States. They've been known to play naked in the past so who knows what's in store for today!

**Family Go Town**
Leamington's Hammond driven popsters scored a Top 75 hit with Turtle before being dropped by Phonogram. They supported the Inspiral Carpets on tour and are currently negotiating a new deal

**Midway Still**
After a succession of indie hits, Midway Still released their debut LP and toured with Mega City Four picking up a big following on the way. After a quiet spell and the departure of drummer Declan, they're back with a new album called 'Life's Too Long'. Get in early if you want to catch them

**Tribute to Nothing**
Three brothers all under 16 (the lead singer is 13!!) who came to prominence when they supported the Neds at Gloucester last year and were declared the best new band of 92 by the Neds themselves. Central TV have filmed their live act and Fabulous offered to put a single out on their Kinglake label after they played with them in Malvern earlier this year.

**Melon**
The only Kidderminster band on the festival, they've just recorded their second demo and have supported Dodgy and Sensitize.

**Weird's War**
Weird's War have been attracting a fair bit of attention from the majors in the last couple of months. Their Seventies influenced style is often compared to Suede, although the Melody Maker opted to call them 'Gloom Glam'. Singer Michael Valentine West is a Hendrix for the '90s and you can expect them to sign on the dotted line before the year's out

**Joyce McKinney Experience**
'Everyone who's heard them thinks they're brilliant' boasts their press release. But I don't doubt it. After taking two years off due to drug problems they're back and ...they're going to take your f*cking head off'!

**Panic Beach**
The arrival of new vocalist Ian has seen a rapid change for Wolverhampton's finest. Gone are the leanings to Indie grunge and now they're being touted in some quarters as the English Metallica! Dates with PWEI sharpened their live act and the lads are currently looking for a new deal

**Emission**
Three young lads from Dudley belting out catchy techno guitar pop. Last year saw them supporting the Neds, this year sees the release of their debut single 'Life's Not Real'

**Scrash**
Scrash started life as 3 lads and a drum machine but have recently added a real life drummer to their ranks. Yet another band at the festival who have supported PWEI, their sound isn't too different from that of Clint and the boys but they're much more than Poppies wannabees

**Bang Bang Machine**
Don't let the CV of Bang Bang Machine's musicians put you off (ex-Wrathchild no less!!), their recent re-release of John Peel's Festive Fifty No 1, Geek Love, featured 8 different ambient remixes by MixMaster Morris and was well received by the critics and audiences alike

**Tanglefoot**
Birmingham's Tanglefoot are signed to Chapter 22 and have played with bands such as Leatherface and The Lunachicks in the years they've been together. Their crowning glory however came when they did a couple low key shows with PWEI earlier this year. They've also had their gig at London's Marquee filmed and shown on Polish TV

# KIDDERMINSTER FREE FESTIVAL

Mark Badgeman "The Tavern became known for its' All-Dayers. The first was the Kidderminster Free Festival of 1993. Festival bands such as Back To The Planet were starting to play the venue and they were selling out. I loved going to festivals, especially free ones, so although I don't remember, I suspect a combination of those two things plus the success of the Save The Tavern benefit gig spurred me into doing one of my own. I knew it needed to be free so that I could convince the bands to play for no fee. If we had to pay them, costs would spiral out of control and it would not be viable. Nobody got paid for doing things like Castlemorton so I thought it was perfectly reasonable.

I managed to get a great line-up by playing the bands off against each other. I'd tell Band One that Band Two had already agreed to do it and that would spur them on to confirm. Then I'd quickly go back to Band Two and tell them Band One was definitely confirmed! Nobody ever wanted to be first to commit. Once one band was onboard, it was easier because at least you were telling the truth about who had confirmed from that point onwards.

The other thing I did was to try and avoid having a headline act. I wanted equal billing to ensure we had people around all day. Fortunately, FMB were agreeable to playing second and they were likely the biggest draw of the day as they were the stars of a Channel 4 TV show called Next Big Thing that had just finished its run. Hair and Skin Trading Company had insisted on playing last but the bill was so strong that it no longer mattered. Having a second stage outside with a vocal PA was a great addition, but we should have done it out the back where there was more space.

By my reckoning, we had 800 people over the day. It was packed all day long. Unfortunately for Hair and Skin, most people were slaughtered by the time they played and they waited far too long to start their set so they played to a handful of drunken idiots and whoever had stuck around to watch them.

Future all dayers never quite matched the strength of the bill but I kept the ethos of not having a headliner and it's a tactic I still employ to this day. I think that's what made them so successful."

## The Market Tavern's One Day Free Festival

## Saturday August 14th

### INFORMATION SHEET

There will be two stages, the normal 'indoor' stage and a small outside stage. The inside stage will have our usual 3k rig whilst the outdoor one will only have a vocal PA due to noise restrictions.

Each band will be allocated 30 minutes with the outside stage running from 12.00 till 8.30 and inside from 4.30 till 11.00. No-one will get a full soundcheck with the exception of the band who lend their drum kit to all the bands playing inside.

It is not intended for there to be a 'headline' act and an 'opening' act, we just want to have good music throughout the day.

No-one will get paid and there will also be no food or drink riders but there will be a barbeque outside along with jugglers, unicyclists etc and the indoor cafe will be open most of the day.

A programme of the event will be produced with an article on each band so you will need to supply a photo, press cuttings and biog. This will act as the advance publicity as well as local press features and hopefully some sort of national coverage from NME, Melody Maker etc.

Bands who have shown interest so far are: Credit to the Nation, Midway Still, Family Go Town, Joyce McKinney Experience, Funbug, Scrash, Wishplants, Bang Bang Machine, Bitter Tears, Panic Beach, Magic, Fretblanket, Another Fine Mess and Madhalibut.

If you want to play then I need to know for definate by 1st June so we can get all the advance publicity out. Remember: someone has to go on first so you can't pick your own time slot, merely whether you'd prefer to be inside or out.

INFO SHEET SENT OUT TO BANDS

# Bands line up in free-for-all!

## MARKET TAVERN HOSTS FESTIVAL

A HOST of bands big and small await you at the first ever Kidderminster Free Festival next weekend.

It takes place at the Market Tavern on August 14, with 17 bands taking part, all playing for free and with no particular pecking order.

For instance, Midway Still have sold out the Tavern in the past and are due on at 6.30pm, while Channel 4 stars FMB play three hours earlier.

And as regards FMB, here's a bit of info you need to know. On safety grounds they are the only band for which you will need a ticket to gain entry to the main room, such is the expected demand.

The tickets are free, but you need to collect them by 2pm from the Tavern on the day.

As well as Midway Still and FMB, the festival also sees the first Jacobites show for eight years with a re-united Nikki Sudden and Dave Kusworth, and the reformed Joyce McKinney Experience.

There are two stages, the main stage which will have a full PA and a smaller, busking-session type stage.

The day starts at 2pm and the full line-up is: Midway Still, FMB, The Jacobites, Bang Bang Mchine, Hair & Skin Trading Co, Family Go Town, Joyce McKinney Experience, Scrash, Panic Beach, Funbug, Madhalibut, Tanglefoot, magic, Bitter Tears, Another Fine Mess, Melon and Emission.

For further details, ring the Tavern on Kidderminster 752590.

■ Madhalibut (above) and Midway Still (right), two of the bands that will be taking part in Kidderminster Free Festival next Saturday.

Andy Price "I wasn't convinced it would work but as usual I left it in Mark's good hands. To give you an idea how well it went, the chip shop over the road later told me that he had never had such a busy day in 20yrs!"

Mark Badgeman "FMB were so popular we had to operate a ticket system. If you wanted to see them, you had to collect a free ticket and once all 300 were taken, that performance was sold out!"

Lamp (Bang Bang Machine) "I remember the all-dayer with the Hair & Skin Trading Company headlining. We were the penultimate band (a slot we always really liked). I think it must have been at the end of a tour as we were firing on all cylinders and the crowd went wild. I was looking forward to seeing Hair & Skin but they locked themselves in their van and said they wouldn't go on as it was impossible to follow us! I can't actually remember whether they did or not."

Jo Deakin "I remember Tom and Dan (my bf at the time) doing 'security' at the '93 all dayer and getting pissed and giggling a lot. Newky Brown, army boots and stripy leggings. We packed a lot into the summer of '93 before going off to Uni - mainly hanging out at the Tavern and going off to free festivals in the back of Badgeman's van - it was a happy time."

Mike Reed "Saw Joyce McKinney Experience have a hissy fit in front of a crowd who wanted noise - the singer screamed, 'We don't play that shit anymore'! I was really looking forward to them and they were awful!"

Andrew Wolfman "Having overseen the death of my musical ambitions, Badgeman tried to kick-start a stand-up career for me, by booking me to compere the first Market Tavern all-day festival. I prepared two gags, and the first one killed.

"Ladies and gentlemen, please give a Market Tavern welcome to your friends not mine, F.M.B. In case you're wondering, their name stands for 'Five Members in this Band' which is literally the only interesting thing about them." Britain's worst band were livid and kicked my football onto the roof of the market.

I followed up this early success with, "I'm Andrew and I'm your compere, so today I'm going to be comparing things. You shout something out, and I'll compare it to something else. Come on... nothing? Alright, I'll start. FMB! They're like all the other bands... but shit! etc."

I tried to launch this solid gold bit every half an hour between bands until someone out of Midway Still begged me to fuck off and Mark suggested that it hadn't been my day, perhaps I should go home. I never got my ball back."

# Mark's major festival coup is a feat to be applauded

Organiser Mark Badgeman pulled off a major coup in obtaining the services of so many fine bands to help constitute the first ever Kidderminster Free Festival.

But while committing bands such as Midway Still, FMB and the Joyce McKinney Experience to leave themselves out of pocket was a feat in itself, getting them all together to play smoothly on an 'ego-free' bill was surely asking too much.

Not so.

If, the reaction of the 800 or so people who visited the Market Tavern on Saturday was anything to go by, the Kidderminster Free Festival of 1993 could well be the first of many.

The 3.25pm performance of recent TV stars FMB epitomised

the spirit of the occasion, and their early appearance attracted a healthy throng.

They were followed by local favourites Scrash.

Teeny sensations Tribute To Nothing, who already boast a support slot to Ned's Atomic Dustbin and a lead singer who is just 13, received a generous response with their punkish material, but it was left to Funbug to really set the outdoor stage alight.

The Redditch three piece have gained a large local following with their energetic powerful guitar-fuelled power pop

The Levellers-like folky music of the Pink Dandelions brought a genuine festival feel to proceedings as they completed the outdoor line-up, while inside activity was reaching fever pitch.

Bang Bang Machine have finally got it right. They offer a combination of a lush voice, mellow guitars and a fusion of organised noise wrapped in an assortment of gorgeous rhythms which delight the ears.

Although they were a hard act to follow, The Hair and Skin Trading Company made an admirable attempt and kept the walls of Kidderminster's Market Tavern ringing out long enough for the Free Festival 1994.

Duncan Bickley: "This was a great day. My main memory however, was that while Hair and Skin Trading Company were playing, this guy in the crowd, who was swilling from a bottle of wine, staggered into me saying 'you know how there is always one c**t at every gig? Well tonight that c**t is ME'. I thought that pretty soon he would be smashing the bottle over my head, but instead he moved a a bit further forward to the barriers and screamed at the band to 'play the next one for Dobbo', and spat into the singers face. He did this continually for about thirty minutes. WTF?!"

## MARKET TAVERN
### KIDDERMINSTER
### tel: 0562 752590

| | | |
|---|---|---|
| Friday 4th June | **ALLOY** + *Funbug* +Tangiefoot — U.S. Hardcore — Ex members of Cro-Mags, Articles of Faith, Uniform Choice, Dag Nasty | £3.00 |
| Friday 11th June | **The Selecter** + IMAGE105 (Ex- International Beat) + Mr Toad | £5.00 |
| Friday 18th June | **LEVIT~~ATION~~** CANCELLED + RUI Refunds from point of purchase | ~~£4.50~~ |
| Saturday 3rd July | **The Mavericks** featuring Ex-Sex Pistol ... Glen Matlock | £3.50 |
| Friday 9th July | **Sweet Jesus** &emission | £3.00 |

### FREE All-Dayer
### SATURDAY 14TH AUGUST 1993

2 stages, food, jugglers, uni-cyclists, face painting...

Bands confirmed so far:- Wishplants, Family Go Town, Panic Beach, Joyce McKinney Experience, Funbug, Magic, Melon, Madhalibut, Pale Kings, Bitter Tears, Scrash.

*More big names to be announced soon!*

 last trains: B'ham 23.02 Worcs 00.01
one minute from the station

*The prices listed are advance prices. It may be more expensive on the night.*
**advance tickets from:** Market Tavern, Sounds Around, Magpie (All shops)
Birmingham outlets: Tempest, Way Ahead, Plastic Factory.

# Levitation

Levitation were a psychedelic indie rock band featuring Terry Bickers from The House Of Love (you know that song - 'Shine On') and Bic Hayes who'd played guitar in the Cardiacs. They'd narrowly missed the Top 40 with their album from the previous year. It should have been a good gig but they didn't get to play it.

Duncan Bickley "They split up the week before the date. Apparently Terry Bickers wanted to devote more time to being an otter, according to NME or MM."

Jo Deakin "I went to the gig in Brum where they split up, I was gutted, totally obsessed with them."

# DISCOS

Anybody could rent the room at the Tavern. Over the years, there's been a variety of 'discos' ranging from ambient to metal to psychedelic. Here's a collection of flyers and posters.

Kevin Baskin "Once a month I used to do alternative disco at the Tavern called th Lysergic Space Dance. It was a joint effor with myself and a guy called Spazzer. Th was late '80s. We supported a few bands. Ou event was a quid on the door and we potat stamped your hand. No photos I'm saddene say but if you were there you'd remember final song being 'Joe 90'. We played acid house, Culture Shock, Napalm Death... it w varied."

The Head Barman "I did a fancy dress DJ event that involved a lot of mushrooms and acid. One guy came in a shower curtain with a chrome ring over his head and had a knife, like Jack Nicholson in Psycho! A pantomime cow had a piss next to me!"

A TACTICAL NEURAL EVENING OF
# INDUSTRIAL & TECHNO

MINISTRY • NIN • FRONTLINE ASSEMBLY • REVOLTING COCKS •
KMFDM • FRONT 242 • PIGFACE • NITZER EBB • SKINNY PUPPY •

SHEEP ON DRUGS • MURDER INC • CASSANDRA COMPLEX •
FINITRIBE • 1000 HOMO DJ'S • AND MUCH • MUCH MORE • MATE!

## Saturday 20th March 1993
## MARKET TAVERN, KIDDERMINSTER
7.30m - 11.00pm                                    £1.50

The Head Barman "After Andy left, there was a Mini Cooper that had been cut in half and was used as the DJ booth. You had to open the door to get in and then the decks were on the dashboard. The rear end was fixed to the wall sticking out halfway up."

The Head Barman "I was DJing one night, one of my mushroom fancy dress parties. I had a large strobe. Warning on back - Do not use in less than 3,000 capacity crowd for more than 10 seconds at a time. I just used to leave it on all night in front of about 80 people. Miffi gave me a bag of mushrooms one night, after a few handfuls while DJ'ing I forgot and thought they were sweets. Came to my senses sitting on the front of the stage dangling my legs staring into the strobe. Everyone was chanting my name to arouse me from my trip and there had been no music on for about 5 mins!"

# Mega City Four + Skyscraper

## Mon 27th Sep 1993

Mark Badgeman "Mega City Four was the beginning of the end. It should have sold out. I loved the band and had seen them loads of times so I'd misjudged the prevailing mood and not noticed they were on a decline. I suppose I should have realised but we'd had 'underplay' shows before such as the Buzzcocks, Carter and Chumbawamba and I felt this was going to be another big band wanting to play a small venue. Unfortunately, instead of selling out, only 135 turned up.

Andy was struggling financially and losing so much money on a show was a big blow. We didn't have enough cash on the night to pay them so he wrote a cheque for the remainder, but told the tour manager to go and cash it in the morning as he was in danger of going bankrupt. Unfortunately, they sat on the cheque for weeks and when they finally cashed it, the account was empty and the cheque bounced.

This happens once in a while to bands. There was no intention to stiff them, but they didn't do what was necessary to get paid and I didn't see quite how that was my fault. Their agent held it against me for a good 20 years or more, trying to tell people not to work with me, albeit to little avail."

● Mega City Four at the Market Tavern on September 27.

## Mega gig with a fab Four

SEPTEMBER sees the arrival at Kidderminster's Market Tavern of a band who have long wanted to play the venue but never quite got round to doing so.

The Mega City Four play on September 27 as part of a national tour taking in smaller venues they have been unable to take in over recent years but which they feel are their ideal setting.

Their pulling power has grown since emerging on the scene in 1989, having supported The Wonderstuff and The Cramps on tour, playing the main stage at the Reading Festival and having a Top 40 hit with *Stop*.

Tickets are £5 in advance and are available from the Tavern.

# FMB + Anna & Joyland

## Fri 15th Oct 1993

FMB (Fuck My Boots?!) were the stars of a Channel 4 documentary called The Next Big Thing. It was actually quite funny, like an Indie Spinal Tap. They were perfect for the Tavern pop-kid crowd and their appearance at the Free Festival was rammed. By the time October came, the novelty had worn off. We sold slightly shy of 100 tickets, hampered by the addition of Anna, a pointless tour support who denied an opportunity for a local band to bolster the bill.

Lindsay Smith "I went to see Joyland support FMB in 1993. I was at college with the guitarist from Joyland so they were the main attraction, but FMB had been on the telly as part of a tv documentary to find the next big thing so obviously we went to see them to take them down a peg or two. I read in the paper that the lead singer won the lottery years later and he was trying to get the band back together a la Creme Brulee. It's a shit business!"

Mark Badgeman "He spent the lot and ended up penniless!"

*By Andy Jones*

**Which town were you based in?** We were spread out all over the place, Birmingham, Malvern, Stourbridge, Bewdley.

**What years were you active?** 1989-1993

**Who was in the band?**
Andy Tomlinson - Guitar, Alan Jones - Guitar, Andy Tucker - Bass, Steve Smith - Drums, Andy Jones - Vocals

**What kind of music did you play?** Gothy Alternative rock

**Who were the influences?** Fields of the Nephilim, Cocteau Twins, Dead Can Dance, The Mission, The Sisters, but also a lot of other things ranging from, The Doors to Pink Floyd, Tangerine dream, and Cardiacs. We were keen on musical variation didn't want to limit ourselves to one genre.

**What level of success did you achieve?** In the great scheme of things Ambelian remained on the cusp of better things and started to be offered good support slots with the likes of Zodiac Mindwarp, Alien Sex Fiend, And Also the Trees, Rosetta Stone, Marshall Law and Dawn After Dark.
We were included in a goth book compiled by Mick Mercer, former editor of Siren magazine, so that was quite a coup. It sold quite well and generated a lot of interest in the band. Ambelian were a firm favourite with many fanzines and were included in many, usually in the form of an interview etc. The band were mentioned in Sounds music paper and even had some airplay on a Radio 1 show at some point.
We were planning a European tour, which would have happened in 1993, but unfortunately the band disintegrated before this could happen.
The band also recorded music at Outlaw studios in Birmingham. Unfortunately it never made it to vinyl, which was the predominant format at the time. I'm almost certain that if the band had continued and sorted out its internal problems, they would have been quite successful.

**What do you remember about playing at the Tavern?** On the whole very friendly and receptive crowds who were appreciative of most bands that played there. Like most people I remember the juxtaposition of a music venue and the smell of cowshit when you went to the bogs, as of course during the day it was still a farmer's market selling livestock.
I remember it was always quite a job stopping people letting their mates in through the fire exit. It was always a good sound at the Tavern and the PA was usually good, although getting people on the dance floor was often difficult, folks from Kiddy are often a bit self-conscious until they let their hair down, then they go fucking mad.

**Any memories of the other bands you played with at the Tavern?** Yes I became great friends with Bliss the Pocket Opera,in particular Dee Davidson the bassist who is still a great friend to this day, but this was probably way back from my days of playing with Omnia Opera. We put on some great anarcho style gigs together that would pull all sorts of strange people out of the woodwork which was great because we fitted in perfectly. We kind of formed an alliance and would do gigs in each other's hometowns supporting each other.

**How did the band end?**
Ambelian came to an end because of infidelity. I'm afraid it was my fault. I had an affair with the guitarist's girlfriend and whilst the band continued for quite some time, the tensions became quite difficult and the band slowly disintegrated. I regret this to this very day. Looking back I want to tell my younger self not to be such a twat. My own desires completely ruined all the hard work and effort that had gone into Ambelian and I can't quite forgive myself However over the years we have remained great friends still, the best in fact.

**Did anyone go on to further success or have a career in the music industry?**
Steve Smith the drummer has been in many bands since Ambelian and is currently playing drums for Rouen. Alan Jones, one of the guitarists and main songwriters, moved to Spain and formed a band in Madrid called Shimo. They had a record deal over there and were doing well but unfortunately that band disintegrated as well. Thing about being in bands, it's actually quite difficult because you're kind of married to 5 other people and that's hard to maintain. I myself carried on performing with Omnia Opera for many years on and off. I've released several albums which were very well received, so that's something I've always been proud of.

# AMBELIAN

Ambelian aim to transport the listener to a world of anthemic riff laden atmospheric songs with strong leanings towards the goth sound, interwoven with wanderings into other realms of musical spheres and influence. Using two guitarists, drums, bass and vocals and masses of effects pedals.

# CYCLORAMA

John Combe recounts the story of how we set up Cyclorama in his Get Your Kicks On The A456 book. But what I can't remember is whether hearing Dreamfish by Mixmaster Morris playing in a record shop in Soho is what convinced me and Sarah Blackband to start the night, or whether we'd been seeking out records because we'd already been going to Oscillate or Megatripolis.

Oscillate was a really busy club night in Birmingham run by Higher Intelligence Agency, who were making some really chilled electronic music that was danceable without resorting to four on the floor beats. Megatripolis was in London at the Heaven nightclub and had the same vibe as the greenfields in Glastonbury, with a musical policy verging towards the kind of new age hippy CDs you get in shops that sell crystals and dreamcatchers. I remember sitting in a circle one night learning to hand massage!

The other clubs that were similar were Whirl-y-gig at Shoreditch Town Hall that had parachutes and balloons as well as an abundance of Solar 250 lights with oil wheels and projections, and the harder-edged Megadog with their Fruit Salad Lightshow that we drooled over because they had Solar 575s! Bringing something this cutting edge to Kiddy seems a huge

risk in hindsight as provincial towns are not known for being at the forefront of new musical movements. But it worked.

The key to Cyclorama was that we were going to be super-chilled and that it took place in what I now know to be the adult version of a babies' sensory room!! We bought white artic cargo netting, an

old parachute, we painted old bedsheets with crazy dayglo UV images, made papier-mache fish with table tennis ball eyes that looked a bit like the cover of the Dreamfish record and started to amass a collection of old Solar 250s, which nobody really wanted at the time because oil wheels had gone out of fashion. We bought the Optikinetics cassettes which had better effects than the glass wheels, and even made one of our own from a cut up polythene bag that rotated slowly whilst a polarising filter rotated at a different speed. If you search "Solar 250 effects" on YouTube, you'll see the video from when I (regretfully) sold it on

SHIP OF FOOLS WERE A GREAT PROG / PSYCH BAND. THE ALBUM Close Your Eyes IS A MASTERPIECE

BANCO DE GAIA     PLANET DOG

Background image is a detail of a Scott Richard painting

eBay. Soundtracked by Dreamfish, of course!

It wasn't just me and Sarah. We roped friends in to help make the decor and props and we had a nice pool of DJs. Ben Willmott from the NME got involved which may or may not be how we got 'Club Of The Week' in the NME.

Our ambition with Cyclorama was huge. Not content with presenting acts like Banco de Gaia and Pentatonik at the Tavern, Ben organised regular nights in London at the Monarch and other places. We did a lot of chillout rooms for people

# VIBES GIG OF THE WEEK

**FRIDAY 7**
**CYCLORAMA POST-CHRISTMAS CHILL OUT**
Resident DJs Tim Bayley and Mega crank their turntables for a post-festive orgy of ambisonic soundscapes. The club mashes ambient noise with harder techno and eye-bending visuals from the Nebula posse.
Cyclorama at The Market Tavern, Kidderminster, Comberton Place (0562-752590), 7.30pm-midnight, £2.50.

PICTURE: DEREK RIDGERS

including one in Brixton at the old piano factory, at least one with Megadog, one with Oscillate in the Que Club, we did other provincial places such as Rugeley and, if memory serves me right, somewhere in Derby or Nottingham, maybe both. We presented Mike Paradinas' first ever live performance as U-Ziq. We did the chill out room for Andrew Weatherall at Lancaster Uni - when the sun came up we realised

the students were all dancing on the roof! We did a strange one with ROC, featuring Nirvana's agent Russell Warby, where all the A&R men wanted to know what time the band were on AFTER they'd

*Duncan Bickley's photo of a Cyclorama at the Tavern. White cargo netting on the ceiling and net curtain projections!*

just watched them! They didn't realise because the vocalist was hidden in the DJ booth behind net curtains that we were projecting onto, whilst the others sat on a sofa on the stage. I remember Bjork coming in one night for a look but she had her shopping with her so she didn't stick around!

As with many things you're reading about in this book, it wouldn't pass muster with the invention of modern day health and safety. Actually, thinking of it now, our UV lights sometimes shattered over the dancefloor if the bass wobbled them out! I think we could have kept it going but I have a feeling I started to get bored and felt like a decor hire business. Ben was living in London, our DJs started to drift or play harder music, Sarah went to uni and it just fizzled out. By contrast, Whirl-y-gig is still going strong, so if you want to revisit the vibe but with more upbeat world sounds, pay them a visit.

# ON GIG OF THE WEEK

**WEDNESDAY 2**
**ROC**
The Brixton-based scarypop collective, whose 'God Willing' single continues to enjoy Radio 1 airplay, make their live debut at the opening night of new ambient techno club, House Of Nuts.
The Monarch, Chalk Farm Road, Camden Town, London NW1, 8pm-1am (band play 10pm), £3 (£2 with flyer).

PICTURE: ANDY WILLSHER

*No idea why the NME called this House Of Nuts - it was Cyclorama!*

DJs - BEN WILLMOTT + OSCILLATE DJs

**cyclorama**

LIVE SET FROM

## HIGHER INTELLIGENCE AGENCY

THE MONARCH • CHALK FARM ROAD • CAMDEN

8pm - 1am : £3.50 (£2.50 with flyer)

**WED 04 MAY 94**

DETAILS 071 916 1049

NEAREST TUBES: CAMDEN OR CHALK FARM

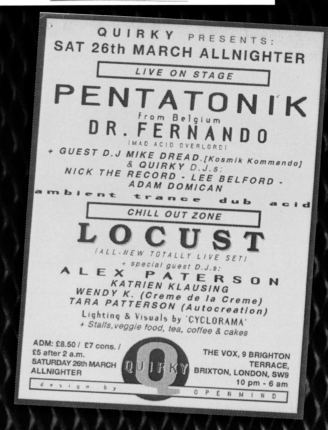

QUIRKY PRESENTS:
SAT 26th MARCH ALLNIGHTER

LIVE ON STAGE

# PENTATONIK
from Belgium
## DR. FERNANDO
(MAD ACID OVERLORD)

+ GUEST D.J MIKE DREAD.(Kosmik Kommando)
& QUIRKY D.J.S:
NICK THE RECORD - LEE BELFORD -
ADAM DOMICAN

ambient trance dub acid

CHILL OUT ZONE

# LOCUST
(ALL-NEW TOTALLY LIVE SET)

+ special guest D.J.s:
A L E X   P A T E R S O N
KATRIEN KLAUSING
WENDY K. (Creme de la Creme)
TARA PATTERSON (Autocreation)

Lighting & Visuals by 'CYCLORAMA'
+ Stalls, veggie food, tea, coffee & cakes

ADM: £8.50 / £7 cons. / £5 after 2 a.m.
SATURDAY 26th MARCH ALLNIGHTER

THE VOX, 9 BRIGHTON TERRACE,
BRIXTON, LONDON, SW9
10 pm - 6 am

design by OPENMIND

● **PENTATONIK**, **ROC** and **BANCO DE GAIA** are among the names headlining a number of nights organised by Midlands ambient techno promoters Oscillate and Cyclorama over the coming weeks.

Oscillate's fortnightly residency at Birmingham Bonds, which saw a rare DJ appearance from Orbital's Paul Hartnoll last weekend, plays host to Pentatonik (February 4), Exquisite Corpse (18) and Biosphere (March 4).

Cyclorama, the irregular club night at Kidderminster's Market Tavern, has Pentatonik (February 11), Banco De Gaia (25) and a Sound Information night with Space and Path (March 4).

The Cyclorama posse also stage evenings at London Camden Monarch with ROC tonight (February 2), Stone Oasis Bar with DJs Tim Bailey and Megga (19), London Camden Monarch with Pentatonik (March 2) and Rugely Red Rose Theatre with Ship Of Fools (11).

*NME*

## CYCLORAMA PRESENT...
### PENTATONIK

CYCLORAMA is the name of the exciting new Ambient Techno club based at the Tavern. It's run by a collective of people who all have an equal input. The venue is decorated beyond belief with white netting, drapes, parachutes and backdrops and an amazing psychedelic light show! As well as beer, you can buy cakes and hot drinks and then chill out on the cushions to watch cartoons on the big screen before getting down to it on the dance floor. There are no dress restrictions and the aim is to achieve a 'festival atmosphere'. The NME were so impressed, they gave the last event 'Gig of the Week' and are going to do a feature in the near future as one of the top 5 'post Megadog' clubs outside of London.

Tonights show will feature a live set from Sim Bowring who is better known as Pentatonik. He's had Top 20 Indie success but the live show is something else. Augmenting the visuals provided by CYCLORAMA with a freaky slide show, Sim also works with a drummer live to give his unique style of dance music that extra edge.

As well as resident CYCLORAMA DJ's Tim Bailey and Megga, sounds will also be provided by Ed Dickens who is Preston's top ambient DJ and has warmed up for the likes of Alex Patterson (The Orb) and MixMaster Morris. He promises underwater ambi-sonic vibes and minimalist techno from his set.

This whole scene is about to go massive with Birmingham's Oscillate Club packing 500 in each time and CYCLORAMA paving the way for Worcestershire. If you like Megadog and Whirl-Y-Gig, The Orb and Orbital, then this is for you.

Admission £3.50 Advance

*PRESS RELEASE*

# PSYCHICK WARRIORS OV GAIA
t o u r

**FRIDAY 30TH SEPTEMBER**
## MEGADOG
THE ROCKET N7
with LFO - SPOOKY - µ-ZIQ

**SATURDAY 1ST OCTOBER**
## CYCLORAMA
ISLE OF WIGHT KEATS

**THURSDAY 6TH OCTOBER**
## GLASGOW QMU

**FRIDAY 7TH OCTOBER**
## PURE
EDINBURGH VENUE

**SATURDAY 8TH OCTOBER**
## MEGADOG
MANCHESTER ACADEMY
with UNDERWORLD

SISTER SAVAGE

## MARKET TAVERN KIDDERMINSTER tel:0562 752590

| | | |
|---|---|---|
| Tuesday 14th Sept | CHUMBAWAMBA CREDIT TO THE NATION | £5.00 |
| Friday 17th Sept | Ambient night. DJ's Ben Willmott (NME) Ed Dickens (Bone) live set from... SHIP OF FOOLS | £2.50 |
| Monday 27th Sept | MEGA CITY FOUR + Skyscraper | £5.00 |
| Friday 1st Oct | Senser (to be confirmed) | £4.00 |
| Friday 8th Oct | CROPDUSTERS MADHALIBUT + Chuck (ex-Resque) | £3.00 |
| Thursday 14th Oct | F.M.B. + Youth Culture Killed My Dog + Joyland | £3.00 |
| Friday 29th Oct | The Tansads | £3.00 |
| Friday 19th Nov | Reggae night with PSYCHASTORM | £3.00 |

Coming soon.. The Sea · Citizen Fish · AOS3...
Also - Back to the Planet / Madhalibut / Poisoned Electick Head...
The Northwick, Worcester on Tuesday 7th September £5.00

last trains: B'ham 23.02 Worcs 00.01 one minute from the station
The prices listed are advance prices. It may be more expensive on the night.
advance tickets from: Market Tavern, Magpie (All shops)
Birmingham outlets: Tempest, Plastic Factory, Odeon (MC4 only)

## MARKET TAVERN KIDDERMINSTER tel:0562 752590

| | | |
|---|---|---|
| Tuesday 7th Dec | CARDIACS + Ship of Fools | £4.00 |
| Friday 10th Dec | CITIZEN FISH + AOS3 + The Gr'ups | £3.50 |
| Friday 17th Dec | The International BEAT CANCELLED | £5.00 |
| Saturday 18th Dec | The Stubble Brothers | £3.00 |
| Friday 24th Dec | The PALE KINGS + Hornblower | £2.50 |
| Monday 27th Dec | All-Dayer with... Funbug · Fever Dream · Sister Savage · Cooler Than Jesus · Melon · Kiwi Feedback · Another Fine Mess · Pale Kings · And special guests | 50p |
| New Years Eve | ALTERNATIVE DISCO | FREE |
| Friday 7th Jan | Post Christmas Chill-Out with... CYCLORAMA | £2.50 |
| Saturday 8th Jan | DUB MERGE + MADHALIBUT | £3.00 |
| Friday 28th Jan | BLYTH POWER + Funbug + Blobnut | £2.50 |

last trains: B'ham 23.02 Worcs 00.01 one minute from the station
The prices listed are advance prices. It may be more expensive on the night.
Advance Tickets: Tavern, Magpie (Kidd & Worcs), Stourbridge Records
Birmingham Outlets: Tempest, Plastic Factory
Or by post from 51 Lea St, Kidderminster, DY10 1SW (enclose a S.A.E.)

## MARKET TAVERN KIDDERMINSTER tel:0562 752590

| | | |
|---|---|---|
| Friday 17th Sept | Ambient night. DJ's Ben Willmott (NME) Ed Dickens (Bone) live set from... SHIP OF FOOLS | £2.50 |
| Friday 24th Sept | omnia opera Kidderminster's original Hawkwind / Ozrics style crusty band | £2.50 |
| Monday 27th Sept | MEGA CITY FOUR + Skyscraper | £5.00 |
| Friday 1st Sept | Wishplants + The Berts | £2.50 |
| Friday 8th Oct | CROPDUSTERS MADHALIBUT + Chuck (ex-Resque) | £3.00 |
| Thursday 14th Oct | F.M.B. + Youth Culture Killed My Dog + Joyland | £3.00 |
| Friday 29th Oct | The Tansads | £3.00 |
| Saturday 30th Oct | GIGOLO AUNTS + Scrash (From USA) | £3.00 |
| Friday 12th Nov | The Sea | £3.00 |
| Friday 19th Nov | Reggae night with PSYCHASTORM | |

last trains: B'ham 23.02 Worcs 00.01 one minute from the station
The prices listed are advance prices. It may be more expensive on the night.
advance tickets from: Market Tavern, Magpie (All shops)
Birmingham outlets: Tempest, Plastic Factory, Odeon (MC4 only)

## MARKET TAVERN KIDDERMINSTER tel:0562 752590

| | | |
|---|---|---|
| Tuesday 11th May | A few tickets left BUZZCOCKS + funbug | £5.00 |
| Friday 14th May | MIDWAY STILL & PANIC BEACH + Elizabeth Jane | £3.00 |
| Friday 21st May | Dr PHIBES and the House of Wax Equations + Tomorrow's Joy | £3.50 |
| Friday 28th May | THE LURKERS + Adorey | £3.00 |
| Friday 4th June | P.S. Hardcore ALLOY + Funbug + Tanglefoot Ex members of Cro-Mags, Articles of Faith, Uniform Choice, Dag Nasty | £3.00 |
| Friday 11th June | The Selecter + IMAGE105 (Ex-International Beat) + Mr Toad | £5.00 |
| Saturday 18th June | LEVITATION + RUMBLEFISH & melon | £3.50 |
| Saturday 3rd July | The Mavericks featuring Ex-Sex Pistol ... Glen Matlock | £3.50 |
| Friday 9th July | Sweet Jesus & emission | £3.00 |
| Saturday 14th August | All dayer - loads of bands Watch this space for details | free |

last trains: B'ham 23.02 Worcs 00.01 one minute from the station
The prices listed are advance prices. It may be more expensive on the night.
advance tickets from: Market Tavern, Sounds Around, Magpie (All shops)
Birmingham outlets: Tempest, Way Ahead, Plastic Factory, H.Q.

## MARKET TAVERN KIDDERMINSTER tel:0562 752590

| | | |
|---|---|---|
| Friday 29th Oct | The Tansads + MONEYGODS + Cantaloop | £3.00 |
| Saturday 30th Oct | GIGOLO AUNTS + SCRASH + Mile High Smile (From USA) | £3.00 |
| Friday 5th Nov | Bang Bang Machine | £3.00 |
| Friday 12th Nov | The Sea + Madhalibut + under a couch | £3.00 |
| Saturday 13th Nov | Ambient night... live set from NEW AGE RADIO Lots of cushions, lights, backdrops etc. | £2.50 |
| Friday 19th Nov | PSYCHASTORM + ye fungus | £3.00 |
| Friday 26th Nov | Avanti (New Age Folk) | £? |
| Tuesday 7th Dec | CARDIACS + Ship of Fools | £4.00 |
| Friday 10th Dec | Citizen Fish + AOS3 + The Gr'ups (from America) | £3.50 |

American Doors Show - Sunday 28th November £5.00
The International Beat - Friday 17th December £5.00

last trains: B'ham 23.02 Worcs 00.01 one minute from the station
The prices listed are advance prices. It may be more expensive on the night.
advance tickets from: Market Tavern, Boars Head, Magpie (All shops)
Birmingham outlets: Tempest, Plastic Factory.

1993 FLYERS & ADS

## MARKET TAVERN KIDDERMINSTER tel:0562 752590

| | | |
|---|---|---|
| Monday 27th Sept | MEGA CITY FOUR + Joyce McKinney Experience | £5.00 |
| Friday 8th Oct | CROPDUSTERS MADHALIBUT + Chuck (ex-Resque) | £3.00 |
| Friday 15th Oct | note new date... F.M.B. + ANNA + JOYLAND | £3.00 |
| Friday 22nd Oct | fretblanket + Family GoTown + Youth Culture Killed My Dog | £3.00 |
| Friday 29th Oct | The Tansads + MONEYGODS + Cantaloop | £3.00 |
| Saturday 30th Oct | GIGOLO AUNTS + SCRASH + Mile High Smile (From U.S.A.) | £3.00 |
| Friday 5th Nov | Bang Bang Machine + very special guests | |
| Friday 12th Nov | The Sea | |
| Friday 19th Nov | Reggae night with PSYCHASTORM | £3.00 |
| Friday 10th Dec | Citizen Fish + AOS3 + Ancient Ones | £3.50 |

last trains: B'ham 23.02 Worcs 00.01 one minute from the station
The prices listed are advance prices. It may be more expensive on the night.
advance tickets from: Market Tavern, Magpie (All shops)
Birmingham outlets: Tempest, Plastic Factory, Odeon (MC4 only)

## MARKET TAVERN KIDDERMINSTER tel:0562 752590

| | | |
|---|---|---|
| Friday 4th June | U.S. Hardcore ALLOY + Funbug + Tanglefoot Ex members of Cro-Mags, Articles of Faith, Uniform Choice, Dag Nasty | £3.00 |
| Friday 11th June | The Selecter + IMAGE105 (Ex- International Beat) + Mr Toad | £5.00 |
| Friday 18th June | LEVITATION CANCELLED + RUI Refunds from point of purchase | £3.50 |
| Saturday 3rd July | The Mavericks featuring Ex-Sex Pistol ... Glen Matlock | £3.50 |
| Friday 9th July | Sweet Jesus & emission | £3.00 |

### FREE All-Dayer SATURDAY 14TH AUGUST 1993
2 stages, food, jugglers, uni-cyclists, face painting...
Bands confirmed so far:- Wishplants, Family Go Town, Panic Beach, Joyce McKinney Experience, Funbug, Magic, Melon, Madhalibut, Pale Kings, Bitter Tears, Scrash.
More big names to be announced soon!

last trains: B'ham 23.02 Worcs 00.01 one minute from the station
The prices listed are advance prices. It may be more expensive on the night.
advance tickets from: Market Tavern, Sounds Around, Magpie (All shops)
Birmingham outlets: Tempest, Way Ahead, Plastic Factory.

TRIBUTE TO NOTHING

# Gigolo Aunts + Scrash / Mile High Smile

Sat 30th Oct 1993

David Rose "Kidderminster?? Well, Clive held a quiz night (which I won) which clashed with the more sensible Bristol date in this potential-loaded new band's tour, so in return, we enjoyed a 1 3/4 hour cross country journey to a dilapidated prefab community centre type building, with a dingy black hall, which actually was the essence of rock'n'roll! Things boded well, especially as the beer was also cheap!

Unfortunately, things didn't start off well musically with the well named, but poor, Mile High Smile, a clumsy middle-aged Ned's Atomic Dustbin rip-off. Better followed, as the dynamic Scrash got the locals' feet tapping. A souped-up version of EMF, with a young vocalist with an acerbic attitude, they certainly warmed the cockles with some incisive rhythms and guitar attack. Their last gig, apparently - but as I told the vocalist afterwards, he's a cocky little bugger who should stick with it, as you never know...

Following a splendid harmonic Reading Festival set earlier this year, the Gigolo Aunts really announced themselves to me with their 'Full On Bloom' CD, which featured a brilliant song 'Walk Among Us'. Not only fantastically anthemic and soaring in its' own right, this number also featured a lyrical homage to my all-time favourite band, fellow Bostonians Big Dipper. So they'd already endeared themselves to me, but upon meeting guitarist Phil Hurley prior to their set,

his greeting of, "so you're the guy who wrote us about the Dipper - and you've got a Dipper shirt on! Wow! Put it there, buddy!" only served to elevate them more!

So, expectation levels were high as the boys took the stage to 'Cope', the fantastic opener from their 'Flippin' Out' LP, and Clive and I were transformed into whirling dervishes as their stunning, whirling, exhilarating, effervescent pure pop belted out. Every one a winner, each song loaded with hooks big enough to land a blue whale with, but with the aforementioned 'Walk Among Us' an outstanding jewel in the set. Brilliant, brilliant stuff, but more amazing was to come with the encore. "This one's for a friend of ours," was the introduction of their version of Big Dipper's 'Mr. Woods'!! This was then followed by an amphetamine-fast cover of The Smiths' 'Ask', climaxing a wonderfully spent hour.

Chatted for ages afterwards with the band, with vocalist Dave Gibbs videotaping Clive and I singing 'Serious Drugs', and also promising to send me a copy of Big Dipper's last album 'Slam'! Smiles and handshakes all around upon departing, and now I can't wait for my next Gigolo Aunts gig! An astonishing night!"

This review originally appeared on https://gigbook.blogspot.com/2010/11/253-gigolo-aunts-scrash-mile-high-smile.html. Thanks to David for allowing us to use it.

## American coup for the Tavern

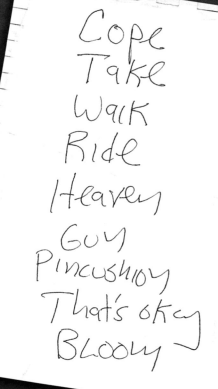

THE Market Tavern claims another musical scalp with the arrival of America's Gigolo Aunts.

They play on there Saturday night, which will be the only Midlands date of their time in the UK.

Playing in a similar vein to Scottish bands such as Teenage Fanclub and BMX Bandits, Gigolo Aunts were last in this country in August, when they played the main stage at the Reading Festival.

They come on the recommendation of fellow Transatlantic Tavernites Redd Kross.

Support comes from Scrash and Mile High Smile of Stourbridge, admission is £3.

Preceding them come The Tansads, who return to the Tavern tomorrow night.

They were last here supporting Radiohead in February and since then have played any festival that would have them, including the Phoenix and nearly all of the Heineken gatherings.

They play a brand of urban folk along the lines of The Levellers and The Pogues, which in their native Wigan pulls in audiences in excess of 1,000 people.

A new single called Camelot was due out Monday on the Musidisc label, the same as The Levellers before they made it.

Support comes from The Moneygods and Cantaloop, house band at Mirage's in Kidderminster and making their Tavern debut. Admission is £3.

■ Gigolo Aunts, playing their only Midlands date at the Market Tavern on Saturday.

Cope
Take
Walk
Ride
Heaven
Guy
Pincushion
That's okay
Bloom

KIDDY SET LIST

# TAVERN MEMORIES

Adam Veevers "I remember seeing Funbug play there as I recall it was on Jase's 21st birthday. They were playing outside. A brilliant gig as I remember it and poignant for me as at the time. I think I'd only just met Tez who shortly afterwards asked me to join him and his brother Kev to form Skimmer. During the few years following we played at the Market Tavern supporting Dr Bison and Bracket. I also remember seeing Mega City 4 and UK Subs there. Probably many other bands too but can't remember. I certainly went there a lot during that time... A brilliant but odd venue as it was right next to the cattle market and I remember having to trudge through cow shit once to get to the toilets!!"

Mike Moore (DJ) "I remember constantly being asked to play the bloody Levellers and I never did."

Dave Morgan "I remember going to get the tank camouflage in Malvern with Badgeman for the first official Tavern backdrop. Bloody thing weighed a ton and stunk of oil. It took us ages to hang it up as well! Think we used tie wraps and duct tape from my work van!"

Tom Watson (Politician / Chair of UK Music) "The Market Tavern? I could tell you some stories." (He didn't - AW)

David Rann "I drove over from Dudley quite a bit. The first time was to see The Groundhogs (my mate was a huge fan) but I seem to remember they cancelled and maybe 'Ice Cold In Alex' were on instead? I loved them so much, I came over to see them the next few times they played there.
The singer was a cool, Robert Palmer-ish chap and the two female backing singers were worth the ticket price alone. It was a cracking little venue."

Lucy Clark "I remember the long corridor to the toilets, stomping down there in my Doc Martin's!"

Paul Chance "The best thing about the Tavern was no one knew you were smoking weed because of the overwhelming smell of cow shit."

Garry Plumley "Played there with Honey Turtles... nice rider food, small crowd... and there was the smell from cattle pens near the toilets"

David McCaskill Elliott (Spike) "I played there two or three times, the one time we were supporting Machine Head, an American group that was passing through, the other times I don't remember the lineup." (Badgeman - It was Crazyhead and they were from Leicester!)

Lee Biggs (Dive / Love Buzz) "I loved the whole drinking on the train, waiting outside, chatting up convent girls vibe. Moody Stan, Satan's midget love child. Dready Jon Blinker, the stench of animal shite and a fantastic UV light on the door that showed every little blemish. Halcyon days."

Woz "Had some great times there with my mate John, first gig was going to be either Dodgy or Radiohead and we went for Dodgy as we had just bought their debut single from Sounds Around the week before."

The Head Barman "I only got told off once whilst I was working. Andy pulled me to one side and asked me if I could do slightly less acid when the pub was really busy!"

Darren Watkins "Great memories of gigs inc Cardiacs, Pale Kings and a few others but being a young lad my memories have faded... there was chaos in the venue... sweat... smiles... such a good vibe. Then outside to sit in the doorways or steps to calm down...
I remember the sadness of when it closed... the feeling of loss to an outlet of our youth... The venue from the outside always looked to be well run and well received by bands and fans... Warm fond memories remain."

Ben Schrieber "I remember someone asking me where the toilets were... just down there mate, if you see cows you've gone too far!"

Joseph Stokes (Delicious Monster / Tolerance Manoeuvre / Scow) "I was there. It had a wobbly concrete roof. A sarcophagus. We were more popular outside of the Midlands so I suppose we played to one man and his dog."

# THE SIMKINS
# PARTNERSHIP
## SOLICITORS

45-51 Whitfield Street, London W1P 5RJ
Telephone 071-631 1050
Fax 071-436 2744
DX No. 7 London Chancery Lane

The Kidderminster Market Tavern
Comberton Hill
Comberton Place
Kidderminster
DY10 1QH

**Your Reference**

**Direct Line**
071 331-2298

**Our Reference**
CWA/des

**Date**
11 November 1993

Dear Sirs

## THE AUSTRALIAN DOORS SHOW

We act for Brandon Saul Management Pty Ltd, an Australian limited company ("the company"), and Steve Griffiths, Steve Lonti, Carston Holroyd and Neil Rankin who perform as and are professionally known as The Australian Doors Show.

The Australian Doors Show have toured extensively in this country during the last three years and have built up a considerable reputation and following as a result.

For the last two years The Australian Doors Show has been promoted by reference to promotional material consisting of (from top to bottom) the following elements:-

(i)     a an image of Jim Morrison;
(ii)    the words "the australian" set in lower case type on either side of the upright of the D of "doors";
(iii)   the word "doors" set in very bold lower case type;
(iv)    the word "show" set again in lower case but in a different type face between two horizontal rectangles which serve to underline the word "doors".

This combination of images, distinctive lettering and artwork ("the logo") constitutes an artistic work within the meaning of section 4(i) Copyright Designs and Patents Act 1988. The copyright in question is owned by the company.

It has recently come to the attention of the company and The Australian Doors Show that another band performing as and professionally known as "The American Doors Show" are touring the United Kingdom and have been promoting proposed gigs at Rugeley Red Rose Theatre on 27th November and Kidderminster Market Tavern on 28th November with publicity material which reproduces the logo devised for The Australian Doors Show and owned by the

Charles Artley, Nigel Bennett, Ian W Burlingham, David Campbell, Tim Curtis, Cyrus Fatemi, David T Franks, Dominic Free, Lee A Goldsmith, Lawrence Harrison, Simon Long, Adrian Nelson, Anthony J Quick, Sara Robinson, Robert C Rutteman, Michael Simkins, Charles Swan, Richard H E Taylor, Julian M Turton, Paul Walker.
Associates: Oliver Fryer, Susan O'Mahony, Nick Rann, Sarah C Rees, Teresa Rogers, Howard Stacey.
Consultant: Michael Mellersh

Regulated by The Law Society in the conduct of investment business.

the american doors show 1993

**Sat 27th Nov - RUGELEY RED ROSE THEATRE** (0889 582390)
Tickets: Killer Sounds. Tudor Tunes (Lichfield). Bridge Records (Walsall)
A&S (Cannock). Lotus Records (Stafford)

**Sun 28th Nov - KIDDERMINSTER MARKET TAVERN** (0562 752590)
Tickets: Market Tavern. Boars Head. Magpie. Tempest. Plastic Factory
**Tickets for both shows £5.00**

Mark Badgeman "The Australian Doors were playing big venues so when I was approached about doing a band called The American Doors, I had an idea of how to sell it. My plan was simple - take the Australian Doors advertising and switch it so it said American Doors. Then I took those flyers up to the Wulfrun Hall and leafletted the Australian Doors audience on the way out!!

It didn't take long to get a cease and desist from the Australian Doors' solicitors. I took that straight down to the Shuttle and got acres of coverage. As a result, we sold 158 tickets and made a good profit. There's a beautiful irony when a tribute band complains they've been ripped off. Ha!"

**THE RETURN OF THE MARKET TAVERN ·ALL-DAYER·**

30th MAY · 30th MAY · 30th MAY · 30th MAY

TRIBUTE TO NOTHING
MILO FADITE
MILE HIGH SMILE
COCKLEPICKERS
FUN BUG
SLOTH
MELON
PALE KINGS
FEVER DREAM
MAD CARSON
ORANGE ALERT

CYCLORAMA CAFE
VEGGIE FOOD & AMBIENT SOUNDSCAPES

ONLY 50p

PLUS INDIE DISCO

FIRST BAND 3pm

29th DEC · 29th DEC · 29th DEC · 29th DEC

MARKET ·····TAVERN·····
XMAS 95 ALL-DAYER
ONLY 50p

HALF TERM
FRETBLANKET
MAD CARSON
SOLO 70
INFO STALLS
SPECIAL GUEST DJs
JACKPOT
BUMPER
STARTS AT 4pm
ANOTHER FINE MESS
SISTER SAVAGE
LOVE BUZZ (NIRVANA TRIBUTE)

POUND A PINT

SAT 29 JULY · SAT 29 JULY · SAT 29 JULY · SAT 29 JULY

**THE RE-BIRTH OF A LEGEND ALL DAYER**

BANG BANG MACHINE
TRIBUTE TO NOTHING
MAD CARSON
LAXTON'S SUPERB
HALF TERM
SOLO 70
TORN BLOODY POETRY
GROUPIE

ALL FOR £1

IN ASSOCIATION WITH ACTIV X FM
COME ALONG & SIGN THE CHARTER

THE FUN STARTS AT 4pm

AT THE MARKET TAVERN
COMBERTON PLACE, KIDDERMINSTER
TEL: 01562 825868

27th DEC · 27th DEC · 27th DEC · 27th DEC

**The MARKET TAVERN'S CHRISTMAS ALL-DAYER**

MELON
FUNBUG
SISTER SAVAGE AND THE BUGGERED NUNS
FEVER DREAM
PALE KINGS
ANOTHER FINE MESS
COOLER THAN JESUS
KIWI FEEDBACK

CYCLORAMA CAFE
VEGETARIAN FOOD & AMBIENT SOUNDSCAPES

DOORS OPEN 5.00PM

PLUS INDIE DISCO

ONLY 50p

·WIN· FREE BEER

# ALL-DAYERS

If you ask anyone now what they remember about the Tavern, there's a fair chance they'll say the all-dayers. It started with the Kidderminster Free Festival in 1993 and I followed that up with a Christmas all-dayer that year. The idea was to do them on holidays such as Easter or Christmas so that fewer people were likely to be at work or college. I kept the ethos of the original one by never allocating a headliner and tried to spread the big hitters throughout the day to ensure we always opened with a decent crowd. Even Danbert from Chumbawamba played ball and went on at 3pm!

Traci Templer "OMGoodness...Orange Alert...*sigh*...I know my loyalties were always tested whenever these played with the Pale Kings...They just had such a great '60s Garage sound though..."

Andrew Wolfman "Laxton's Superb were a rare occurrence of rotten fruit being lobbed at an audience, not the other way around."

Sarah Fawsitt "I particularly loved the 'mother of all Christmas parties one'."

## Easter bonanza

FORGET your chocolate eggs and get yourself out to an all-day pop festival in Kidderminster if you want an Easter with a difference.

Eight bands are lining up for the show at The Market Tavern on Monday with fast-rising county group Jackpot head-lining the show.

Also on the bill is indie band Burst and heavy metal monsters Fibrestream, who are both from Stoke.

Completing the line-up are Wolverhampton bands Frisbee and Roseville, Cordial from Birmingham and Kidderminster bands New Artic Set and Intense.

For tickets and more information phone Mark

Dan Brown "My overriding memory is playing there, Christmas All Dayer, Dec 95. I remember it clearly as they had closed the A449 as they found the body of a missing French women in a layby and we had to detour. I was the drummer in a band called Lovelier at the time, and think we went on 1st... there were probably 15 people there... still can't work out if they clapped quietly or didn't clap at all! Anyway, it was insane playing on the same stage as some huge bands of the time and I treasure the memories fondly."

Lucinda Jayne Allen "Market Tavern all dayers. A happy distant memory."

Baron Webb "One memory that stands out was meeting a beautiful albino girl outside on an all dayer, SMASH and Tribute To Nothing playing."

Lee Wood "I remember an all dayer. Tribute To Nothing blew everyone away as they were just kids. FMB thought they were rockstars but really weren't."

### EASTER ALL-DAYER
#### Monday 8th April 1996
I've come to see
## JACKPOT
+ nine other totally cool bands for £2.00 starting at 3pm
## MARKET TAVERN
### KIDDERMINSTER

## The All-Dayers:
### Mon 27th Dec 1993
### Mon 30th May 1994
### Sat 29th Jul 1995
### Fri 29 Dec 1995
### Mon 8th Apr 1996
### Sat 13th Jul 1996

Mark Badgeman "I used to like Cooler Than Jesus. Simon White later joined Brit-poppers Menswear. After I'd lost touch with him, I found out he's my distant cousin. What's the chances?!"

# PRESS RELEASE

The Market Tavern in Kidderminster goes back to it's Indie / Alternative roots starting on May 30th, with a Bank Holiday all-dayer featuring the cream of local talent. There will be live bands in the main room, a Cyclorama ambient cafe and for the first time since the take-over, the front bar will be in operation.

The theme of the event is awareness of the forthcoming Criminal Justice Bill and what you can do to show your opposition to it. If the bill becomes law, you will become a criminal by merely attending an event such as last year's legendary Kidderminster Free Festival. The bill also criminalises the homeless by making squatting illegal and abolishes the ancient right to remain silent when arrested. Other 'goodies' contained in the bill include the non-bail detention of 10 - 13 year olds, electronic tagging and the re-introduction of prison ships. It is the first piece of legislation to ever outlaw a lifestyle by recinding the councils duty to provide sites for travelling people. Amongst the groups affected by these wide ranging new measures are New Age Travellers, environmental protesters, the Caravan Club, Hunt Saboteurs, Shelter and the Ramblers Association!

A huge noticeboard will carry information on the bill and explanatory leaflets will be handed out to everyone attending.

On the music side, there will be no headliners as such, to ensure quality entertainment across the day. The running order will be displayed inside the venue.

## A LOWDOWN ON THE BANDS

### TRIBUTE TO NOTHING
Just confirmed for the Phoenix Festival, these young punksters from Worcester have made the Tavern their adopted hometown gig. Singer Sam was still just 13 years old at the last count - and the eldest is 17! They're all brothers and have been together for a couple of years. Their big break came when they supported the Neds in Gloucester and since then they have released two singles on the Kinglake label. They've also just recorded a John Peel session so catch them while you can.

### MILO FADITE
A new band from Kidderminster playing their first live gig even though they already have a single ready to be released by Revolver.

### MILE HIGH SMILE
Hot new Stourbridge contenders, tagged by some as the new Mega City Four. (As if there's any need for that!)

### MELON
Another Kidderminster band with a record on the blocks, featuring live favourites 'August' and 'Hit The Road To Hard Brake', due to be released in the very near future. Influenced by the beat poets of the sixties, their sound clocks in somewhere between Julian Cope and The Bunnymen.

### PALE KINGS
After being tipped to play the ill-fated Foley Park festival last summer, the band have been locked away in the rehearsal studio writing new material. Expect an even bigger rock sound from this big local band.

### FEVER DREAM
Completing the Kidderminster contingent, these local indie rockers also have an EP on the cards. It's been picking up airplay on Radio Wyvern and has been a hit with the local paper.

### MAD CARSON
Crazy indie sounds from this Wolverhampton four-piece, playing their first Tavern gig.

### ORANGE ALERT
Sixties garage grooves and the ghost of the Stooges kept alive by this Stourbridge based outfit. The band are also politically active and will no doubt be speaking out on the injustices of the proposed Criminal Justice Bill.

### SLOTH
Hailing from Redditch, these noise merchants were a big hit at last years Malvern Fringe festival. Who said grunge was dead?

### FUNBUG
Another Redditch band, these local heroes have finally found some big name management and have a new album and video in the pipeline. Their poppy punk has won them much acclaim locally, and their current single on cult label 'Lookout' has been selling steadily. There has even been talks of a compilation CD with all their previous singles lumped together with the last album. But in the meantime they're one of the most exciting live bands on the circuit, so don't miss them.

### COCKLEPICKERS
Two female buskers, Lindsay and Beff who can often be seen in the town centre bring their show to the Tavern for the first time

## CYCLORAMA

The ambient-techno crew will be providing the decor and sounds for the veggie cafe before going to Birmingham on the 3rd to do the chill-out room for the Big Oscillate all-nighter. Re-Hab from Brum will be playing live alongside the regular CYCLORAMA DJs. Admission for this fantastic event is a mere 50p on the door and the fun starts at 3pm

# Monday 30th May
## Market Tavern
Comberton Place, Kidderminster
tel: 0562 752590

## The J.S.A. Awareness Day

# CHUMBAWAMBA'S DANBERT NOBACON
(Rare solo show starting at 3pm)

# SPIDER SIMPSON
(Featuring ex-members of Neds Atomic Dustbin & Babylon Zoo)

# AURA
(Live tribal-trancey-techno. Supported Dreadzone, Loop Guru etc.)

# OTO & FACEACHE & DAN

Look out for....

# SPECIAL GUEST DJs

Also DJing...

## FRAGI • THE MONKEY BROTHERS

# OUTSIDE SOUND SYSTEM
(Depending on the weather)

## INFO STALLS • FOOD • CHEAP BEER
PUPPET SHOW • CONTEMPORARY DANCE DISPLAY • JUGGLING
UNICYCLING • TRIBAL FACE PAINTING • DRUMMING

# SATURDAY 13TH JULY
# MARKET TAVERN, KIDDERMINSTER
SPECIAL ADVANCE TICKETS ONLY £1.00 • DOORS OPEN AT 2PM

---

MY FIRST EXPOSURE TO POLITICS CAME THROUGH MUSIC. AS SPRINGSTEEN SAID, WE LEARNT MORE FROM A 3 MINUTE RECORD THAN WE EVER LEARNED AT SCHOOL. GROWING UP AT THE TAIL END OF THE PUNK DAYS MEANT IT WENT HAND IN HAND. I USED TO PHOTOCOPY SchNEWS, A DIRECT ACTION NEWSLETTER WITH A USEFUL GUIDE TO FREE FESTIVALS AND LEAVE THEM ON THE DOOR AT THE GIGS. WHEN I HAD A CHANCE TO SPREAD THE WORD, I WENT FOR IT. THE JSA DAY WAS THE MOST POLITICAL OF THE EVENTS AND I THINK IT WAS THIS ONE THAT WAS COMBINED WITH THE RECLAIM THE STREETS ROAD CLOSURE, ALBEIT OF A ROAD THAT ONLY WENT TO THE MARKET WHICH WAS SHUT ANYWAY. THE ALL-DAYERS HAD A PROPER FESTIVAL ATMOSPHERE. I LOVED THEM! X

---

# INTRODUCING THE BANDS

**DANBERT NOBACON**
Chumbawamba's lead singer Danbert Nobacon needs no introduction to those who remember the Tavern's finest hour. After two sold-out gigs they returned with Credit To The Nation in tow on the back of the 'Enough Is Enough' single and promptly sold the venue out in five minutes! Around 200 people crowded around the stairs outside and peered through the door and we turned the jukebox off in the bar and opened the dividing door so people could see. From there they went on to sell out the 1000 capacity Northwich in Worcester! With the sustained success of Chumbawamba, Danbert has very little time to persue his solo career - he has two gigs this year and they're both today, which is why he's on first.

**OTO**
Oto are Kidderminster's finest purveyors of soul - jazz - funk fusion.

**PAZ**
The lead singer of local band Jackpot, Paz is going to do an acoustic set, possibly drawing on the experience he gained whilst jamming with Evan Dando in Australia a couple of years ago.

**FACEACHE**
Kidderminster and Worcester based hard-edged indie-rock.

**OBLIVIOUS PIG**
Acoustic drug induced trance music featuring the extraordinary vocal talents of lead singer Dan.

**SPIDER SIMPSON**
The first of the new projects from the ex-members of Neds Atomic Dustbin to see the light is Spider Simpson featuring Dan, and Floyd who stood in for Rat on the last American tour. So far they have supported Spacehog and done a few low-key shows around the Midlands. They've also got a guitarist who used to be in Babylon Zoo!

**AURA**
Live trancey-techno from London who have supported Dreadzone amongst others. Their first release was a big underground hit in Croatia! The debut album 'Oranges Are Blue' is due out at the end of the month and they have collaborations with Greg Hunter (The Orb and System 7) and Pentatonik under way.

## WHATS ON AT THE TAVERN

| MONDAYS | TUESDAYS | THURSDAYS | LIVE BANDS |
|---|---|---|---|
| **DJ FRAGI** | **STUDENT NIGHT** | **MONKEY BROS** | **WEDDING PRESENT** (tbc) |
| AMBIENT DUB • TECHNO | INDIE • ALTERNATIVE | JUNGLE • HIP-HOP | **STEREOLAB** (tbc) |
| **FREE** | **FREE** | **FREE** | **ASTRALASIA** Friday 25th October |

---

# RUNNING ORDER

## INSIDE

| | |
|---|---|
| 2.00 - 3.00 | DJ FRAGI |
| 3.00 - 3.45 | DANBERT NOBACON |
| 3.45 - 4.00 | PUPPET SHOW |
| 4.00 - 4.30 | DJ VICKI |
| 4.30 - 5.15 | OTO |
| 5.20 - 5.40 | PAZ |
| 5.40 - 6.00 | DJ LAMP |
| 6.00 - 6.30 | FACEACHE |
| 6.30 - 7.00 | DJ LAMP |
| 7.00 - 7.30 | OBLIVIOUS PIG |
| 7.30 - 8.15 | DJ LAMP |
| 8.15 - 9.00 | SPIDER SIMPSON |
| 9.00 - 10.00 | GUEST DJ |
| 10.00 - 11.00 | AURA |

## OUTSIDE

The Monkey Brothers Sound System
+ guest DJs
Drumming and Didg workouts

(Just make your own entertainment like the old days)

# MARKET TAVERN
## KIDDERMINSTER
### tel: 0562 752590

| | | |
|---|---|---|
| Friday 28th Jan | **BLYTH POWER** + Funbug + Blobnut | £2.50 |
| Friday 4th Feb | **MIDWAY STILL** + **THE BERTS** + **GENIUS FREAK** | £3.00 |
| Friday 11th Feb | *CYCLORAMA* presents... **PENTATONIK** | £3.50 |
| Friday 18th Feb | **S*M*A*S*H** + Casino + Tribute to Nothing | £3.00 |
| Sunday 20th Feb | **DOPPELGANGERS** THE OFFICIAL U2 TRIBUTE BAND | £5.00 |
| Friday 25th Feb | *CYCLORAMA* presents... **BANCO DE GAIA** | £3.50 |
| Friday 4th Mar | *CYCLORAMA* presents... A Sound Information Night with **SPACE + PATH** | £2.50 |
| Friday 25th Mar | **BLESSED ETHEL** PLUS VERY SPECIAL GUESTS!!! | £3.50 |
| Coming soon ? | **PANIXSPHERE** | |
| Coming soon ? | **HIGHER INTELLIGENCE AGENCY** | |

**last trains: B'ham 23.02 Worcs 00.01**
one minute from the station

*The prices listed are advance prices. It may be more expensive on the night.*
**Advance Tickets:** Tavern, Magpie (Kidd & Worcs), Stourbridge Records
**Birmingham Outlets:** Tempest, Plastic Factory
Or by post from The Market Tavern, Kidderminster, Worcs (enclose a S.A.E.)

# Blyth Power

Fri 28th Jan 1994
w/ Funbug & Blobnut
Sat 18th Jun 1994
Fri 25th Aug 1995
w/ Manifest & Downward Thing
Fri 9th Feb 1996
w/ Funbug & Boing

Joseph Porter (Blyth Power) "I have the warmest recollections of The Market Tavern - a great venue and always a pleasure for me due to the proximity of Kidderminster station and the Severn Valley Railway. I was always wanting to finish the soundcheck as soon as possible and get off to the railway. Happiest memories are of the former Central Trains class 150 sets, which I was always keen to pick up when in the West Midlands. That and Funbug, who we played with on one occasion, and one of whose stickers 'Keeping Live Music Shit' is still on my bass drum case. Great band and great people as I recall..."

Mark Badgeman "The design of this book was inspired by the iconic typewriter cut n paste page layout of the Kill Your Pet Puppy fanzine, an early 80s anarcho publication (if I lent you my copies and you still have them, I'd like them back!). Their world encompassed bands like The Mob and Blood & Roses, the Better Badges shop and the All The Madmen record label. When The Mob split, Joseph and Curtis joined with Neil from Faction to form Blyth Power.

They recorded a cassette in the basement of 96 Brougham Road in Hackney, a squatted street with an old bus station at the end, where the peace convoy parked their vehicles. Rob Challice from Faction released the tape on his cassette label, 96 Tapes. I still have my original copy and the accompanying train engineer's manual lyric booklet. Rob later ran All The Madmen records and is now a highly respected booking agent for acts such as Billy Bragg and Ezra Furman.

I first saw Blyth Power live in 1985 at Peacocks in Birmingham. For me, that was their classic line-up, although precious little memory of that gig remains. I bought all their records when they started releasing vinyl and saw them as often as I could. As far as I'm aware, there is not another band with the lyrical dexterity to shoehorn Shakespeare, cricket, British history and trainspotting into a song and deliver it on the back of joyous folk-influenced punk rock singalongs.

When I had the chance to book them, I was more than happy to overlook the fact they weren't a big draw by the mid-nineties. I mean, what's the point of putting bands on for a living if you can't book one of your favourites? I'd bolster the bill with local bands and push the shows as hard as I could, highlighting things like the fiddle player from the Wonder Stuff used to be in the band, although things like that are pretty tenuous and don't tend to translate into sales.

It'd be entirely remiss of me at this point to not implore you once more to go and seek out Blyth Power. The most glorious of their output is the 'Do The One About The Horse' video on YouTube. Then you can buy all their back catalogue, although '10 Years Inside The Horse', which is essentially the greatest hits, is nothing to do with the band so best to start with any of the first five albums. The barbershop quintet's expenses cannot be defrayed!"

150275

# S*M*A*S*H +
## Tribute To Nothing & Catalyst

## Fri 18th Feb 1994

The music press created a scene around this band which they dubbed The New Wave Of New Wave and lumped in These Animal Men and Compulsion. S*M*A*S*H were closer to punk than new wave and it was a good booking for the Tavern as it was busy and the band were on Top Of The Pops the following month. The bassist, Salv, was back at the Tavern a couple of years later playing with Carter USM on their ill-fated 3rd gig.

Roland Link "I've seen thousands of bands, but only a handful at what I consider the perfect moment in their careers. The Wonder Stuff throughout '88 springs to mind. Another one is S*M*A*S*H in the early '90s. For me, the Kiddy Market Tavern was the perfect venue to catch them at what I consider their furious, glorious peak. Ram-packed and then some, the place was blisteringly hot and the audience was way past rabid in its anticipation. The band hit the stage and performed with righteous fury. They looked the business, they commented on important issues and they had the hooks, melodies and choruses. Perfect."

Katie Wilson "We were so grateful for the Market Tavern, as there was really nowhere else to see live indie music in the Worcestershire area. I think the first time I went was for the Kidderminster Free Festival when I was 16. We were all over the moon that we could get served in there and I think Diamond White was our main tipple. We would have probably pre-loaded on 20/20, and I have mental images of a friend of mine lying on the floor refusing to get up when someone's parents arrived to collect us.

I remember there always being straw on the floor from the cattle market and sometimes some smells you wouldn't normally associate with a music venue. It was really the first place where, as countryside teenagers, we finally got to taste the world of Melody Maker and the NME, very exciting. We also saw FMB, Fretblanket, Bang Bang Machine and countless others, but I remember being insanely excited about S*M*A*S*H. I bought a t-shirt, and the bassist, Salv, gave me his blood-flecked plectrum."

THE NEW WAVE OF NEW WAVE...
# S*M*A*S*H
## + TRIBUTE TO NOTHING
### + CATALYST (EX JERK FRENZY)
# FRIDAY 18TH FEBRUARY
# MARKET TAVERN
## KIDDERMINSTER
£3.00 Advance                    7.30 - 11.00

# ANDY PRICE LEAVES

In February of 1994, 18 months after the council first tried to evict Andy Price, the Tavern went bankrupt and Andy moved to the Boars Head. We ran the gigs for another 6 weeks before Andy sold the Tavern to David Cox, who somehow managed to quickly book a solid run of local bands such as Ballroom Glitz, Fred Zeppelin and the Red Lemon Electric Blues Band.

Unfortunately, that was doomed to fail as those bands were a tough sell at the Tavern, probably because the pub still had a reputation for being a bit rough and wasn't the sort of place their fans would voluntarily go to. I started promoting at The Stage in Worcester, a venue owned by the Jolly Roger brewery, so it was of little concern to me.

As an interesting aside, I used to work for Brian and Val from Ballroom Glitz. They had a small printing company inside Burgage Lodge on the Franche Road and I ran their sole printing press, which was in an outbuilding. I think I lasted about three months but leaving that job coincided with my avowed intention to work in the music industry. I just hadn't figured out how I was going to do it when I walked out of their door!

I don't remember but I must've done a deal with David to put some gigs on as I did a May bank holiday all-dayer and headline gigs for Blyth Power, Compulsion and The Tansads. Then it got boarded up and was empty until Jolly Roger took it over in the summer of 1995. We reopened with an all-dayer called 'Rebirth Of A Legend' and I booked some great bands for it such as Bang Bang Machine and Robert from Birdland's new band, Torn Bloody Poetry.

Andrew Wolfman "With Andy Tavern off to the Boar's Head and Badgeman engaged elsewhere, the Tavern quickly scurried back to its default setting, gruesome blues bands every night. I scarpered to the South West and hid in the Exeter Cavern until someone said that Stereolab were on, and it was safe to come back."

TAVERN REGULARS CUM TO BEDLAM WERE THE SELF-STYLED BLACK COUNTRY MACC LADS

Nick McCarthy "In the late 80s I formed a band, initially called Full Circle, that became Blind Lemon and we are still going to this day. We rehearsed at the Market Tavern in the main room for a few years. After its demise we switched rehearsals to The Corn Exchange, New Road, Kidderminster.

The Blind Lemon line-up has changed little over the past 30 years. We have played literally thousands of gigs in the local area including regular venues such as Kidderminster Town Hall, Stourport Civic, The Wyre Forest Glades and all the local hotels, live music venues etc. I would suggest we must have the record locally for the longest continually established band."

# Those 3... RedBeards From Texas

Derek Eynon "The original idea was by Mark Breecher, who was the 'guitar doctor' at Birmingham's Muzos store, along with Mick Hayes (True Grit, Rev Brown and the Earlybirds) etc. Mark, a guitarist went by the name of Nathan Fury and played bass. This early lineup changed from that to:
Morton Pinkley (Ian Allen) - Guitar, Vocals
Wild Hoss Maverick III (David 'Kink' Keates) - Bass, Vocals
Bud Weiser (Craig Fenney) - Guitar
Duke Delight (Colin) - Drums

This line-up known as The RedBeards From Texas and later The RedBeards, went on to some minor success, with strong followings at JB's Dudley and the like. The ongoing joke was the faux American accents, and the fact that most or all band members were not playing what was their first instrument, for example, Craig was actually a bassist and Ian Allen a drummer.

This line-up split up in the late 1980's. In mid-1994, Mark Breecher decided to resurrect 'Nathan' and form a new band Those 3...RedBeards From Texas, with the rhythm section from the recently split Company Of Strangers, Derek Eynon on bass and vocals (Bullshit J Haugwash III) and Ray Horton (Jailer Rayboy) on drums. These people were highly skilled musicians and on their own instruments. The new band, unlike Fenney's line-up, played almost entirely ZZ Top covers, and higher octane versions than ZZ could muster live.

Those 3...RedBeards From Texas played Robin 1 in Brierley Hill, JB's Dudley, Limelight Club Crewe , Market Tavern Kidderminster, The Railway in Birmingham, The Stage Worcester always ripping the piss out of the audience and current affairs, and bizarrely always taking a foreigner's view of England. The band toured the UK, inc Devon and Cornwall finally playing the massive Colosseum in St Austell.

By the end of 1999, the run was at an end, nowhere to go with it, although a few shows took place in 2000. Ray Horton now plays for Legend, and Derek Eynon for English Electric Lightning and folk group Red Shoes. Mark handbuilds valve amps at Sheldon Amplification."

Mark Badgeman "I remember seeing The Redbeards From Texas with the fake beards when they just did ZZ Top covers. They released an album, did a Peel session and were on the telly a couple of times. They were surely the perfect band for the Tavern's front bar biker crowd!"

# Compulsion

COMPULSION appear tonight (Friday) at Market Tavern, Comberton Place, Kidderminster. The exhilarating guitar rock quartet are being tipped as "the next Therapy?". London-based, but with members from Ireland and Holland, they're signed to One Little Indian and their album Comforter was an indie chart hit. Support comes from Done Lying Down and Swat Tang.

Compulsion were lumped in with the New Wave of New Wave scene and had mastered the Nirvana trick of quiet and loud in the same song. They claimed to have been threatened by bikers at one of their gigs and didn't enjoy themselves.

## Offbeat gig coming to new Tavern

COMPULSION are in the county tomorrow for a show at the newly revitalised Market Tavern, Kidderminster.

The band, formed in early 1993, created their own label, fabulon, to release their first two EPs which were recorded in two one-day sessions.

Their mini-album was recorded in the same way — one take. Not only did this method suit the budget restrictions Compulsion found themselves with but it also helped to capture the original atmosphere of the songs.

The band are now signed to One Little Indian and are building on their early successes.

Now out gigging around the country their live show has been described as deranged and hyper-tense.

As Compulsion themselves point out, if you're not going to give 100 per cent of yourself to what you do, you shouldn't do it!

Karen Barker "I was deaf for 3 days after that gig... stood right at the front... right in front of the amps."

COMPULSION

A = 1. RAPEJACKET
    2. BASKETCASE
    3. MALL MONARCHY
    4. ARIADNE
    5. LATE AGAIN
    6. AIR RAID FOR THE NEIGHBOURS
    7. YANCY DANGERFIELD DELUSIONS
B = 1. LOVERS
    2. I AM JOHN'S BRAIN
    3. BAD COOKING
    4. DICK, DALE, RICK AND RICKY
    (CONT...)

*ONE LITTLE INDIAN*
TEL: 071 924 1661

Valentines Day special...

# Compulsion
+ JACKPOT + support

## Wednesday 14th February 1996

# MARKET TAVERN
### COMBERTON PLACE, KIDDERMINSTER
tel: 01562 825868

Tickets £3.00 from Magpie, Stourbridge Records, Plastic Factory, Tempest or the venue.
Doors open 7.30 · Last Trains... B'ham 22.52 Worcs 23.36 · Only 1 minute from the station.
••• IT MAY BE MORE EXPENSIVE ON THE NIGHT •••

MARKET TAVERN
KIDDERMINSTER
tel: 0562 752590
COMPULSION
+ DONE LYING DOWN
Friday 10th June 1994
£3.00 Adv          7.30-11.00

Baron Webb "I saw Jackpot play with Compulsion who I'd seen support PWEI only months before at Villa Leisure and sat in the back room with them sharing their rider cans with a few of us."

Ian Passey (Jackpot) "Compulsion were on The Big Breakfast in the same week they played at The Tavern. I remember being very impressed at the time!"

Woz "The singer climbed on the lighting rig and almost pulled it down"

# Stereolab + Mouse On Mars

## Thu 28th Sep 1995

This was a big deal. Melody Maker called them one of the most important bands since The Smiths. Daytime Radio One playlisted them and they'd had two Top 40 hits. The Mars Audiac Quintet album had been Top 20. This tour saw them stepping up to bigger venues... with the exception of Kidderminster where they deigned to play at the Tavern. It should have sold out but it was hard to sell gigs at the Tavern in 1995. We only did 178 and lost a bit of money but it was a nice busy room and a great gig.

Andrew Wolfman "As classy Gallic surprises go, getting Stereolab to play at The Market Tavern is the indie rock equivalent of convincing David Ginola to track back for a corner."

Katie D "Early autumn 1995. One year before I left home to go to University, meaning my parents were running out of reasons why I was not allowed to go out to gigs, at least nearby. I won.

Stereolab were a band I'd heard regularly via my radio favourites of John Peel, Mark Radcliffe, Marc Riley and the Evening Session (drinking... I mean evening. I'll stop there as I've lost 90% of my audience), and it seemed a bit mad that a part-French band had even heard of Kidderminster, let alone agreed to play a gig there on a Thursday night.

Mouse on Mars opened up to a pretty sparsely-filled room. I'm not sure I knew what to expect (I'd probably heard one song via John Peel. Probably in one of those late night 'has he finally lost it?' segments), but I remember being blown away by ridiculously loud bass-heavy electronica and (at least in one case of) slightly unruly hair. I still know I liked it.

For those who like to place things, or listen along, this was Stereolab in the era of Mars Audiac Quintet & Refried Ectoplasm (Ping Pong & French Disko getting the most radio play, which mattered back then before things all went digital and stream-y).

After 25 years I'd be lying if I said I remembered a lot. But I remember being totally focused on every single thing that happened in that room, to the exclusion of everything else. I knew I'd found my place at gigs and that I wanted to keep going into dark and sweaty rooms filled with strangers and noise, to lose my mind, sense and hearing time and again. Reader, I did this. Vehemently and repeatedly.

Fast forward to a year ago when I saw Stereolab again at a festival in the Netherlands (my current home), and it all came flooding back. Last Christmas I was back in the area visiting my parents, walking to Aggborough to watch Harriers and again trying to recall where the Market Tavern once stood.

Another year on and my 25-year long gig-going 'career' hit its first pause (having even managed gigs during travelling breaks in Tibet & Patagonia before). First a pause only for me via a serious concussion (mosh pit injury. Another story), now to us all, via coronavirus.

All I can say is that I whole-heartedly wish a speedy return to having live music in our lives for all those who love, support and / or work in the industry. To some of us, it means everything. Shine on, you crazy diamonds."

167

By Ian

**Which town were you based in?** Bewdley

**What years were you active?** September 1994 – December 1996

**Who was in the band?**

Chris Guillaume - bass, Steve Watkins - drums and myself (Ian Passey aka Paz) – vocals and guitar.

**What kind of music did you play?**

We were an up-tempo indie guitar band, or as it became commonly known at the time, ' Britpop'!

**Who were the influences?**

The Jam, The Stone Roses, Supergrass and The Small Faces - although, sadly, we didn't sound anything like any of them!

**What level of success did you achieve?**

We played a lot of gigs across The Midlands, building up a great following locally. Our biggest shows were two headliners at The Northwich in Worcester. We took three coach loads of fans to each one which was a pretty amazing feat, in hindsight! We released several EPs on the ' classic' cassette format but never quite managed to put out the album that would document the band properly.

**What do you remember about playing at the Tavern?**

I loved it! I'd been to see lots of gigs there from 1990 onwards (and played there with indie-pop janglers Smedley) but then went to Australia for a year, from August 1993.
As soon as I returned I put Jackpot together (I think The Tavern was our second gig) and we went on to play there several times over the next couple of years.
Looking back, bands were so lucky in those days – they only had to get one size of T-shirt printed because everyone seemed to wear XL (preferably long sleeve!)

**Any memories of the other bands you played with at the Tavern?**

We supported both Duffy and Compulsion there, and headlined one of the all-dayers. I seem to recall Duffy smashing his guitar, initially accidentally, and getting a bit peed off with some of our followers being noisy during his set. I can't say I blame him, to be honest!

**How did the band end?**

We had a fair bit of record company interest and went down to London to speak with a couple of labels. When nothing concrete materialised we seemed to think we'd reached our level and eventually called it a day. Looking back, it was a real shame that we split up when we did, as we all loved playing together and had such fun doing it.
I then put another band together called Swagger. We only got to play The Tavern once, in 1997, although we were rebooked for a second date. I remember taking the posters to the venue ahead of the show to find it boarded up. Sadly, it never reopened.

**Did anyone go on to further success or have a career in the music industry?**

I still perform regularly as The Humdrum Express. I've released six albums and racked up over 40 plays on BBC 6-music, gigging with many of my favourite acts such as John Cooper Clarke, Half Man Half Biscuit and Bob Mould along the way. I love it just as much as ever – song writing, playing live, recording and making music videos – and I'd like to think I'll still be doing it for a good while yet!
I also promote a few gigs and can now fully appreciate how time consuming and stressful it can be, and what a massive achievement it was to get so many great acts come to play in our town.

**BAND FILE**

# JACKPOT

JACKPOT JACKPOT JACKPOT JACKPOT

**JACKPOT**

| | | |
|---|---|---|
| THUR 21st Sept | BANBURY, Marwells | |
| FRI 29th Sept | KIDDERMINSTER, Market Tavern | ( Supporting DUFFY ) |
| TUES 24th Oct | DUDLEY, J B's | |
| THUR 26th Oct | BIRMINGHAM, Flapper & Firkin | |

AT THE TAVERN

Baron Webb "My first live solo performance was supporting Jackpot. I was nervous as hell. I only played 5-6 songs acoustically but surprisingly went down well, I just remember buzzing afterwards having played there."

● Jackpot: Playing on home turf.

## Lads play at home

BEWDLEY-based Jackpot will be playing close to home on Valentine's Day following a hectic series of gigs around the Midlands.

But guitar-based Britpop will be in the air rather than love when the trio appears at Kidderminster's Market Tavern.

The band, known for its catchy vocals and upbeat tunes, is supporting Compulsion.

**Duffy** (Market Tavern, Comberton Place, Kidderminster). Stephen 'Tin Tin' Duffy (remember his 1985 hit Kiss Me?) returns to his old Midland stamping ground to launch his new album, simply called Duffy. A highly-rated pop songsmith, Duffy's admirers include Blur and his album was produced by former REM cohort Mitch Easter. Support from Britpop outfit **Jackpot**.

**Mark Badgeman** "I don't know why I have such a limited recollection of this gig because I'm a big fan of everything Duffy has done. He was a founder member of Duran Duran along with Simon Colley, Nick Rhodes and John Taylor, and whilst I don't think they'd have achieved the same level of success with Duffy as the singer, the Devils 'Dark Circles' album of original Duran songs that he made with Nick Rhodes is one of my favourites. (Duffy: "We'd have ended up supporting Echo & The Bunnymen.")

When TV Eye (Birmingham's first punk band) split, a musical chair shuffle took place. The singer, Andy Wickett, became the new singer of Duran Duran whilst Duffy and Colley left to form a new band called the Subterranean Hawks with ex-TV Eye guitarist, Dave Kusworth. The Hawks released a 7" in 1980 featuring Duffy's song 'Words Of Hope' with 'Sense Of Ending' by Duffy and Kusworth on the flip. I have the 7" and as I write, the original 16 demos they recorded are being collated by Duffy for an album release.

By the mid 80s he'd become Stephen 'Tin Tin' Duffy and had a hit with, what I presume is, the old Hawks song of the same name, 'Kiss Me'. Two years later, he was releasing pioneering sample-based electronic dance music (with trumpets) as Dr Calculus with Roger Freeman of Pigbag.

In 1987, Duffy resurfaced as The Lilac Time with his older brother Nick and released an astonishingly brilliant timeless folk-rock record on Birmingham's Swordfish label. Success cruelly eluded them but they kept on making records until Duffy decided to release Britpop records under his own name and take a band on tour.

A year after he played the Tavern, he formed a Britpop supergroup with Alex James from Blur, called Me Me Me, and scored a Top 20 single with 'Hanging Around'. Major commercial success came when he wrote songs for Barenaked Ladies and then in 2005, he co-wrote Robbie William's 'Intensive Care' album which was No 1 in 15 countries and sold over 8m copies.

There's a film about him called 'Memory & Desire: 30 Years in the Wilderness.' His autobiography is going to be called 'What The Fuck Was I Thinking?'. That's genius I can't wait "

**Baron Webb** "I saw Jackpot support Stephen 'Tin Tin' Duffy. Myself and best pal Wayne J Barber (local legend) spoke to him for some time, he asked for my Midlands mods pin badge which I handed to him. He told me Alex James from Blur had photos of him on his bedroom wall. I asked how he still looked so young as he was old =)) then he started to become a bit of a penis by actually saying out loud 'yeah, it's the sex, drugs and rock & roll' as we were walking off in disgust!"

**Lunchtime For The Wild Youth** "Duffy played and was sullen and moody. The wayward boy got through the best he could, but was obviously cheesed off as at one point he raised his guitar and shattered the strip light above the stage (classy venue, The Tavern), seemingly oblivious to the hot broken glass showering down on him. Looking back now it seems obvious drugs were the cause of all this. But not all memorable shows need to be brilliant, it's no bad thing to watch things fall apart now and again."

**Dale Von Minaker** "Having turned up late to this gig I found the atmosphere charged; Stephen 'Tin Tin' Duffy had reinvented himself as a Britpop icon and the place was jumping. Spurred on by his roadie at stage right, he held aloft his telecaster above his head and in a perfectly-timed accident, proceeded to shatter the fluorescent light in the low ceiling, which erupted in a fantastic explosion of light and noise. The crowd thinking this was planned went wild with euphoria as he proceeded to smash his guitar to pieces on the glass-covered stage. 25 years later and I've never seen anything like this before or since."

**AUTECHRE** - Friday 27th October

Warp's experimental techno duo are no stranger to the Top 40. Normally they can be found selling out huge dance venues such as Birmingham's Que club but for this tour they're taken it upon themselves to adopt a 'punk rock' approach and let the music do the talking. The upshot of this is that there will be no lightshow, no decor, no jugglers, no go-go dancers - just a bare stage and Autechre's music.

Whether this will work remains to be seen but it will fit in nicely with their stripped down minimalist techno experimentation.

The new EP, 'Anvil' takes a harder, more industrial approach but is bound to score them another hit so if you're in it for the music and not the clothes, this is the place to be!

Doors 8.00 and admission £4.00 advance

*THE PRESS RELEASE*

Martin Noble "I remember that Autechre gig - no one knew what had hit them..."

Steven Norgate "It was Freeform who supported Autechre that night, with Rob Hall (Skam Records, Gescom) providing DJ services inbetween. My favourite memory (apart from Ae, of course) is when we very first arrived and the Spice (Original mix with notes) was being played - always a good start to an evening. I don't remember too much about Freeform to be honest. Autechre were of course on their 'Tri-repetour' in support of Tri Repartae. It was the old days, which meant they actually played tracks off of albums semi-faithfully, rather generate a whole album of new material on the spot. The Juno 106 was front and centre with the dual MMT8s driving things. 'Eutow' was the highlight from that night and I can still picture them performing it weirdly. I guess because it features the Juno so heavily, so the action was right there. Not many other memories of the evening other than finding it hilarious that Ae would be playing in such a place."

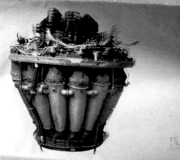

## Autechre. tri repetour.

october
26 manchester granada studios
27 kidderminster market tavern
29 nottingham sam fayes
november
01 sheffield hallamshire
02 newcastle riverside
03 aberdeen pelican
04 glasgow arena
05 edinburgh art college
07 hull the room
08 stoke wheatsheaf
09 cardiff clwb ifor bach
12 cambridge boat race
13 ipswich golden lion
14 margate cobblers
15 southampton joiners arms
16 brighton the joint
17 harlow square
18 london dublin castle
19 manchester roadhouse
22 belfast queen's university
24 dublin tivoli
25 cork art hive

new album. tri repetae

SENTIENT BEAN
& D.Js
LOVE HERTZ
SPOOK
ACID FREUD
Seer

10.30pm - DOOR
RESERVE
TICKETS
ONLY

AVAILABLE
FROM COMET @ £6
or contact E-MAP
& (021) 559609

THIS IS PROBABLY MY FAVOURITE OF ALL MY TAVERN POSTER DESIGNS. THE GAMBLE FOR AUTECHRE WAS REMOVING THE 'CLUB' ELEMENT FROM THEIR NORMAL SHOWS, SO INSTEAD OF SELLING OUT, IT DID 138 BUT I WAS HAPPY WITH THAT.

NOT TO BE MISSED....
# LIVE TECHNO.......
£4.00 adv
# AUTECHRE
WARP
## FRI 27TH OCT
# MARKET TAVERN
### KIDDERMINSTER
Tickets from Magpie, Tempest & Plastic Factory

Autechre. anvil vapre.

# DOWNWARD THING

Which town were you based in?
Kidderminster

What years were you active?
1994-2000

Who was in the band?
Steve Wigley - Vocals / Guitar
Justin Bodley - Lead Guitar
Tim Norris - Bass
Paul Keating - Drums

What kind of music did you play?
Alternative rock

Who were the influences?
Soundgarden, Quicksand etc

Mark Badgeman: Downward Thing were one of the more successful of the Market Tavern bands, although I wasn't aware quite how much so until I started this book. Steve and Tim were previously in Freek and had played with Cake at the Market Tavern in 1991. They also played a gig at a wine bar in Church Street with future Downward Thing guitarist, Justin Bodley, in the audience. Justin said "I went to see them with Nick Townsend from Weak13 whilst we were still at school. We were blown away! Little did I know at the time, I would be in a band with them and record an album and tour etc!"

After Freek disbanded, Steve, Tim and Paul had been jamming together for a while and decided they needed another guitarist. Justin auditioned and introduced the band to the (relatively new at the time he tells me) drop C# guitar tuning. The songs started coming together then.

Their first gig for me was supporting Blyth Power in 1995. Not really musically compatible but a lot of the local bands had split at this point and I wanted to find some new ones. Their second gig for me at the Tavern was supporting Peace Sanctuary, an American hardcore band who pulled absolutely nobody except their record company execs from MIA Records. They watched Downward Thing open the show and signed them on the spot!

I gave them more gigs afterwards and they played with Face Down and Cecil as well as some local band bills and some headlines.

172

Justin remembers "We had a great fanbase and I enjoyed seeing the same old faces, banging their heads!"

The album was recorded in Worcester at The Old Smithy but various delays meant it didn't see the light of day until 2000, when Dave Juste from XLs in Birmingham licensed it to his Sucka-Punch label. It was released in the UK, the US and several other countries. Comparisions to Soundgarden, Foo Fighters and Kyuss cropped up in reviews and the band embarked on two UK tours to promote it, including a support to Lacuna Coil in London.

They had plenty of press coverage in Kerrang! and Metal Hammer. Morat gave the album four K's in Kerrang! and Metal Hammer put a track on one of their cover-mounted CDs.

Phil Anselmo from Pantera was a big fan! He called them the 'fuck you band' from the lyrics of the first track on the album,

'Canned'. He used to listen to it on his tour bus (He had his own as he didn't get on with the rest of the band). The Downward Thing album was played as the walk-in music for one of their tours. This was thanks to their sound engineer being Alan 'Doof' McCann who used to do the sound at the Tavern for a lot of gigs. He also engineered a lot of Downward Thing's gigs around the Midlands.

The band ended when Justin decided to go travelling for a year. They initially continued without him but eventually decided to call it a day. Steve Wigley formed a band called Underdog and gigged for a couple of years. He now plays a lot of acoustic sets around the Midlands. Justin was in a band called Mahoney with Cobb Webb (Weak13, Pornch), Kriss White (Girls Love Ponies) and Karl Brian Melville (Kill Johnny Rockstar). He now records guitar instrumental music under the name 'The Bodster' which can be found on most streaming sites and YouTube.

**DOWNWARD THING**
**Downward Thing**
(MIA, 1002-2)
**KKKK**

Stoner/grunge debut is released two years after it was recorded.

IT'S NO secret that the so called stoner scene always owed a debt to grunge in general and Soundgarden in particular. So it hardly comes as a surprise, that there should be a band out there that falls slap bang between the two styles.

The rather oddly monickered Brit mob Downward Thing have obviously been digging the 'Garden, so to speak, but there are also traces of Kyuss laced throughout this impressive debut. The interesting thing is that this was recorded two years ago so it's quite likely they're absolutely awesome by now.

Gimme that 'Thing, indeed.

*MÖRAT*

JUSTIN & NICK TOWNSEND PLAYING IN INCISION AT THE TAVERN IN 1993

# The Wedding Present + Spectrasonic

## Thu 30th Nov 1995

Keith Evans "Somewhat surprised the semi-legendary The Wedding Present would be making an appearance a few miles away from my hometown, Stourbridge, I eagerly rang the venue about a week before to ascertain how best to get a ticket. I was told by the lady who answered the phone to just turn up on the night, it would be okay. I'd never been to the pub before, but knew where it was, so I relaxed in her assuredness and awaited the day.

None of my immediate mates liked the Weddoes, so it was almost always a case of go alone, as was the case here. I decided that I would drive, and turned up in good time. I wasn't prepared however for what awaited me as I swung into the front bar! There played out in front of me a calamitous scene, that included people lurching over the bar, waving of £5 notes in the air and shouting. It took a minute for it to sink in, and I wasn't alone, an old work colleague, Jamie and his girlfriend were there too. Yes, the last ticket for the gig had just been eagerly snapped up by one of the baying crowd! Evidently the lady on the phone had slightly underestimated the hotbed of Indie guitar fandom that was North Worcestershire!

Gloom and despair hung heavy in the air, however it was good to see Jamie and we chewed the dilemma over between us to try and ease our disappointment - we got a beer, and you could make your way through to an area to the left of the bar, this was a narrow space, taken up with around 12 or so other disappointed, ticketless fans and the merch table. We hung around, then suddenly David Gedge lead singer/songwriter of the band came in and stood behind the merch table.

I'm not normally the go up and start talking to people that I've never spoken to before type, but needs must! Egged on by Jamie, I introduced myself and attempted to break the ice with a shared love of Superhero comics. It quickly degenerated into me trying to shoehorn me and my mate and his girl into the gig! Unfortunately, David's hands were tied as the capacity was reached, so on Health and Safety grounds he couldn't afford us the luxury, he was very apologetic. He told us were were welcome to stay where we were.

The only thing between us and the stage were about 15 yards, two security guards and a set of flimsy, old style smoked glass doors. From here we were able to catch an occasional glimpse of the band when the doors frequently opened, and the soundproofing was practically non-existent. We settled for this. As always, the band were great, and we danced and nodded with approval.

The evening was ultimately made worthwhile when David, early in the set, dedicated a song to us fans stuck in the corridor who couldn't get in! Unfortunately I can't remember the song, but you know it was a great one, so on we bounced surrounded by smiles."

### press release

The Wedding Present will be playing at The MarketTavern in Kidderminster on Thursday November 30 as part of their 16 date tour of towns somewhat off the traditional touring map. Other places visited will include Buckley (North Wales), Cheltenham, Harlow, Hebden Bridge, and Shepton Mallet.

The group have just recorded two songs for a strictly limited 7" single, which will only be available at concerts on this tour. The a-side, *Sucker*, is a new, previously unrecorded song, featuring the group's current two-drummer line-up. The b-side, *Waiting On The Guns*, is a cover version of a song originally by Butterglory, a group from Kansas who joined The Wedding Present on their recent US tour.

Meanwhile, on Monday 6 November, Manifesto Records (through Virgin) release **"Step Right Up : The Songs of Tom Waits"** featuring 10,000 Maniacs, Tindersticks, Drugstore, Pete Shelley, The Violent Femmes, The Pale Saints, Jeffrey Lee Pierce, Alex Chilten, Tim Buckley, Frente!, and The Wedding Present, who have recorded a version of *Red Shoes By The Drugstore* for the project.

Finally, the group appear alongside The Troggs on "The Esther Programme" (BBC2, Friday 17 November) when they perform a track from their latest LP, "Swimming Pools, Movie Stars", **"Watusi"**.

Steve Tuffy "I remember being booted out of bed by my very angry father at 5.00am the next morning to go to work after getting completely trollied at the Wedding Present gig. I fell asleep at my workstation and the guys on the line had to stand in a ring around me to stop the directors from spotting me on their daily walkaround!"

Dale Von Minaker "When The Wedding Present played there I thought the walls were gonna come down they had squeezed SOOOOO many people in there! One of the best gigs I ever saw, even to this day!"

## Poster 1 (top left)

# MARKET TAVERN
# KIDDERMINSTER
## Telephone:  01562 825868
### FRIDAYS  &  SATURDAYS

CHARLATONS MEET BLACKGRAPE
FRI. MAR. 7TH. GRAND CENTRAL + FUSED  £2.50

SAT. MAR. 8TH. EDWIN AVENUE  £2.00

FRI. MAR. 14TH. DOWNWARD THING + AMETHYST + JONAS  £3.00

U.S. WEST COAST ROCK
SAT. MAR. 15TH. EVERBLOWN  £2.00

ELASTICA WITH MELODIES
FRI. MAR. 21ST. MARNIE + SUBTERRA  £2.50

PUNCKERS
FRI. MAR. 28TH. JAYNE DOE + BAM BAM  £2.50

EASTER SPECIAL
SAT. MAR. 29TH. XPERNATE  £2.00

MANICS MEET GREENDAY
FRI. APRIL 4TH. PREFONDO ROSSO + DELETE  £2.50
THE MAINFRAME VIRUS

DOORS OPEN 7.30PM.
ALL THE ABOVE PRICES ARE ON THE DOOR

THE MARKET TAVERN IS ONLY ONE MINUTE WALK
FROM THE RAILWAY STATION

1997

## Poster 2 (top middle)

# MARKET TAVERN
## COMBERTON PLACE, KIDDERMINSTER
### tel: 01562 825868

A cross between The Levellers, Wonderstuff and Squeeze!!!!
FRI 29 MAR  THE DHARMAS + BEEM

Welsh punky pop indie stars....
FRI 5 APR  CATATONIA + SPACE + CAIN

Another legendary Tavern All-Dayer with 10 bands....
MON 8 APR  EASTER ALL-DAYER
JACKPOT - FRISBEE - BURST and more

Indie / Rock....
FRI 20 APR  SKYSCRAPER + MAD CARSON

Psychedelic ambient space rockers who supported the Clarics on tour.....
FRI 3 MAY  PORCUPINE TREE + OMNIA + Fruit Salad Lights

Tickets for all shows are available from this venue or Magpie, Tempest, Stourbridge Records or Plastic Factory
Doors open at 7.30. 1st band at 8.15          Last train to B'ham is 22.52 and Worcs 23.36
Any local bands wishing to play at the Tavern should send a demo to Mark at the above addr
THE MARKET TAVERN IS ONLY 2 MINUTES WALK FROM THE STAT

## Poster 3 (top right)

# MARKET TAVERN
## COMBERTON PLACE, KIDDERMINSTER
### tel: 01562 825868
#### .... 1996 ....

Totally mad Rollins-style metal mayhem....
SAT 3RD FEB  CECIL + DOWNWARD THING + PORNCH

Trainspotting punk folkies....
FRI 9TH FEB  BLYTH POWER + FUNBUG + BOING

The return of....
SAT 10TH FEB  CUM TO BEDLAM
The Black Country Macc Lads!!!

Valentines Day special....
FRI 14TH FEB  COMPULSION
JACKPOT + SUPPORT

Jesus Jones meets Nine Inch Nails....
FRI 16TH FEB  PAPA BRITTLE
DAWNERA + BROKEN

Rescheduled date for The Godfather Of Ska....
FRI 1ST MAR  LAUREL AITKEN
(original tickets still valid)

Tickets for all shows are available from the venue or Magpie, Tempest, Stourbridge Records or Plastic Factory

## Poster 4 (middle left)

# MARKET TAVERN
## COMBERTON PLACE, KIDDERMINSTER
## 01562 825868

Local bands indie night....
THE MURMUR + NEW ARTIC SET + more
Saturday 16th March  £2.50

Levellers / Stuffies style roots pop....
THE DHARMAS + BEEM
Friday 29th March  £3.00

Welsh punk-pop indie stars....
CATATONIA + SPACE + CAIN
Friday 5th April  £3.00

Another legendary....
ALL-DAYER
with Jackpot and loads more
Easter Monday 8th April  £2.00

Indie / rock....
SKYSCRAPER + MAD CARSON
Saturday 20th April  £3.00

Psychedelic ambient space rockers....
PORCUPINE TREE + OMNIA
Friday 3rd May  £3.50

ALL PRICES ARE ADVANCE PRICES. IT MAY BE MORE EXPENSIVE ON THE NIGHT

## Poster 5 (middle centre)

# The Market Tavern's
# Christmas Countdown

Thu 30th Nov - The Wedding Present + Spectrasonic £5.00

Fri 1st Dec - Dubmerge £3.50

Sat 2nd Dec - Bracket (USA) + Skimmer + Pornch + Dawn Era £4.00

Sat 9th Dec - The Jacobites + Harry's Game + New Artic Set £5.00

Fri 15th Dec - R.D.F. (original line-up) + Rhythm Killers £3.50

Sat 16th Dec - Omnia & Pod £2.50

Thu 28th Dec - Dr Bullfrog + My Brother Jake £3.00
(a FREE tribute band)

29th Dec - The Christmas All-Dayer with loads
bands including Fretblanket and Mad Carson 50p

can get tickets from Magpie, Stourbridge Records, Tempest or Plastic Factory. It
be more expensive on the night. The Tavern is one minute from the train station
the last train to B'ham is 22.52 and the Worcester one is 23.36. Doors open at
and bands finish at 11.00 but ring on 01562 825868 to check before you travel.

## Poster 6 (middle right)

# MARKET TAVERN
## COMBERTON PLACE, KIDDERMINSTER
### ☎ 01562 825868

Punky guitar from ex Leatherface & The Abs....
DR BISON + Another Fine Mess
Friday 10th November  £3.00

Ex Soft Machine....
KEVIN AYERS + The Wizards of Twiddly
Wednesday 15th November  £5.00

Hardcore punk trio....
TRIBUTE TO NOTHING + The Glory Strum
Friday 24th November

Top Indie band....
THE WEDDING + Spectrason
Thursday 30 November

From America....
BRAC + Skimmer
Saturday 2nd December

XMAS AL
LOADS OF BANDS, ST
Friday 29th December

ALL PRICES ARE ADVANCE PRICES. IT MA

## Poster 7 (right, tall)

# DUFFY + The Diggers + Jackpot
Friday 29th September

Global grooves and live techno from....
LOOP GURU + Stop + CYCLORAMA DJs
Thursday 5th October

The return of the Stourbridge faves....
FRETBLANKET + Walrus + Dummie + Half Term
Friday 6th October  £2.0

5 local bands raising cash for....
World Mental Health Day
Saturday 7th October  £???

Melodic punky noise from Malvern's....
Blessed Ethel + SOLO 70 + New Artic Set
Friday 20th October  £3.00

Crusty-Dance festival veterans....
Tribal Drift
Saturday 21st October  £3.50

Experimental Top 40 techno duo....
AUTECHRE
Friday 27th October  £4.00

Top reggae band with new vocalist - Dennis from Progression....
RHYTHM-ITES + DJ Dread Lester
Friday 3rd November  £4.00

Punky guitar stuff from ex Leatherface & The Abs....
DR BISON + Another Fine Mess
Friday 10th November  £3.00

Ex Soft Machine....
KEVIN AYERS + The Wizards Of Twiddley
Wednesday 15th November  £5.00

Worcester's groovy rapragga collective....
Dubmerge + Dub DJ
Friday 17th November  £3.50

Robert Plant's fave Led Zep covers band....
Fred Zeppelin
Saturday 18th November  £3.00

Hardcore Skatepunk....
TRIBUTE TO NOTHING + MAD CARSON + THE GLORY STRUMMERS
Friday 24th November

## Poster 8 (bottom left)

# MARKET TAVERN
# KIDDERMINSTER
## tel:0562 752590

Friday 10th June  COMPULSION + Sack + Swat Tang  £3.00

Saturday 18th June  BLYTH POWER + support  £2.50

Friday 8th July  THE TANSADS + Under A Couch  £3.00

At The Northwick - Worcester

Sat 18th June  FISH - UNPLUGGED  £8.50

Thu 30th June  BLESSED ETHEL + BANG BANG MACHINE  £3.50

Friday 5th Aug  CHUMBAWAMBA  £5.00

Coming soon  THE STRANGLERS

Coming soon  SUNS OF ARQA

Coming soon  More bands at The Tavern!!!

last trains: B'ham 23.02  Worcs 00.01
one minute from the station

The prices listed are advance prices. It may be more expensive on the night.
Advance Tickets: Tavern, Magpie (Kidd & Worcs), Stourbridge Records
Birmingham Outlets: Tempest, Plastic Factory
Or by post from The Market Tavern, Kidderminster, Worcs (enclose s S.A.E.)

THE FINAL GIGS IN THE DAVID COX DAYS

## Poster 9 (bottom centre)

# MARKET TAVERN
## COMBERTON PLACE, KIDDERMINSTER
### ☎ 01562 825868

Melodic punky noise from Malvern's....
BLESSED ETHEL + SOLO 70 + New Artic Set
Friday 20th October  £3.00

Crusty-Dance festival veterans....
Tribal Drift + Munch
Saturday 21st October  £3.50

Warp's experimental Top 40 techno duo....
AUTECHRE
Friday 27th October  £4.00

Top reggae band with new vocalist - Dennis from Progression....
RHYTHM-ITES + DJ Dread Lester
Friday 3rd November  £4.00

Punky guitar from ex Leatherface & The Abs....
DR BISON + Another Fine Mess
Friday 10th November  £3.00

Ex Soft Machine....
KEVIN AYERS + The Wizards of Twiddly
Wednesday 15th November  £5.00

ALL PRICES ARE ADVANCE PRICES. IT MAY BE MORE EXPENSIVE ON THE NIGHT

# PORNCH

By Jon Roberts

**Which town were you based in?** Kidderminster

**What years were you active?** 1994 to 1996

**Who was in the band?**

Jo Allard, Wayne "Cob" Webb, Simon Record, Jon Roberts

**What kind of music did you play?**

Heavy rock / metal

**Who were the influences?**

Lots. Of that era. Metallica, Megadeath, Sepultura to Smashing Pumpkins, Green Day and Beastie Boys.

**What level of success did you achieve?**

Supported Bracket and Cecil. Mainly just local gigs. No record deal.

**What do you remember about playing at the Tavern?**

A massive group of friends pretty much spent all our youth there, irritating the guys on bikes, and pretty much annoying everyone.

I remember lending my drum kit to RDF who then proceeded to trash it! The heaviest dub band I know of!

Carter USM in 1997 was a great memory. Some uncouth individuals graffitied the tour bus - the driver was not happy!!

**Any memories of the other bands you played with at the Tavern?**

Not really just memories of people crowd surfing to us and having a reasonable following for a bunch of kids.

**How did the band end?**

We all progressed onto other things, creative differences and life.

**BAND FILE**

FROM AMERICA...

# BRACKET

## + SKIMMER + DAWN ERA + PORNCH

### Saturday 2nd December

# MARKET TAVERN

## COMBERTON PLACE, KIDDERMINSTER

### tel: 01562 825868

Tickets £4.00 from Magpie, Stourbridge Records, Plastic Factory, Tempest or the venue.
Doors open 7.30 · Last Trains... B'ham 22.52  Worcs 00.01 · Only 1 minute from the station
*** IT MAY BE MORE EXPENSIVE ON THE NIGHT ***

# SKYSCRAPER

### + Mad Carson
#### + PORNCH

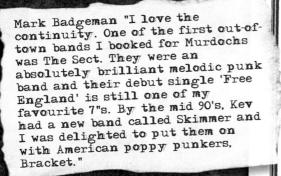

Silver

**Saturday 20th April**

**Market Tavern KIDDERMINSTER**
Tickets from the usual places

**Doors 7.30**
**£3.00 / £3.50**

punk
rock

# DR
BISON

(ex Leatherface & The Abs)

ANOTHER FINE
MESS
*Friday 10th Nov*

## MARKET TAVERN
COMBERTON PLACE, KIDDERMINSTER
tel: 01562 825868

£3

DICKIE HAMMOND

# The Jacobites - 9th Dec 1995

The first proper club / pub gig I ever went to outside of Kiddy or Stourport was the Rag Dolls at Peacocks in Birmingham in 1984. I'd read about them in Brum Beat and it was suggested they sounded like Hanoi Rocks. They didn't but the guitarist looked like he could have been in Hanoi Rocks. That same guitarist also opened the show as a duo with another scarf-laden, velvet-jacketed Stones clone - both on acoustics playing a set of originals that sounded like you should already know them, really classic English songwriting. I'd just seen The Jacobites - Dave Kusworth and Nikki Sudden.

I also saw them at the Barrel Organ and then I'd see them busking in the subways around Brum. I bought their two albums, I had the What A Nice Way To Turn Seventeen fanzine album and noted that Mike Scott from the Waterboys played piano on the Rag Dolls track. Nikki had a couple of earlier solo albums and I later realised that Mike Scott had pretty much stolen his musicians to form the Waterboys. I made a point of trying to see the Jacobites as often as possible but they split in about 1985 and Kusworth formed the Bounty Hunters who eventually signed to Creation and made the record Dogs D'Amour should have made!

I spoke to Nikki about doing a one-off Jacobites acoustic set at the Kidderminster Free Festival and whilst he initially agreed, they later cancelled because they were in Lithuania. That was a shame because I was sure by putting them in front of a big crowd, they could pick up some new fans. Then, in 1994, the Jacobites reformed properly and made a full band record with Glenn Tranter from the Bounty Hunters on guitar, Mark Williams from Suicide Blonde on drums, Carl Picot on bass and Terry Miles on piano. Surely I had to get them to come and play a show for me?

The problem with 'vanity bookings' is that you're blinded by your own love of the act and can't judge how well they'll do. I knew that they traditionally didn't pull a big crowd but I thought that I could 'do a Redd Kross' and just make people love them as much as I did. My press release was crammed with every detail I could muster that could potentially pique interest: Nikki Sudden was in the Swell Maps who were widely regarded as the first indie band, Kusworth had been in a band with Stephen Duffy and was apparently first choice as Duran Duran's guitarist, Kusworth had also been in an early incarnation of Dogs D'Amour who made an album in Finland, Nikki had made an album with REM after Peter Buck had seen him backstage and asked his wife to go and find out 'who that guy is who looks like Nikki Sudden', the Lemonheads (and later Mercury Rev) had covered Jacobites songs on their records, they sounded like Sticky Fingers era Stones, Neil Young and Dylan - what more did people want? Who doesn't want to see that band?

It didn't work, numbers were low but I loved the gig. Sadly, Nikki died in 2006 and Dave died in his sleep whilst I was writing this book.

Photos taken at the Tavern by Katriina Etholen

DAVE KUSWORTH AND NIKKI SUDDEN IN THE TAVERN'S DRESSING ROOM

Dave Kusworth & Nikki Sudden...
# THE JACOBITES
+ Harrys Game
## Saturday 9th December
# MARKET TAVERN
COMBERTON PLACE, KIDDERMINSTER
tel: 01562 825868

By Tom

**Which town were you based in?** Wolverhampton

**What years were you active?** 1991 to 1996

**Who was in the band?**

JD (drums), Andy Quinn (Bass), Tom Law (Guitar, Vocals)

**What kind of music did you play?**

Punky punk

**Who were the influences?**

Fugazi, Angelic Upstarts, SLF, UK Subs

**What level of success did you achieve?**

We got signed to Rough Trade Publishing and released a single, John Peel played us a couple of times, and we appeared in a porn mag (Club International) and supported Supergrass, Ned's Atomic Dustbin, 999, Captain Sensible, Daisy Chainsaw, PWEI, Back to the Planet, King Prawn.

**What do you remember about playing at the Tavern?**

There are all those roundabouts in Kidderminster like Milton Keynes and every single time we came off the wrong roundabout and got lost. However it was always a gig you were excited to play. You always got an enthusiastic crowd, the sound was great and everyone hung around outside between the bands chatting so it became a real social club too. It was such a unique venue though and it didn't matter where else you gigged and who you gigged with, everyone knew the Market Tavern.

**Any memories of the other bands you played with at the Tavern?**

We played a couple of all-dayers there, we played with Tribute To Nothing and we played with Skyscraper. Sony Publishing came to see us play at the Tavern. We went there as gig goers too though.

**How did the band end?**

We kind of ground ourselves down really. It was around the time of heightened activity for the IRA on the mainland and we were driving around in a dodgy looking white van so kept on and on getting stopped - unload van - load it back up again. On our way back from playing London once we got surrounded by armed police and then got stopped a further two times before we got back to Wolverhampton. We wrote to the police to tell them to stop harassing us but it didn't make any difference. All that and just general frustrations kind of took the thrill out of it.

**Did anyone go on to further success or have a career in the music industry?**

We all did local crewing at gigs helping to set up and take down productions. We worked a lot at the Civic and Wulfrun Halls in Wolverhampton and worked at Milton Keynes Bowl, and London too. One day you could be working at a Joe Longthorne gig and the next day it could be Pantera. Tom now works for Jagermeister as their Music Manager.

**What else do we need to know about the band?**

Well a couple of years ago, not sure what kickstarted it but the band got back together, now called MC16 and loving it again. Would have been really special to play the Tavern again. (www.facebook.com/MC16band)

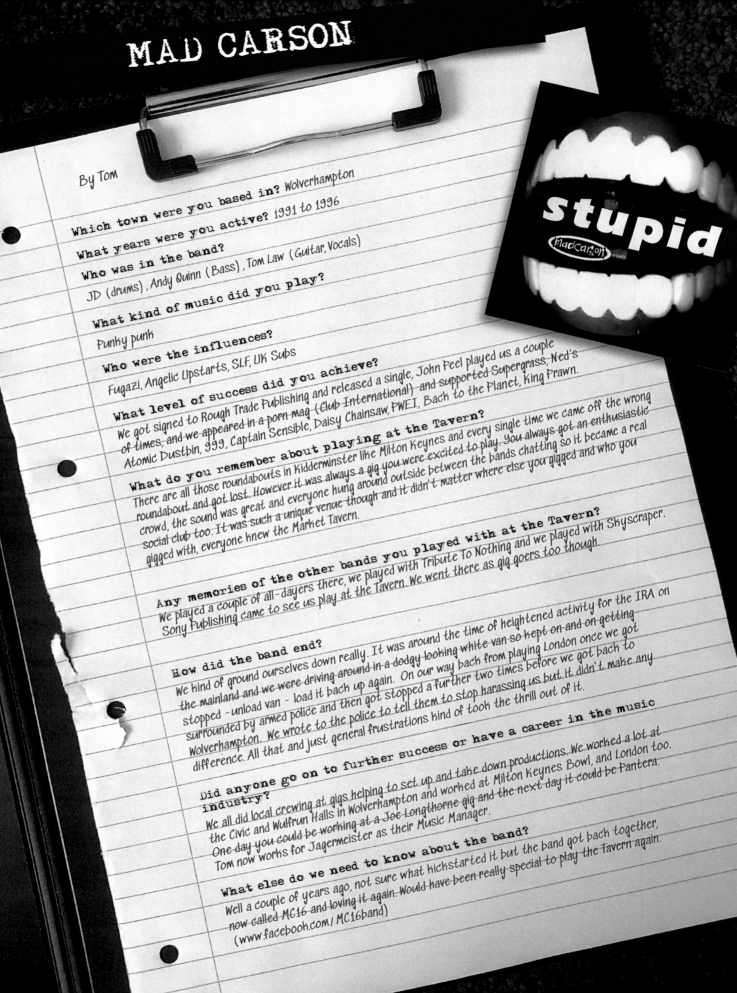

stupid
madcarson

# PRESS RELEASE

# LAUREL AITKEN
## 18th JANUARY 1996

### The Market Tavern, Kidderminster

Widely acknowledged as both the Godfather Of Ska and the High Priest Of Reggae, Laurel Aitken is a living legend as far as Jamaican music is concerned.

Although born in Cuba in 1927, he emigrated to Jamaica with his family when he was eleven years old, and quickly became involved in the local music scene - busking in the streets, entertaining tourists and singing in the talent contests of the day.

His recording career began in 1958 and the following year he became the first local artist to top the Jamaican charts with the double A - sided **Little Sheila** and **Boogie In My Bones**. In 1960, he left Jamaica as one of the country's top artists and emigrated to England where he was to record hundreds of tracks, including **Mary Lee** for the newly formed *Melodisc* label, and **Boogie Rock**, the first release on the now famous *Blue Beat* label. He then worked with a variety of labels throughout the Sixties, moving from Ska to Rock Steady and eventually to reggae.

Not only was he one of the most successful reggae artists of the time, packing out clubs and selling thousands of records, he was also one of the top producers of reggae in the UK, working mainly with *Pama* and its many subsidiaries.

He continued to work throughout the Seventies, but it wasn't until the coming of 2 Tone that he once again found himself in the limelight. His **Rudi Got Married** reached number 60 in 1980 and incredibly remains Laurel's only appearance in the UK charts to date, although he was widely acknowledged as one of the key influences of the whole movement. He also toured with **The Beat** and **Secret Affair**.

When the 2 Tone era ended, so did the mainstream's interest in Laurel's work, but he was given a new lease of life in the mid-Eighties when he teamed up with **The Potato 5** for some of the best British ska and reggae of all time and in 1985 Laurel's **Landlords & Tennants** featured in the film *Absolute Beginners*.

He continues to spread the gospel of Jamaican music to this day, covering everything from boogie to reggae and touring all over the world. His career spans an amazing five decades and Laurel remains one of the most popular performers on todays ska scene.

For the Kidderminster gig he will be joined by this regular band the *Pressure Tennants* and tickets priced £3.50 are on sale now from Magpie, Tempest, Stourbridge Records, Plastic Factory or the venue itself.

*I wrote press releases for every gig to try and get local press coverage. By 1995, even The Selecter were only pulling 150. This gig didn't do anywhere near as well as it should. By rights it should have sold out.*

# HI-ON MAIDEN

*By Dean*

**Which town were you based in?**
Members were from Kidderminster and Birmingham at the time we played the Tavern

**What years were you active?** 1995 to present

**Who was in the band?**

Dean Moraity - Speed Harris

Elias Aboud - Brisk Dickinson

Steve Parry - Adrian Swift

Simon Bradley - Dave Hurry

Steve Bennett - Quicko McBrain

**What kind of music did you play?**
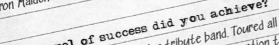
Iron Maiden tribute band

**What level of success did you achieve?**
We were the official Iron Maiden tribute band. Toured all over Europe.
Played on the official Iron Maiden fan club convention tour in 2001, joined on stage throughout by various
members of the real Iron Maiden.

**What do you remember about playing at the Tavern?**
The Tavern was my local and I'd played there several times in a previous band, but the APS support was Hi-on
Maiden's first ever gig, so it was special. We had decided that we wanted to go the whole hog with the tribute
thing and dress up; being our very first outing, we hadn't refined the wigs... So my main memory from that gig was
Bradders (Dave Hurry) in a ridiculously long blonde wig that kept getting stuck in his strings. That and his face
when I produced the electric blue spandex I had bought for him to wear. He refused to wear them stating that
they were made for a 9 year old girl and there was no way he could even get his arm in there, let alone his legs...

**How did the band end?**
Still going strong to this day, just with completely different members

**Did anyone go on to further success or have a career in the music
industry?**
Bradders left the band to go and write for Guitarist Magazine. The rest of us are still playing in bands
in some form or other. I have joined up with ex Iron Maiden members Paul Di'Anno, Terry Wapram, Terry
Dance and Doug Samson in a band called The Ides of March; there has never been an ex-bass player
from Iron Maiden since it is Steve Harris' band, so they asked me.

**What else do we need to know about the band?**
www.hi-onmaiden.com

BAND FILE

HI-ON MAIDEN

# TAVERN MEMORIES

Sand Palmer "I went on to run the Boars Head in 2011 for 6 years and had a lot of the old Tavern customers and put on a lot of bands that had played such as RDF, Citizen Fish, Inner Terrestrials, Interrobang (Dunstan from Chumbawamba) who remembered the Tavern really well. He went to look at the site when he got off the train... We also did a Tavern Legends Gig. So the Tavern was well talked about in The Boars."

Kim "I remember collecting the empty Newcastle Brown Ale bottles at the Tavern then taking them to the off-licence and getting the deposit back to buy cheap wine."

Keri-Jane Herman "I remember someone who worked for Jolly Roger being held hostage with a nail gun in the back room overnight!!!"

David Watkins "It was the mix of genuinely scary bikers in the front bar, no-nonsense farmers in the back. And then a bunch of indie kids in the evenings. I really loved it. All united by a love of, and complete cultural approval for, getting absolutely wangered on ale."

Lucy Clark (barmaid in the Jolly Roger days) "The bar never had any hot water, we had to wash all the glasses under the cold tap! Half the time we were running out of beer and we just sold out of date bottles for a quid!"

Jim Vickrage "I worked behind the bar for a couple of years while at the college. When I went for my 'interview' I was greeted by Tom, the then manager, who was wearing a sombrero, poncho and wellies with nothing underneath."

Roy Davies (about Engine) "A bit of Scouse boogie was always welcome!! They used to crash at my cousin Di's house. If I recall they were part of a 'Hamsters Sweepstake', where to win the kitty, all participating bands had to play a venue The Hamsters had never played before... it was a few years before anyone won it!!"

Jim Vickrage "Monty was a cleaner there while I was a barman. Horrendous. One of the bikers used to use the seat rather than the pan just to make him earn his crust!!"

Dr Marc Price "Unfortunately, the toilets stick in my mind. They were worse than Edwards No 8 (where a pair of waders was advised). If one needed a number 2, then the bushes outside would be more, er, possible."

Rebecca Griffin "Through a haze of Newcastle Brown Ale, I'm remembering how I wasted my youth. Brilliant."

Keri-Jane Herman (manager in the Jolly Roger days) "Two good friends I mistakenly locked in one night, they spent all night there (no mobile phones in those days) they wrote down everything they drank & consumed so they could reimburse, but I wouldn't let them!"

Clive (Fretblanket) "I loved the Tavern. A short hop on the train from Stourbridge, this was a proper venue. A good sized room with a good PA, decent lights and an actual stage. I loved seeing local bands and trying to figure out how they made their noise. Mark had a good handle on which bands would work/turn up to the venue and we got to see some great up and coming acts. I'll never forget The Gigolo Aunts playing an absolute blinder, a gig so good I wrote a song about how jealous I was. When Radiohead postponed their gig we stepped up from support into the headline slot and played to a full house. That was just one of many great gigs for Fretblanket at the Tavern, the venue which we played more often than any other. By the time we were proper headliners, we even got a rider! Thank you guys for the lovely veggie lasagne and the terrible continental lager.
Reading the list of gigs brings back so many happy memories. I never felt out of place and always went home happy, with my ears buzzing and my head full of songs."

Keri-Jane Herman "I stayed there until it closed because I remember all goods & chattels being stripped out. It was still run by Jolly Roger, they slowly ran it into the ground, but it was the last pub standing in their chain of doom, I think. We had nights with no electricity because Jolly hadn't paid the bill, also I remember often sending some of 'the students' down to the off licence, with the cash from the till, to get crates of beer, because Jolly sent us no stock. They ruined the Tavern. It would obviously have closed one day but it didn't need to slide into nothingness."

Mark Badgeman "There's something odd about The Dharmas. I'd seen them live and they were an absolutely brilliant festival act, replete with the requisite fiddle, bongos and big dancey tunes but sporting a clean cut indie pop-kid look with long sleeved t-shirts and not a dreadlock in sight. Then they put out a single called 'Channel Hopper' that sounded like it was by a different band. Only the logo on the cover gave me the confidence it was actually them. Fast forward to 1998, they'd dropped the fiddle player, changed labels, changed their name to Steadman and were churning out workaday indie fare. Search The Dharmas at Kingston Green on YouTube for a flavour of what they used to be."

# The Dharmas

+ ANOTHER FINE MESS
+ ROOSTERVELT

## FRIDAY 8TH SEPTEMBER
## MARKET TAVERN
### KIDDERMINSTER

£3.00 adv from Magpie   info 01562 825868   Doors 7.30

LEVELLERS·WONDERSTUFF·SQUEEZE·BOUNCY ROOTS COLLISION STYLE POP
**Debut Single RUNAWAY - out now**

Mark Badgeman "In the Jolly Roger days, I acquired a doorman. I say 'acquired' because I never asked him to do it, he just told me he was my doorman from now on! I liked Mad Mik. He was a slightly terrifying skinhead with a tattoo of a cross on his head but he had a heart of gold. We were chatting one day and he's telling me about the time he glassed himself. Yeah, you read that right. But suddenly I'm putting two and two together - it was Mik who'd got glassed at the Sweet Xtasy gig which ended up with me being banned from the Tavern! He told me that he needed both hands to adjust his trousers so he put his pint glass in his mouth but bit too hard and it smashed into his face. He also told me he refused to go to hospital because he thought he might have to pay for the ambulance.

When researching for this book, I found out he'd died in 2018. Such a shame. He was very funny, far more intelligent than people gave him credit for and I think he might have remembered some stuff from back in those days. I've still got the Ex Pistols 12" he insisted I buy from him. We'd sit in his flat and his records would be chucked all over the floor, not in their sleeves, which horrified me. He had some good punk ones but they were wrecked. I always looked after mine but he just didn't care! Rest easy Mik."

Steve Cooper "I remember Mad Mick being looked after by an ambulance crew and returning later, still drinking, blood everywhere and enjoying the rest of the gig with the ambulance driver's hat on his head."

Dave Lane "When Seven Dead Astronauts supported Sweet Xtasy someone known as (I think) Mad Mick managed to glass himself after one song. (We weren't that bad!)"

# Catatonia + Space + Cain

Kidderminster!! What were you thinking? This is the gig that killed it for me. Two great bands, Catatonia were nudging towards the Top 40, Space were gaining traction and hardly anyone bothers to come. This is when you're wasting your time. There's hardly any money to be made from gigs at what is now called 'grassroots venues' (used to be called the toilet circuit) but when you're booking the right bands, putting the effort in on the marketing and tickets aren't selling, that's the time to knock it on the head. We had a good run, we put Kiddy on the map but ultimately you have to use it or lose it.

Stan The PA Man "Another person I remember not being over impressed with the Tavern was Cerys Mathews who, when Catatonia played, would only come in to the venue to soundcheck, which she did in dark glasses and a hoodie. Before the show we had to build a walkway from the fire door to the stage so she could get in."

Lucy Clark (barmaid) "I remember Space and Catatonia playing and Space doing a really short set and I kind of told them off!!"

Mark Badgeman "Space were a bit lairy. They nicked the lampshade and wrote their set list on it! By September of 1996 that was probably worth some money as they were Top 10 with 'Me and You Versus The World'."

Helen Hipkiss "I thought both bands were great. Cerys was very drunk!"

Tom Cooke "I was walking by the back room and hearing a band playing a song called 'Neighbourhood' - turned to my mate John to say that band was shit hot on covers as it was only on that morning on the Chartshow on TV. A few days later realise it was Space, just before they got big :("

Keri-Jane Herman (manager in the Jolly Roger days) "My most re-told memory is asking Cerys Matthews who the feck she thought she was, trying to be a diva in my pub!"

Bev Pagett "Bloody hell. 3 quid to see Catatonia lol"

Kerry P "The Catatonia & Space gig was pretty rowdy. It was really exciting seeing bands that you had read about in NME playing the local pub. I may or may not have still been at school at the time."

CATATONIA - KIDDERMINSTER MARKET TAVERN - 05.04.96
Here's how you end up seeing bands before they are famous, just go to loads of gigs. Catatonia and Space were on the road together and at the small Market Tavern. Catatonia had the Sweet Catatonia single out, I don't think Space had released much at all. In fact I'm not sure that I was aware of them prior to this gig. And they were good, interesting and weird.
Catatonia were just getting into their stride, knocking out loads of catchy indie singles. It was a fun night, but my abiding memory of it was of Big Steve haranguing Space after the gig. I think he was repeatedly trying to tell them how ace he thought they were, but it seemed to come off as a tad aggresive, possibly due to his stature and drunkeness. All ended well though, as I'm sure being Scousers they were pretty tough lads and had seen worse before.

LUNCHTIME FOR THE WILD YOUTH FANZINE

*Catatonia*

BLANCO Y NEGRO

PHOTO CREDIT: STEVE DOUBLE 1996

# Porcupine Tree + Omnia

There's a proper bootleg album of Porcupine Tree from this gig with a very nice cover. I don't have the figures to hand but I've a feeling the gig didn't do so well. That's madness because Richard Barbieri had previously been in Japan (the band, not the country) for all of their hits, and Porcupine Tree had built up a great reputation on the prog scene. Adding Omnia to the bill should have ensured queues around the block but the Tavern was a tough sell during this period.

Mark Badgeman "One of the best local bands in the mid to late 80s was space rockers Omnia Opera. I remember their Market Tavern gigs being packed. They were the real deal, playing gigs all over the country, lots of festivals, regulars at the Mermaid in Brum, support slots to Cardiacs, The Pink Fairies, Here And Now and many others. They had a great psychedelic trippy lightshow, loud guitars, quelchy synths and two fabulous female backing singers with great outfits called the Drone Clones. They released two cassette albums which sold thousands. Their silver machine was 'Space Bastard', a great tune that everyone went wild for. I really liked that band."

Andy Jones "Out of the ashes of Omnia Opera, the acid rock band who were Kidderminster's answer to Pink Floyd, Hawkwind and Cardiacs came a more hard hitting guitar orientated version of the band, simply called Omnia.

The Omnia ship's crew were Rob Lloyd - Guitar, Steve Smith - Drums, Andy Jones - Bass & Vocals and Captain Bagley adding the elements of synthy weirdness associated with all things Omnia. The band existed for about 3 years in the mid 1990s. Mainly gigging around the Midlands blasting out the old Omnia Opera anthem 'Space Bastard'.

This version of the band struggled to gain enough momentum in some ways, always living in the shadow of Omnia Opera. The band recorded and produced a self-released cassette album titled 'Seeking the Elusive' and indeed, like most bands that have ever existed, bigger and better things evaded them. The cassette album is quite rare as only a handful were ever produced.

The morale and motivation to carry on finally took its toll and the band called it a day to pursue other projects. Omnia's epitaph could be taken from their song 'Second Skin' "Habitual creatures are we, adorning ourselves within life's tapestry, senses thirsting, seeking the elusive good time".

Still seeking, Omnia is dead, long live Omnia."

OMNIA

IDIOT PRAYER
THE SKY MOVES SIDEWAYS (PHASE ONE)
WAITING (PHASE ONE)
THE NOSTALGIA FACTORY
MOONLOOP
DISLOCATED DAY
RADIOACTIVE TOY
BURNING SKY
VOYAGE 34

PORCUPINE TREE SETLIST FROM KIDDY

porcupine tree
+ FruiT Salad LighT Show

Friday 3rd May - KIDDERMINSTER MARKET TAVERN
with special guests OMNIA + DJ Fragi

Saturday 4th May - WOLVERHAMPTON VARSITY
with special guests Cosmic Generator

OMNIA OPERA

*By Neil Phillips*

**Which town were you based in?** Worcester / Bridgnorth / Stourbridge – but we all went to Kiddie college together doing music.

**What years were you active?** I think we started around 1995 – played locally for a few years then I left to join the Yo-Yo's. The rest of the guys kept it going to a degree then I re-joined in 2001 – we carried on until 2007.

**Who was in the band?**

Neil Phillips (guitar / vocals) Dave Halloran (bass), Scott Garrett (drums) and Dean McCreadie (guitar / vocals)

**What kind of music did you play?**

Poppy / punky / rock kinda stuff

**Who were the influences?**

At this early point it would have been Green Day, the Wildhearts, Terrorvision, Therapy?

**What level of success did you achieve?**

Not so much in the early days but after I returned from the Yo Yo's we released 2 full albums ( Anthems for the Underdog on Spank records and Calibrate on Undergroove records) and several EP's. We made some videos (on YouTube) and released a few singles. Absolutely shit loads of touring nationally – sometimes going out on 70 date tours around the UK to promote albums. Always had great reviews in Kerrang! and other press but never really sold a lot! We had a really dedicated but small fan base. We played with absolutely loads of bands: The Wildhearts, Terrorvision, My Ruin, GU Medicine, Buckcherry, Carbon / Silicon to name a few.

**What do you remember about playing at the Tavern?**

I may be wrong but wasn't there a cage around the stage at some point? I just remember it being really cool that there was a decent venue with cool bands playing so close to college. I also remember that it was fairly easy to get into a scrap if you wanted one!

**How did the band end?**

After all of our touring etc I think we just got a bit burnt out and wanted to do different things. We're all still good buddies and Dean and I are making music together again at the moment – just for shits and giggles really.

**Did anyone go on to further success or have a career in the music industry?**

During my time in the Yo-Yo's I was lucky enough to sign to Subpop records in the States and tour the world for a couple of years. It was a pretty mental and chaotic experience but we toured the States with The Bachyard Babies and with the Murder City Devils – big long tours that took us all over the country for months. I've got a million stories from that. We went to Japan when we signed to EastWest records over there. Another mad couple of days. Over here we toured relentlessly and were nominated for Best New British Band at the 1999 Kerrang Awards. Bands we played with over the years: Bachyard Babies, The Hives, Therapy?, Clutch, Terrorvision, The Reverend Horton Heat – to name just a small few.

Scott and Russ from B Movies played in a band called the Culprit for a while and toured the States after releasing their album. Scott now runs the MAS records project at Kiddie college and Russ is a filmmaker. Dean has continued to make music and plays all over the country still – he's also a guitar teacher. Dave played in a few bands after leaving B Movies in 2003 and now lives in America, having spent some time as a prison guard in New Zealand!

I now manage a national music project that supports talented young musicians from low income families. We try to support them getting into music education and establish some better progression routes into the music industry. We're all still in touch and good mates.

**What else do we need to know about the band?**

Despite not selling a million records we all still get people regularly coming up to us to tell us how much our albums meant to them, which is always a treat to hear.

The other guys seem to think we were still called Bam Bam at the time we played the Tavern.

## BAND FILE

B★Movie Heroes

The Yo-Yo's were formed in 1998 by ex-The Wildhearts bassist, Danny McCormack and Tom Spencer (ex-Sugarsnatch / The Lurkers), after the two met at a Toy Dolls recording session. The Yo-Yo's recruited Andy Selway (Bladz) (ex-Sugarsnatch) on drums and guitarist Neil Phillips (B★Movie Heroes) to the band.

Amethyst

The Murmur & New Artic Set
+ support bands: FUZED
54 Amethyst    Live at the
MARKET TAVERN
Fri 15 March    Tickets: £2.00

Andy Price "Cage? Pathetic."

Amethyst in the cage

# MISSY HATE

Ella Mullins "We were an all-girl alternative band from Redditch/Studley, who formed in 1992 while at school. Pictured are Jayne Travis on vocals and bass, Kelly Bogan on drums and Ella Mullins on guitar, supporting Full Tilt. I can't remember who booked this gig and we didn't know Full Tilt at all. Their sound was classic rock, so quite different to us!"

Mark Badgeman "I'm gutted to find out after all these years that Redditch was harbouring an all-girl guitar band who I didn't know about and who were active during the Tavern's golden years. We could have done with a bit of gender balancing as the audience was fairly evenly split. I can't help feeling they'd have gone down a storm."

MISSY HATE help thousands of elderly KIDDERMINSTER people to get out and about.

AND Full Tilt 24th February AT market Tavern

# The
# MARKET TAVERN
### Comberton Place
## KIDDERMINSTER
Tel: 01562-825868

## ·PRESENTS·

# STRAPPING YOUNG LAD

Featuring ex-Wildhearts guitarist/Steve Vai vocalist
Devin Townsend and ex-Death drummer
Gene Hoglan

## with  RIVERS EDGE

## plus BAMBOO PUNCTURING

# SATURDAY 19th APRIL
## Tickets £3.50 in advance £4 on the door
Available from Market Tavern and Magpie Records
WORCESTER

Mark Badgeman "I had no idea what was going on at the Tavern in these later years but let's not under-estimate the importance of this gig. Devin Townsend is a big name and Strapping Young Lad had played lots of major festivals such as Ozzfest and Download. Whoever booked this had landed a great gig. They were touring the album called 'City' which is widely accepted to be a benchmark of the industrial metal genre these days."

Nick J Townsend "I am the singer & guitarist from British band WEAK13. One of the first gigs I ever played was at the Market Tavern. We supported world famous Canadian band Strapping Young Lad in 1997. The very short lived Kidderminster college band I was in back then was called Bamboo Puncturing (it only did about 5 live shows) which eventually, years later, became the springboard for me creating my own band WEAK13.

I was young at the time and quite naive but it was a real fantastic experience playing live at The Market Tavern. It was the first venue that I as a musician performed at and the happy memories of that particular show there with Strapping Young Lad spurred me on years later to consider beginning a music career and start my own band. When my college band (Bamboo Puncturing) finished, I was going to quit music but that gig at The Market Tavern kept reminding me how special rock 'n' roll is. The Market Tavern was as rock 'n' roll as they come, the real deal.

It was perfect like a movie set. Natural. Raw. The toilets at times seemed to resemble a crime scene but I don't think anyone minded. I was drawn to the place and there was always a good reason to go there. Meet a friend, make friends, watch a band or just simply hangout. I was there during its final years and if I'm honest saw sights that few could ever possibly imagine or forget."

Mark Badgeman "When the Tavern hit its peak around '91-'93, I had no idea what we were creating. Or even that we were creating anything at all. I was just putting gigs on, finding my feet, people were coming and I didn't need to bother getting a real job. Years later, in 2008, Rich Morley from the Pale Kings called me about John Combe's second 'Get Your Kicks On The A456' book. He suggested I joined Facebook to have a look at the Market Tavern page and that was the first time I realised how much it had meant to people. Up until that point, I had no idea that we'd actually created a scene based around the venue.

After Andy Price left, I started putting gigs on at The Stage in Worcester, which was run by the Jolly Roger brewery. It used to be called Druids and didn't have a good reputation. I booked some corkers for the first few shows. I remember we had The Bluetones supporting Supergrass and Reef played a show just as they were about to break off the back of the Sony Minidisc advert. But the numbers weren't right. Shows that should have sold out just didn't quite make it. My advertising was the same, I still knew how to use the most effective local bands as supports, there was nothing intrinsically wrong with the venue - it had good sightlines, a good PA and sold decent beer - but it just wasn't as good. I was on a salary and booking all sorts of acts but nothing was working as well as it should.

Paul Sodon from Jolly Roger called me in for a meeting to find out why I wasn't replicating the success of the Tavern. I had no idea. I wasn't getting anything wrong, (apart from when he'd asked me to book a reggae night and then complained that none of the acts were 'proper reggae' because they didn't have steel drums and grass skirts). I didn't really have any answers. So Jolly Roger decided to buy the Market Tavern for me so we could do it all over again.

Unfortunately, it just didn't work a second time around. Lots of people had moved on and gone to university or drifted away. I was actually booking decent acts such as the The Selecter, Stereolab and Catatonia but they weren't all selling out. Something just wasn't quite right and I didn't know why. Around '96, I started booking into The Varsity at Wolverhampton and that really took off straight away. I had bands on the same tour playing both venues and Wolves was doing better numbers. In the end, I picked up a pay packet from the Tavern and just felt bad that I was getting paid and not getting the results, so I said that was the last one and I wasn't coming back because it wasn't working for either of us. Market Tavern Phase II had only lasted a year for me.

I'm not a sociologist so if I try to analyse what was so magic the first time, I can't quite put my finger on it. Second time around, so many things were the same. The room was the same, people still piled out after the bands and hung around outside, people still watched from the stairs without paying to get in, the toilets were still terrible, the front bar still had the bikers, it still stank of cow shit, the farmers still didn't like it but something was missing. I don't really know what it was. There's obviously a lot of people who felt at home there during my 'second phase' and it may still have defined some lives but the original scene had gone and left an indelible mark on a lot of lives. Or was it just having the same effect on me that it had on the later generations? We all move on eventually.

I've spoken with other promoters from the small venue circuit of the 1990s and they too feel that their venues made a huge impact on the lives of those who went. There's definitely a book in it from the sociological angle as those types of venues are few and far between now, destroyed by the corporate soulessness of the O2 Academies. But I find myself thinking whatever happened at the other venues, it was nothing like the Tavern. It really was something special."

Mark Badgeman "When I put this book together, I was fascinated to see that most of the local bands split around the time that the Tavern entered its decline. When I booked The Varsity in Wolverhampton, there were hardly any local bands to start with but as that venue became hugely successful in the late 90s, we had hundreds of local bands wanting gigs and ran a very popular weekly local band night called Sound As A Pound (a pound on the door!). What does that tell us? That small venues where local bands have the chance to play, not just to their mates but also as support to touring acts, are absolutely essential. If there's nowhere to play, there's no bands. We can all curse the farmers and the council for killing off the Tavern but there was definitely a drop in support from punters around 1995 - 1996. We need to support live music but we also need to make sure local bands get regular opportunities to play with touring bands. It's what made the Market Tavern such a vibrant and exciting place."

Andrew Wolfman "Bands are like toddlers. Sure, they're cute and funny to be around, but they can't do anything for themselves, and are always tired or crying. Build them a playroom and they'll have a whale of a time, but left to their own devices, they'd just be smearing jam up the walls and eating crayons."

# THE MARKET TAVERN'S GREATEST HITS

| HIGHEST CHART PLACING | ARTIST / TRACK / YEAR |
|---|---|
| 1 | **DOCTOR AND THE MEDICS** <br> Spirit In The Sky - 1986 |
| 2 | **CHUMBAWAMBA** <br> Tubthumping - 1997 |
| 2 | **TERRORVISION** <br> Tequila - 1999 |
| 3 | **CATATONIA** <br> Mulder & Scully - 1998 |
| 3 | **RADIOHEAD** <br> Paranoid Android - 1997 |
| 4 | **DODGY** <br> Good Enough - 1996 |
| 4 | **SPACE (FEAT CERYS)** <br> The Ballad Of Tom Jones - 1998 |
| 5 | **THE PRIMITIVES** <br> Crash - 1988 |
| 7 | **CARTER USM** <br> The Only Living Boy In New Cross - 1992 |
| 8 | **THE SELECTER** <br> On My Radio - 1979 |
| 9 | **JOHN OTWAY** <br> Bunsen Burner- 2002 |
| 10 | **CLIMAX BLUES BAND** <br> Couldn't Get It Right - 1976 |
| 10 | **THE WEDDING PRESENT** <br> Come Play With Me - 1992 |

Some might say that the charts don't mean anything but it's still the yardstick by which we measure success. It was always a thrill to see a band we'd promoted going into the Top 40. Some of these hits in our chart pre-date the band playing the Tavern with the biggest disparity being Doctor & The Medics hitting number one but pulling relatively few to their gigs. Conversely, Back To The Planet sold out both their Tavern gigs but couldn't crack the singles chart.

I've disqualified Echo & The Bunnymen for not being the real version of the band. I've also disqualified the massive number one hit by Babylon Zoo on the grounds that they didn't actually play!

Trevor Burton probably played Blackberry Way at his gigs and although he was in The Move, that particular number one can't be counted because it's not the actual band. Same applies to Eric Bell who played Thin Lizzy's number six hit, Whiskey In The Jar.

Our chart takes the highest placed single by each band to avoid it being dominated by Radiohead and Terrorvision. Radiohead have also had six albums go to number one. At least Back To The Planet managed to scrape a chart placing with their album, which reached 32. Carter's 1992 Love album was a number one hit as were two of Catatonia's albums.

Mark Badgeman "I'm still working in the entertainment industry, as a production manager. That's a job I didn't even know existed for the entirety of the time I was promoting at the Tavern! When I have to explain it, I tell people I'm the glue that holds an event or tour together. I've production managed things as diverse as the Sundance film festival in London, the festival stages of the annual C2C country music event at The O2 Arena, world tours for Erasure, outdoor festivals, big orchestral shows for Rick Wakeman and lots of crazy things such as WWE wrestling, which I've done all over the world.

I didn't make this book on my own - I've 'production managed' it! I've been thrilled to still be collaborating with people such as Steve Cooper, whom I first met at Murdochs in the mid 80s when he was in the Vital Organs with Neil Archer, with Dave Morgan from Spiny Dogfish whom I've known since school, with Stan the PA Man who did his first ever solo PA gig at my Shark Taboo gig at Murdochs in the 80s and of course, Andrew Wolfman, who I still think of as 'Wag from Cake'. There's many many more that I haven't got room to list. I love that continuity.

Some bits for the book were like getting blood out of a stone but I don't seem to have lost the tenacity that landed me the first Carter gig. I've corralled a massive cast and channeled the output into something coherent, useful and worthwhile - the book you are holding. I realised this is exactly the same thing I do in my day job as a production manager and that this must be where my biggest skill lies. The Tavern was definitely a collaborative effort and so is this book. Thank you all! I'm still counting my lucky stars that nobody ever made me go out and get a proper job!"

# SOLD OUT!
# THE MOST POPULAR GIGS

**CHUMBAWAMBA**
Sold out all three times

**BACK TO THE PLANET**
Sold out both gigs

**CARTER USM**
Sold out the second gig

**THE WEDDING PRESENT**
Sold out

**BUZZCOCKS**
Sold out

**ROBERT PLANT**
Sold out

**THE 1993 FREE FESTIVAL**
FMB and others sold out

**THE SELECTER**
Sold 297 and then 287

**SAVE THE TAVERN BENEFIT**
Sold 286

**GOD MACHINE**
Sold 281

**MIDWAY STILL**
Sold 273

The official capacity might have been 99 but the room looked empty and wasn't financially viable on those numbers. So I used to sell 300 tickets because that's how many people you could fit in the room. There were only ten sold out shows during my time there but The Selecter came close twice (what I like to call a TSO - technically sold out!). The Buzzcocks and the 1993 Chumbawamba / Credit To The Nation one were the only gigs to sell out in advance. By contrast, the first Chumbawamba one only did 60 in advance and we sold the other 240 on the door!

Only two of my gigs were ever oversold, Carter (by accident) and one of the Chumbawamba ones (oops!) but that was only by a handful. I couldn't possibly comment on what happened during the Robert Plant gig but I don't recall anyone asking to borrow my clicker! Other gigs might have felt sold out because once you had 200 in there, that room was rockin'!

Nick J Townsend "I was one of the few in the back room in 1997 on the night of the... let us say 'the incident' or biker gang civil war. After that night, most were afraid to go there again. There was a band from London booked and about to play but the gig never started as the fight broke out dead on the hour, either 9 or 10pm, just before they were about to play.

I was there with my bassist at the time, Stuart. I promised him a good Saturday night out in Kidderminster (think it was Saturday night), bizarrely the place was empty, which was very strange. Just me and Stuart plus 4 or 5 others at the bar and the band from London, who we saw soundcheck, were the only ones there.

As the band was supposed to start, the back door flew open and about 20 people with baseball bats, chains, knives and a sawn off shotgun (which I believe wasn't fired) entered the room and fought the four at the bar.

I'm still amazed me and my bassist were not harmed. It was all over in two minutes. We were both sat in the corner with our drinks, frozen, witnessing the end of The Market Tavern as far I know. Police arrived seconds after the incident and all who arrived earlier had disappeared.

Stuart and me were questioned by police and all we could say was that it all happened so fast that we were unable to identify anyone, (me and Stu kind of agreed to keep our mouths shut anyway) blood was everywhere and I've never seen anything like it. Both me and Stuart never talked about that night but years later we still can't believe what we saw."

# THIS IS THE END
## BEAUTIFUL FRIEND

David Wright "How dare they build flats on this sacred ground. I curse them to be disturbed by loud music by night, by day the clinking of glasses and pool balls being potted. But Tuesdays shall be the worst of their woes with the smell of shit, the mooing of cows and the spectral figures of the horrific farmers arguing about their change!"

# THE INDEX

WHY WASTE SPACE WHEN YOU CAN USE A PIC OF CAKE?!

# Gig Guide

This gig guide is as accurate as possible but is bound to contain errors and definitely has omissions. If you're aware of a missing gig, please post it in the Market Tavern Facebook group. The Badgeman gigs are in yellow, although it's been hard to remember exactly which were mine. The gigs after July 1996 aren't included because it's too hard to find out who played.

| DATE | HEADLINE | SUPPORT / NOTES |
|---|---|---|
| Thursday, 5 July 90 | Cheap n Nasty | |
| Saturday, 28 July 90 | Citizen Fish | |
| Friday, 31 August 90 | Unfinished Bizness | Stop The World |
| Wednesday, 3 October 90 | Carter USM | Seven Dead Astronauts |
| Saturday, 27 October 90 | Giant International | Stomp Disco |
| Saturday, 3 November 90 | Helter Skelter | Paintbox |
| Wednesday, 7 November 90 | Shark Taboo | Bathchair Suicide |
| Tuesday, 13 November 90 | Family Cat | Polarbug, The Kilbaines |
| Saturday, 17 November 90 | Nik Turner & His Fantastic Allstars | |
| Wednesday, 21 November 90 | Dr Phibes & The House Of Wax Equations | Head In The Heavens |
| Friday, 23 November 90 | International Resque | Swamp Donkeys |
| Wednesday, 28 November 90 | Snuff | Sink, Psychedelia Smith |
| Saturday, 1 December 90 | The Telescopes | Slowdive |
| Sunday, 2 December 90 | Joolz & Rev Hammer | |
| Thursday, 6 December 90 | Frank Sidebottom | Bathchair Suicide |
| Thursday, 13 December 90 | Citizen Fish | Kitchen Police |
| Sunday, 13 January 91 | Shrine | |
| Friday, 18 January 91 | Wyche | |
| Saturday, 19 January 91 | Pretty Tame | Nod |
| Sunday, 20 January 91 | West Edge | |
| Friday, 25 January 91 | The Kilbaines | Stomp Disco |
| Saturday, 26 January 91 | Tubilah Dog | Satyrs |
| Friday, 1 February 91 | Senseless Things | Genius Freak, Elegy |
| Saturday, 2 February 91 | Kurt | (A French band) |
| Wednesday, 6 February 91 | Carter USM | Family Cat, Pop Am Good |
| Friday, 8 February 91 | Priest Town | |
| Saturday, 9 February 91 | Metal Monkey Machine | (snowed off) |
| Friday, 15 February 91 | Giant International | |
| Saturday, 16 February 91 | UXB & Warning | |
| Friday, 22 February 91 | The 1000 | The Stairs |
| Saturday, 23 February 91 | Jacknife Disciples | |
| Wednesday, 27 February 91 | Hayz Three | |
| Friday, 1 March 91 | County High | |
| Saturday, 2 March 91 | Fatima Mansions | King Woderick & The Yogots |
| Friday, 8 March 91 | Kernel Clarke | |
| Saturday, 9 March 91 | Ginhouse | |
| Thursday, 14 March 91 | Metal Monkey Machine | |
| Friday, 15 March 91 | Progression | DJ Lester's Skyline Radio Disco |
| Saturday, 16 March 91 | Ambelian | Your Icon |
| Friday, 22 March 91 | Band Of Gypsies | |
| Saturday, 23 March 91 | Power | |
| Thursday, 28 March 91 | Otherside | |
| Saturday, 30 March 91 | The Megas | |
| Monday, 1 April 91 | Christmas Trees Stomp | Stomp Disco |
| Tuesday, 2 April 91 | Cake | Freek, Dive, Stroke Bagpuss |
| Friday, 5 April 91 | Beatriders | |
| Thursday, 11 April 91 | John Otway | Atilla The Stockbroker |
| Friday, 12 April 91 | The Hamsters | |
| Friday, 19 April 91 | The Sandmen | |
| Friday, 26 April 91 | Nature Things | |
| Saturday, 27 April 91 | Haze III | |
| Thursday, 2 May 91 | Demented Are Go | |

# Gig Guide

| DATE | HEADLINE | SUPPORT / NOTES |
|---|---|---|
| Friday, 3 May 91 | ~~25th Of May~~ | Cake |
| Saturday, 4 May 91 | Bang Bang Machine | |
| Friday, 10 May 91 | Bleach | Cake |
| Saturday, 11 May 91 | Tubilah Dog | |
| Sunday, 12 May 91 | Genius Freak | |
| Friday, 17 May 91 | Scorpio Rising | |
| Thursday, 23 May 91 | UK Subs | |
| Friday, 24 May 91 | (International) Resque | |
| Tuesday, 28 May 91 | Panic Beach | Manic Thing |
| Friday, 31 May 91 | Blow Up | |
| Friday, 7 June 91 | Honey Turtles | |
| Tuesday, 11 June 91 | Wench | Mad Cow Disease |
| Friday, 14 June 91 | Drop | |
| Friday, 21 June 91 | Hope Springs Eternal | |
| Tuesday, 25 June 91 | Giant International | Cake |
| Thursday, 27 June 91 | The Vibrators | Another Fine Mess |
| Friday, 28 June 91 | The Primitives | Emma Gibbs Loves Badges |
| Friday, 5 July 91 | The Hamsters | |
| Tuesday, 9 July 91 | Jain Faith | Mercenary Tree Freaks |
| Friday, 12 July 91 | Cake | Genius Freak |
| Saturday, 13 July 91 | The Moonflowers | |
| Friday, 19 July 91 | Hover Chairs | Elegy |
| Tuesday, 23 July 91 | Scumbug | |
| Friday, 26 July 91 | Honey Turtles | Mercenary Tree Freaks |
| Thursday, 1 August 91 | ~~Dogs D'Amour acoustic~~ | |
| Friday, 2 August 91 | Korova Milkbar | Box 'Em Domies, Dive |
| Tuesday, 6 August 91 | Panic Beach | Tomorrow's Joy |
| Thursday, 8 August 91 | Rhythm-ites | |
| Friday, 9 August 91 | Prunes | |
| Friday, 16 August 91 | Crazyhead | Pop Am Good, Stop The World |
| Friday, 23 August 91 | The Primes | Fretblanket |
| Friday, 30 August 91 | Trevor Burton Band | Funny Daze |
| Sunday, 1 September 91 | Impact | |
| Friday, 6 September 91 | Top | Cake |
| Saturday, 7 September 91 | Ambelian | Ye Fungus |
| Friday, 20 September 91 | Pop Am Good | Stop The World, Another Fine Mess |
| Saturday, 21 September 91 | Radical Dance Faction (RDF) | |
| Tuesday, 24 September 91 | Cake | Dive, Pale Kings, Stroke Bagpuss |
| Friday, 27 September 91 | Scorpio Rising | Spiral Eye, Bitter Tears |
| Saturday, 28 September 91 | Citizen Fish | |
| Thursday, 3 October 91 | Trevor Burton Band | |
| Friday, 4 October 91 | Venus Beads | Fretblanket, Teenage Mess |
| Saturday, 5 October 91 | Indian Angel | |
| Thursday, 10 October 91 | Steve Gibbons Band | |
| Friday, 11 October 91 | Drop | Panic Beach, Bathchair Suicide |
| Saturday, 12 October 91 | Cruella de Villa | |
| Thursday, 17 October 91 | The E Numbers | |
| Friday, 18 October 91 | Family Cat | Bill Pritchard, Elegy |
| Saturday, 19 October 91 | Red Lemon Electric Blues Band | |
| Thursday, 24 October 91 | The Lurkers | Stop The World |
| Saturday, 26 October 91 | Bushfire | |
| A Friday night! Date unknown | Robert Plant | |
| Friday, 1 November 91 | Flowerdrum | Belch Pop Frenzy |
| Saturday, 2 November 91 | Four On The Floor | |
| Saturday, 9 November 91 | Rhythm-ites | |
| Friday, 15 November 91 | BOB | Liberty Thieves |
| ~~Saturday, 16 November 91~~ | ~~Leatherface~~ | ~~Genius Freak~~ |

# Gig Guide

| DATE | HEADLINE | SUPPORT / NOTES |
|---|---|---|
| Thursday, 21 November 91 | Unfinished Bizness | |
| Friday, 22 November 91 | Bollweevils | Fretblanket |
| Saturday, 23 November 91 | The Climax Blues Band | |
| Sunday, 24 November 91 | The E Numbers | |
| Thursday, 28 November 91 | Steve Gibbons Band | |
| Friday, 29 November 91 | Midway Still | Panic Beach, Sloth |
| Saturday, 30 November 91 | Band Of Gypsies | |
| Sunday, 1 December 91 | Tin Drum | |
| Thursday, 5 December 91 | Trevor Burton Band | The Ripps |
| Friday, 6 December 91 | Echo & The Bunnymen | Twiggs |
| Saturday, 7 December 91 | Wolfsbane | The Wildhearts |
| Wednesday, 11 December 91 | John Otway | |
| Thursday, 12 December 91 | UK Subs | Stop The World |
| Saturday, 14 December 91 | Dead Ringer & The Clones | |
| Sunday, 15 December 91 | Dangerous | |
| Wednesday, 18 December 91 | The Selecter | Tribe |
| Friday, 20 December 91 | Cake | Fretblanket, Panic Beach |
| Saturday, 21 December 91 | The Ripps | |
| Monday, 23 December 91 | The Roosters | |
| Tuesday, 24 December 91 | The E Numbers | |
| Sunday, 12 January 92 | Egypt | |
| Thursday, 23 January 92 | The Mingers | Another Fine Mess, Lost Soul |
| Saturday, 25 January 92 | Eric Bell | |
| Friday, 31 January 92 | The Pale Kings | Smedley, Spike |
| Saturday, 1 February 92 | UXB | Ransom |
| Friday, 7 February 92 | Scorpio Rising | Fretblanket |
| Saturday, 8 February 92 | Pointed Sticks | |
| Tuesday, 11 February 92 | Uncle Ian's Oral Circus | |
| Thursday, 13 February 92 | Dr & The Medics | |
| Saturday, 15 February 92 | Dangerous | Crazy Little Sister |
| Thursday, 20 February 92 | Doppelgangers (U2 tribute) | |
| Friday, 21 February 92 | Panic Beach | Jain Faith |
| Saturday, 22 February 92 | Cum To Bedlam | |
| Thursday, 27 February 92 | Ruthless Blues | |
| Friday, 28 February 92 | Crazyhead | Scumpups, Spike |
| Sunday, 1 March 92 | Wyche | |
| Tuesday, 3 March 92 | Cardiacs | Pietra Rosa, Conch |
| Friday, 6 March 92 | Drop | Ambelian, Bathchair Suicide |
| Friday, 13 March 92 | Resque | Real Simon Pure, The Flimmers |
| Friday, 20 March 92 | Fretblanket | Pale Kings, Dive |
| Saturday, 21 March 92 | Stop The World | |
| Monday, 23 March 92 | Citizen Fish | |
| Friday, 27 March 92 | Pop Am Good | Scrash, Another Fine Mess |
| Saturday, 28 March 92 | Bushfire | |
| ~~Tuesday, 31 March 92~~ | ~~Daisy Chainsaw~~ | |
| Tuesday, 31 March 92 | Dr Robert | Indian Summer |
| Friday, 3 April 92 | The Telescopes | |
| Saturday, 4 April 92 | D Block | Bob's Last Band, The Ripps |
| Friday, 17 April 92 | Sofahead | Cake, Reverse |
| Monday, 20 April 92 | Ballroom Glitz | |
| Tuesday, 21 April 92 | Smedley | Teenage Mess, Farter (The Unstoppable Bowel Movement) |
| Saturday, 25 April 92 | The Roubelles | |
| Tuesday, 28 April 92 | Birdland | Sugarblast, Pietra Rosa, |
| Thursday, 30 April 92 | Big Foot & Wyche | |
| Friday, 1 May 92 | The Selecter | Stop The World |
| Saturday, 2 May 92 | Tanglefoot | |

# Gig Guide

| DATE | HEADLINE | SUPPORT / NOTES |
|---|---|---|
| Friday, 8 May 92 | Jon 'Fat' Beast | |
| Saturday, 9 May 92 | Eric Bell | |
| Friday, 15 May 92 | Machine Gun Feedback | Scrash, Dive |
| Saturday, 16 May 92 | Robin George's World | |
| Monday, 18 May 92 | Airstream | |
| Wednesday, 20 May 92 | Illustrious | |
| Friday, 22 May 92 | Extreme Noise Terror | Headcleaner, Scumbug |
| Saturday, 23 May 92 | Tanglefoot | |
| Sunday, 24 May 92 | Rhythm-ites | |
| Friday, 29 May 92 | DF118 | Stratosphere soundsystem |
| Saturday, 30 May 92 | Ruthless Blues | |
| Thursday, 4 June 92 | Flaming June | |
| Friday, 5 June 92 | Midway Still | Panic Beach |
| Sunday, 7 June 92 | Redd Kross | Pop Am Good, Identity |
| Wednesday, 10 June 92 | Save The Tavern | Scorpio Rising, Scrash, Panic Beach, Stranglmartin, PWEI DJs (A rave) |
| Friday, 12 June 92 | Stratosphere | |
| Saturday, 13 June 92 | Cum To Bedlam | |
| Thursday, 18 June 92 | Dr & The Medics | |
| Friday, 19 June 92 | Sensitize | Sugarblast, Melon |
| Saturday, 20 June 92 | Dubmerge | Not For Babies sound system |
| Friday, 26 June 92 | Shadowland | |
| Saturday, 27 June 92 | Dumpys Rusty Nuts | |
| Wednesday, 1 July 92 | Whiskey Priests | |
| Friday, 3 July 92 | Fretblanket | Wishplants, Ludicrous Lollipops |
| Saturday, 4 July 92 | Mean Red Spiders | |
| Friday, 10 July 92 | Scorpio Rising | Manic Thing, Genius Freak |
| Saturday, 11 July 92 | Frank Boff Big Band | Stop The World |
| Friday, 17 July 92 | The Faith Healers | |
| Friday, 24 July 92 | Adorable | Wishplants, Pietra Rosa |
| Saturday, 25 July 92 | Stratosphere | (A rave) |
| Friday, 31 July 92 | Illustrious | |
| Saturday, 1 August 92 | Ambush | |
| Wednesday, 5 August 92 | The Wishplants | Private gig for A&R |
| Friday, 7 August 92 | Pale Kings | Kayak |
| Friday, 14 August 92 | Scumbug | |
| Saturday, 15 August 92 | Bushfire | |
| Friday, 21 August 92 | Back To The Planet | Scrash, State Of The Groove |
| Tuesday, 25 August 92 | Panic Beach | |
| Friday, 28 August 92 | Tin Drum | |
| Friday, 4 September 92 | Cerebral Fix | |
| Saturday, 5 September 92 | Korova Milkbar | |
| Friday, 11 September 92 | Chumbawamba | Credit To The Nation |
| Friday, 18 September 92 | Honeyblades | |
| Saturday, 19 September 92 | Cum To Bedlam | |
| Friday, 25 September 92 | Newcranes | Dive, Melon |
| Friday, 2 October 92 | Stop The World | |
| Saturday, 3 October 92 | Another Fine Mess | Funbug |
| Friday, 9 October 92 | Scumpups | Scumbug, Teenage Mess |
| Saturday, 17 October 92 | Engine | |
| Friday, 23 October 92 | Rhythm-ites | Credit To The Nation |
| Saturday, 31 October 92 | Scottish Sex Pistols | Crystal Injection, Another Fine Mess |
| Friday, 6 November 92 | Mike Peters | Pigs From A Gun |
| Saturday, 7 November 92 | Dumpys Rusty Nuts | |
| Wednesday, 11 November 92 | Genital Deformities | |
| Friday, 13 November 92 | Terrorvision | Teenage Mess, Shutdown |
| Saturday, 14 November 92 | Sebadoh | Cooler Than Jesus |

# Gig Guide

| DATE | HEADLINE | SUPPORT / NOTES |
|---|---|---|
| Sunday, 15 November 92 | The Enid | |
| Thursday, 19 November 92 | Radio Moscow | |
| Friday, 20 November 92 | Benefit Show | Small Mercies, Stop The World, Pale Kings |
| Saturday, 21 November 92 | Dubmerge | |
| Wednesday, 25 November 92 | Cardiacs | Honey Blades |
| Thursday, 26 November 92 | John Otway & Wild Willy Barrett | |
| Friday, 27 November 92 | Eat | Pietra Rosa, Various Vegetables |
| Saturday, 28 November 92 | Bushfire | |
| Thursday, 3 December 92 | Progression | |
| Friday, 4 December 92 | Georgous Space Virus | |
| Saturday, 5 December 92 | Cerebral Fix | |
| Friday, 11 December 92 | GBH | Genital Deformities |
| Wednesday, 16 December 92 | ~~Back To The Planet~~ | Madhalibut (headlined) |
| Friday, 18 December 92 | Wraith | |
| Saturday, 19 December 92 | Dead Ringer & The Clones | |
| Friday, 25 December 92 | Frank Boff Big Band | |
| Saturday, 16 January 93 | Sister Savage | Mr Breezy Trousers, 20th Century Hymn |
| Friday, 22 January 93 | The Pale Kings | |
| Saturday, 23 January 93 | Pseudo Hippies | Another Fine Mess, Funbug |
| Friday, 29 January 93 | Big 5 | Stop The World |
| Saturday, 6 February 93 | Tapanzee | |
| ~~Friday, 12 February 93~~ | ~~Radiohead~~ | ~~Fretblanket, Melon~~ |
| Friday, 12 February 93 | Fretblanket | Melon |
| Saturday, 13 February 93 | Eric Bell | |
| Friday, 19 February 93 | Chumbawamba | Papa Brittle |
| Saturday, 20 February 93 | Canaan | |
| Saturday, 27 February 93 | Israel Movements | |
| Tuesday, 2 March 93 | Radiohead | Tansads |
| Friday, 5 March 93 | Dodgy | Pietra Rosa, Emission |
| Saturday, 6 March 93 | Vincent Flatts | |
| Sunday, 7 March 93 | Dubmerge | |
| Friday, 12 March 93 | God Machine | Bathchair Suicide, Appleberry Crescent |
| Saturday, 13 March 93 | Cum To Bedlam | |
| Thursday, 18 March 93 | Tin Drum | |
| Friday, 19 March 93 | Radical Dance Faction (RDF) | Ancient Ones, Jerk Frenzy |
| Saturday, 20 March 93 | Industrial & Techno evening | DJs |
| Friday, 26 March 93 | Pop Am Good | Funbug, Sister Savage & The Buggered Nuns |
| Saturday, 27 March 93 | Blab Happy | |
| Friday, 2 April 93 | Citizen Fish | Spitboy, Preacher |
| Saturday, 3 April 93 | Panic Beach | Melon, Emission |
| Thursday, 8 April 93 | Ballroom Glitz | |
| Friday, 9 April 93 | Back To The Planet | Madhalibut |
| Saturday, 10 April 93 | Small Mercies | |
| Friday, 16 April 93 | Stourbridge Big Night Out | Fretblanket, Scrash, Babylon Zoo, Indigo Jane |
| Saturday, 17 April 93 | Another Fine Mess | Funbug, The Advocacy |
| Friday, 23 April 93 | Leatherface | Guns n Wankers, Pale Kings, China Drum |
| Saturday, 24 April 93 | Bathchair Suicide | Madhalibut |
| Saturday, 1 May 93 | Fun-Da-Mental | Credit To The Nation |
| Friday, 7 May 93 | Bushfire | |
| Saturday, 8 May 93 | Dubmerge | |
| Tuesday, 11 May 93 | Buzzcocks | Funbug |
| Friday, 14 May 93 | Midway Still | Panic Beach, Elizabeth Jane |
| Friday, 21 May 93 | Dr Phibes & The House Of Wax Equations | Tomorrow's Joy |
| Friday, 28 May 93 | The Lurkers | Advocacy |
| Wednesday, 2 June 93 | The Moonflowers | Madhalibut, Jeffrey's Velvet Jacket |
| Friday, 4 June 93 | Alloy | Funbug, Tanglefoot |
| Saturday, 5 June 93 | Cum To Bedlam | |

# Gig Guide

| DATE | HEADLINE | SUPPORT / NOTES |
|---|---|---|
| Friday, 11 June 93 | The Selecter | Image105, Mr Toad |
| Saturday, 12 June 93 | The Pale Kings | |
| Friday, 18 June 93 | Levitation | Rumblefish, Melon |
| Saturday, 26 June 93 | Progression | |
| Saturday, 3 July 93 | Glen Matlock & The Mavericks | The Advocacy |
| Friday, 9 July 93 | Sweet Jesus | Emission |
| Saturday, 14 August 93 | Kidderminster Free Festival | (see feature) |
| Tuesday, 14 September 93 | Chumbawamba | Credit To The Nation |
| Friday, 17 September 93 | Ship Of Fools | |
| Friday, 24 September 93 | Omnia Opera | |
| Monday, 27 September 93 | Mega City Four | Skyscraper |
| Friday, 1 October 93 | The Wishplants | The Berts |
| Friday, 8 October 93 | Cropdusters | Madhalibut, Chuck |
| Saturday, 9 October 93 | Preacher | |
| Friday, 15 October 93 | FMB | Anna, Joyland |
| Friday, 22 October 93 | Fretblanket | Family Go Town, Youth Culture Killed My Dog |
| Friday, 29 October 93 | Tansads | Moneygods, Cantaloop |
| Saturday, 30 October 93 | Gigolo Aunts | Scrash, Mile High Smile |
| Friday, 5 November 93 | Bang Bang Machine | Tribute To Nothing, The Berts |
| Friday, 12 November 93 | The Sea | Madhalibut, Under A Couch |
| Saturday, 13 November 93 | New Age Radio / Space | |
| Friday, 19 November 93 | Psychastorm | Ye Fungus |
| Friday, 26 November 93 | Avanti | |
| Sunday, 28 November 93 | The American Doors | |
| Tuesday, 7 December 93 | Cardiacs | Ship Of Fools |
| Friday, 10 December 93 | Citizen Fish | AOS3, Gr'ups |
| Friday, 17 December 93 | The International Beat | Cantaloop |
| Saturday, 18 December 93 | The Stubble Brothers | Planet Bob & The Satellites |
| Friday, 24 December 93 | The Pale Kings | Hornblower |
| Monday, 27 December 93 | All Dayer | Cooler Than Jesus, Funbug, etc |
| Friday, 28 January 94 | Blyth Power | Funbug, Blobnut |
| Thursday, 3 February 94 | Andy Price moves to the Boars Head | |
| Friday, 4 February 94 | Midway Still | The Berts, Genius Freak |
| Friday, 11 February 94 | Pentatonik | |
| Friday, 18 February 94 | S*M*A*S*H | Tribute To Nothing, Catalyst |
| Friday, 25 February 94 | Banco De Gaia | |
| Saturday, 26 February 94 | The Stubble Brothers | Vincent Flatt's Final Drive, Electric Blues Revue |
| Friday, 25 March 94 | Blessed Ethel | |
| Thursday, 7 April 94 | Steve Gibbons Band | |
| Friday, 8 April 94 | Red Lemon Electric Blues Band | |
| Saturday, 9 April 94 | The Stubble Brothers | |
| Thursday, 14 April 94 | Strange Brew | |
| Saturday, 16 April 94 | The Dick Tracy Band | |
| Thursday, 21 April 94 | Jean Genie | |
| Friday, 22 April 94 | The Climax Blues Band | |
| Saturday, 23 April 94 | Four On The Floor | |
| Sunday, 24 April 94 | Ballroom Glitz | |
| Thursday, 28 April 94 | The Roger Bromley Blues Revue | |
| Friday, 29 April 94 | The Back Street Boys | |
| Saturday, 30 April 94 | Fever Dream | |
| Thursday, 5 May 94 | The Stubble Brothers | |
| Friday, 6 May 94 | Custom Built | |
| Sunday, 8 May 94 | Ballroom Glitz | |
| Wednesday, 11 May 94 | The Rhythm Steelers | |
| Saturday, 14 May 94 | Red Lemon Electric Blues Band | |
| Wednesday, 18 May 94 | The Roger Bromley Blues Revue | |

# Gig Guide

| DATE | HEADLINE | SUPPORT / NOTES |
|---|---|---|
| Friday, 20 May 94 | Cum To Bedlam | |
| Saturday, 21 May 94 | Fred Zeppelin | |
| Sunday, 22 May 94 | Ballroom Glitz | |
| Friday, 27 May 94 | The Stubble Brothers | |
| Monday, 30 May 94 | All Dayer - the last gig | TTN, Mad Carson, Melon, Funbug etc |
| Friday, 10 June 94 | Compulsion | Done Lying Down, Sack, Swat Tang |
| Thursday, 16 June 94 | The Stubble Brothers | |
| Saturday, 18 June 94 | Blyth Power | |
| Friday, 8 July 94 | Tansads | Under A Couch |
| Wednesday, 15 February 95 | Jackpot | |
| Saturday, 3 June 95 | Gorilla | |
| Thursday, 22 June 95 | Tribute To Nothing | Full Tilt |
| Friday, 28 July 95 | Al Boden | |
| Saturday, 29 July 95 | Rebirth Of A Legend | BBM, Torn Bloody Poetry etc |
| Friday, 4 August 95 | Dubmerge | |
| Saturday, 12 August 95 | Free's Company | |
| Thursday, 17 August 95 | Fred Zeppelin | |
| Friday, 18 August 95 | Bulltaco | Baby Silverskins, Gouge |
| Thursday, 24 August 95 | Weknowwhereyoulive | |
| Friday, 25 August 95 | Blyth Power | Manifest, Downward Thing |
| Saturday, 26 August 95 | Jess Roden | |
| Friday, 1 September 95 | The Selecter | Dr Bullfrog |
| Saturday, 2 September 95 | The RedBeards | |
| Friday, 8 September 95 | The Dharmas | Another Fine Mess,Roostervelt |
| Saturday, 9 September 95 | Tyla (from Dogs D'amour) | |
| Friday, 22 September 95 | Black Star Liner | |
| Saturday, 23 September 95 | Cum To Bedlam | |
| Thursday, 28 September 95 | Stereolab | Mouse On Mars |
| Friday, 29 September 95 | Duffy | Jackpot |
| Thursday, 5 October 95 | Loop Guru | Stop |
| Friday, 6 October 95 | Fretblanket | Walrus, Dummie, Half Term |
| Saturday, 7 October 95 | World Mental Health Day | Local bands for charity |
| Friday, 20 October 95 | Blessed Ethel | Solo 70, New Artic Set |
| Saturday, 21 October 95 | Tribal Drift | Munch |
| Friday, 27 October 95 | Autechre | Freeform |
| Saturday, 28 October 95 | Junction 22 | |
| Friday, 3 November 95 | Rhythm-ites | DJ Dread Lester |
| Saturday, 4 November 95 | Peace Sanctuary | Downward Thing |
| Friday, 10 November 95 | Dr Bison | Another Fine Mess, Skimmer |
| Saturday, 11 November 95 | Face Down | Downward Thing, Above All, Deliverance AD |
| Wednesday, 15 November 95 | ~~Kevin Ayers~~ | Wizzards of Twiddly |
| Friday, 17 November 95 | Dubmerge | |
| Saturday, 18 November 95 | Fred Zeppelin | |
| Friday, 24 November 95 | Tribute To Nothing | Downward Thing, The Glory Strummers |
| Saturday, 25 November 95 | Cum To Bedlam | |
| Thursday, 30 November 95 | The Wedding Present | Spectrasonic |
| Friday, 1 December 95 | Dubmerge | |
| Saturday, 2 December 95 | Bracket | Skimmer, Dawn Era, Pornch |
| Saturday, 9 December 95 | Jacobites | Harrys Game, New Artic Set |
| Friday, 15 December 95 | Radical Dance Faction (RDF) | Rhythm Killers |
| Saturday, 16 December 95 | Omnia | Pod |
| Wednesday, 20 December 95 | Downward Thing | Pornch, Broken |
| Thursday, 28 December 95 | Dr Bullfrog | My Brother Jake |
| Friday, 29 December 95 | Christmas All Dayer | Fretblanket , Mad Carson, Jackpot, etc |
| Friday, 5 January 96 | Pale Kings | Omnia, Downward Thing |
| Thursday, 18 January 96 | Laurel Aitken | Spithead |
| Friday, 26 January 96 | Bang Bang Machine | Frisbee, Iris |

# Gig Guide

| DATE | HEADLINE | SUPPORT / NOTES |
| --- | --- | --- |
| Saturday, 3 February 96 | Cecil | Pornch, Downward Thing, Broken |
| Friday, 9 February 96 | Blyth Power | Funbug, Boing |
| Saturday, 10 February 96 | Cum To Bedlam | |
| Wednesday, 14 February 96 | Compulsion | Jackpot |
| Friday, 16 February 96 | Papa Brittle | Dawnera |
| Saturday, 24 February 96 | Full Tilt | Missy Hate |
| Thursday, 29 February 96 | Apes, Pigs & Spacemen | Hi-on Maiden |
| Friday, 15 March 96 | The Murmur | New Artic Set, Amethyst, Fuzed |
| Friday, 29 March 96 | The Dharmas | Beem |
| Friday, 5 April 96 | Catatonia | Space, Cain |
| Monday, 8 April 96 | All Dayer | |
| Sunday, 14 April 96 | Downward Thing | Amethyst, Jonas |
| Saturday, 20 April 96 | Skyscraper | Mad Carson, Pornch |
| Friday, 3 May 96 | Porcupine Tree | Omnia |
| Friday, 10 May 96 | Benefit Gig | |
| Saturday, 25 May 96 | Here & Now | |
| Saturday, 13 July 96 | All Dayer | JSA Awareness Day |

# SPOTIFY PLAYLISTS

If you have a Spotify account, try these three playlists to relive the Market Tavern days

### TAVERN ESSENTIALS
The headliners

### THE STOMP
A typical playlist

### CYCLORAMA
A typical playlist

WOLVERHAMPTON PUNK BAND CONTEMPT PLAYING ON THE ORIGINAL STAGE IN ABOUT 1990

"Market Tavern's loss was gravely felt, in much the same way as the Boar's Head was. Kiddy has got this rich heritage of being a bit wild and providing puck as fuck venues that seem to work there, the Tavern was a marvel, stunk of shit on many occasions, room size was perfect for an intimate gig, I saw so many bands there. Having something that was on the alternative circuit was brilliant for us West Midders, it was perfect that there was a big car park outside, we just used to roll up in our trucks mob handed and park up, off to the offie for a load of Merrydown, party in the car park before and after the gig, was wild and wonderful and I really miss those times, it's like a knife when I drive by there now and see it gone. I wonder if the folks living there have any idea of the serious good karma on that spot! Thanks to the brave souls that made those times happen, we salute you x"

Libbertine Spragg